Parent to Parent: Experience, Strength, and Hope Shared by Parents of Young Drug Addicts and Alcoholics

© **Copyright 2011 by Meek Publishing**

The Twelve Steps as adapted by Al-Anon with permission of Alcoholics Anonymous Services World, Inc. ("AAWS") are reprinted with permission of Al-Anon and AAWS. AAWS' permission to reprint Al-Anon's Steps does not mean that AAWS has reviewed or approved the contents of this publication, or that AAWS necessarily agrees with the views expressed therein. Alcoholics Anonymous is a program of recovery from alcoholism only - use or permissible adaptation of A.A.'s Twelve Steps in connection with programs and activities which are patterned after A.A., but which address other problems, or in any other non-A.A. context, does not imply otherwise.

The Twelve Steps are reprinted with permission of Alcoholics Anonymous World Services, Inc. ("AAWS") Permission to reprint the Twelve Steps does not mean that AAWS has reviewed or approved the contents of this publication, or that AAWS necessarily agrees with the views expressed herein. A.A. is a program of recovery from alcoholism only - use of the Twelve Steps in connection with programs and activities which are patterned after A.A., but which address other problems, or in any other non-A.A. context, does not imply otherwise.

Preface

This book came about because one mother of a young alcoholic and drug addict wanted to create a daily reader for other parents of youth abusing drugs or alcohol. She enlisted contributions from other parents whose children are in one of the Enthusiastic Sobriety Programs throughout the United States. Each entry is based on one parent's or family's viewpoint and experience. We come from all walks of life and all kinds of families: married parents with biological or adopted children, single mothers, single fathers, divorced parents with shared parenting time, blended families, mothers who work outside the home, and homemaker mothers.

The purpose of the book is to help parents whose child may be abusing alcohol or drugs. You are not alone. We have been through the experience. We know it is hell. We also know that the Twelve Steps are a program of recovery, for our children *as well as for ourselves.* There is hope. By sharing our stories and how we have used the Twelve Steps to help us deal with our kids, we offer our ideas and hope to others.

The book can be read daily to gain strength and ideas for coping with a teenager or young adult who is abusing drugs or alcohol. You may also read this book by finding topics in the index. You will learn what other parents have done to cope in similar situations. Using the index is especially helpful at 3 a.m. when you are worried sick about your kid and are reluctant to call another parent.

There are a two terms, "walls" and "shots," which are used frequently in the book. "Shots" refers to absolute, nonnegotiable rules whose violation results in serious, nonnegotiable consequences. An example would be, "No drug or alcohol use is permitted by anyone in this home. Any use will result in your being asked to leave the home until it is clear that you are willing to abide by our household rule." Willingness might be shown by staying sober for a specified period of time. The term, "walls," refers to less severe rules or boundaries that parents set with their teens. Walls are flexible and may be negotiated *in advance of a violation*. For example, a wall may be, "You may play only a half hour of video or computer games a day. If you exceed that time, you will not be able to play the games the next day."

At the end of the book there are appendices giving contact information and listing the Twelve Steps for each of three relevant programs: the Enthusiastic Sobriety Programs (for young people and their parents), Al-Anon (for families and friends of alcoholics), and the first Twelve Step program, Alcoholics Anonymous (for problem drinkers).

We wish the best to all parents struggling with this problem.

Introduction

How does a parent know if his child is abusing alcohol or drugs? In some cases, it may become obvious. The youth is caught by law enforcement officials selling or using, or he or she receives a series of DUI (driving under the influence) citations. Sometimes a parent sees signs of a problem but thinks it is simply teenage experimentation or a "phase."

Some signs of substance abuse that many parents have seen are: missing school or classes (when you thought he or she was in class), a drop in grades, a loss of interest in activities the youth enjoyed in the past, a lack of goals, a change of peer group, being more secretive than before, requesting more money than before, spending every weekend "partying," using Visine or mouthwash or mints often (to clear bloodshot eyes or clean the breath), and becoming irritable or angry when asked questions about friends or whereabouts. Also you may discover money, valuables, liquor or prescription medications are missing or that your teen's bank account is suddenly empty. No one of these is conclusive evidence that your child is abusing drugs or alcohol, but our experience has been that a cluster of these signs probably indicates a substance abuse problem.

If you suspect your child is abusing alcohol or drugs, we urge you to take action. Consult a *substance abuse* counselor as soon as possible. It is very difficult for a parent to know if it is merely a "phase" or if the child is actually predisposed to and on the road to addiction. If you consult a professional and no problem exists, you have protected your child. While you may be concerned about the expense or the wrath of your teen when you insist on such a visit, please understand that consulting someone with appropriate expertise early can save you much heartache and expense later. We recommend that you take your child to a professional who has *specific experience and knowledge dealing with young people who have abused drugs or alcohol.* Some family physicians, general therapists and mental health professionals may not be able to properly assess the situation. Most youth who are abusing drugs or alcohol try to hide their condition and are not honest with doctors and mental health professionals. This often prevents an accurate diagnosis. Therefore, a parent cannot be assured that his child has no problem simply because the child has seen a generalist.

JANUARY

Let It Begin with Me   January 1

When I first discovered my son was addicted to drugs and alcohol, I was lucky to already know about AA and Al-Anon. I also remembered that kids learn best by example. I knew what I had to do: go to Al-Anon meetings, get a sponsor, read Twelve Step literature, telephone other parents, and work the steps. I raced through those steps, just the way I wanted my son to "hurry up and get sober."

However, as I continued to work the program, I saw that recovery is a slow process. No one can change behavior patterns overnight. I had to be patient with myself for my many parental slips—e.g. apologizing for his being late, waking him up in the morning, or rescuing him by paying for his obligations. I began to be gentler with myself. When I realized I had "slipped," instead of condemning myself, I was glad to be conscious of the bad habit and accepted that I had to work to change. For example, I realized that waking my son to get to work on time was preventing him from learning how to do this. So the next time, not having the emotional strength to watch him oversleep, I left the house and telephoned my sponsor who encouraged my letting my son learn his own lessons. As a result, I felt stronger. When I returned home, I discovered that my son learned more about getting up on time when his boss called him.

Today's Reminder
I do my best to refrain from standing in between my teen and the consequences of his poor choices. The more I learn restraint, the more he learns about life.

Letting Go is Not Doing Nothing   January 2

When my husband and I began attending parent meetings, we frequently heard that we had to "let go." Irritated, my husband would ask me, "How can we let go? He is only in high school."

After a while, we finally understood that "letting go" does not mean doing nothing. It means no longer helping your kid use drugs and drink alcohol. We got rid of alcohol in our home. We didn't give him money when he was likely to use the money for drugs or alcohol. We stopped excusing his absences from school. We reported his theft to the police. We let him suffer consequences for his choices. As a result he became more willing to stay in treatment.

Letting go also means to stop worrying constantly and to direct our attention to more productive pursuits. Also, as we focus on taking care of our own needs, we are better able to set boundaries with our kids. When he was sober but not passing all his classes, we told him that he couldn't socialize—outside the mandatory Enthusiastic Sobriety Twelve Step meetings and functions—until he pulled his grades up. When he stopped working the Twelve Step program and relapsed, we told him that he could not live in our home again until he had thirty days of sobriety. We didn't give him money or let him use our car. Letting go did not mean we stopped being parents; it meant we stopped our actions which unwittingly helped our kid continue in the downward spiral of drug and alcohol abuse. Now we act in ways to support sobriety and responsible living.

Today's Reminder
I will let go of enabling my kid to continue abusing drugs and alcohol; I will stop rescuing him from consequences of his behavior. I will take care of my own needs and set boundaries about acceptable behavior in my home.

A Predictable Process   January 3

Addiction is a process and so is recovery. Typically kids suddenly change their friends, their grades tank, and they start getting into trouble which may result in legal action. I found drug paraphernalia in my kid's backpack and confronted him. He told me that he had only tried marijuana once but was holding the pipe for a friend. Later I spoke with a police officer who explained that once parents find paraphernalia in a relatively open place such as a back pack, their kid has been using for a while; a first-time user would be much more secretive.

Before recovery, we parents often try to excuse our kids' behavior and may allow our kids to be verbally abusive and disrespectful. We cover up for our kids' mistakes and feel like martyrs. But at some point we start to recognize the problem, realize that we can make better choices, and intervene to see that our kids get treatment. Good alcohol and drug treatment counselors hold up a mirror for us to see the reality of the situation. While our kids begin to accept treatment, we can pursue our own recovery. By reading about addiction and attending meetings, we see other parents who have peace and serenity whether their kids are still using or not. Learning from others' experiences, we begin to feel better ourselves.

Today's Reminder
I am aware that many parents face a child's drug addiction; I am not alone. Because recovery takes time, I will be patient and take actions for my *own* healing.

Accepting the Unacceptable January 4

How do I love my kid when he is high on drugs and alcohol, cursing loudly, punching walls, and stealing? It was very embarrassing for me to have a police car drive up to our residence. What would the neighbors think? I had visions of the officer taking my kid away in handcuffs, just as I had seen another teen in handcuffs at his high school.

Yet, we lived through it. I learned to love my son, the person hidden deep underneath the disease of alcoholism and substance abuse, and set boundaries to protect all of us from his unacceptable behavior stemming from the disease. I had to take a stand against destructive behavior to others and to him. I set boundaries. My son knew that if he crossed these boundaries by using, drinking, fighting, or committing a crime, he would not be able to live in my home. He did, and he had to leave. Only when he wanted to turn over a new leaf and *showed* me by taking positive action and "working" a Twelve Step recovery program, did I open my home to him again. Since I learned to set boundaries and—most important—implement them, my family life has been much better. I accepted that I *could not* control my son or his disease, but I *could* decide who would live in my home. By refusing to accept unacceptable behavior from my son but keeping the line of communication open, I could eventually welcome home my repentant, "prodigal son." I was able to love the person while keeping my distance from the disease.

Today's Reminder
I cannot control my child's behavior, but I can control my own. May I be guided by my Higher Power to speak and act in ways that show respect for myself, and others.

A Change of Focus — January 5

Before we joined an Enthusiastic Sobriety program, I read Bob Meehan's *Beyond the Yellow Brick Road* and identified with "The Guilt Game" of parents. I had high expectations for my children, felt that I had failed because my son was abusing drugs and alcohol, and blamed myself for everything that my teens did wrong. I kept reviewing the past and seeing things I could have done differently. I dwelled on the past, criticized everyone—especially myself, and tried to rewrite the past. This was an exercise in futility and stress exacerbation.

After getting our son into the program and attending parent meetings, my husband and I began to change our focus from the past to the present. I asked, "What can I do, right now, to improve my life?" As a homemaker I looked at what I could do to make our home healthy, safe, and tranquil. Sometimes this included keeping quiet instead of criticizing my teens. I recognized that I could briefly and sincerely acknowledge them for their current actions, such as "thank you for helping clear the table." I realized that I had been giving my teens no credit for what they did right and simultaneously heaping on blame for any way in which they fell short of my high expectations. By letting go of excessive criticism and embracing acknowledgement of my teens' positive efforts, I changed my focus to the present and also added more encouragement and even levity—which usually coincides with spontaneity—into our home. The result has been extremely positive; everyone in the family now focuses more on the present, makes more positive statements, and jokes. The atmosphere in our home has become much lighter, simply by changing our focus to the present.

Today's Reminder
I let go of guilt and the past. Instead, I focus on the good in the present. I acknowledge my teens' positive efforts and let go of excessive criticism.

Having My Son Take Ownership   **January 6**

My son has a habit of text messaging me to wake him up at different times each morning. Recently, I started looking for a new job and realized how inconvenient it was for me to be his human alarm clock. At the same time I remembered the importance of letting our kids take ownership of their lives. So I decided to take care of myself and let him take responsibility for getting himself up. Having reasoned this out, I did not feel bad about this decision. The next time he texted me to wake him, I replied by text that he would have to find another way to wake up and that I am not going to wake him anymore. The more I am in program, the more I can see how, in simple ways, I can let my son take ownership of his life and simultaneously free myself to take ownership of mine.

Today's Reminder
In the morning I will consider my tasks for the day. How many of these belong to me? Are there any that belong to my kids that they can do for themselves?

Unique Paths to the Twelve Steps — January 7

Both of my daughters are in our local Enthusiastic Sobriety program, but their paths were different. One's behavior changed for the worse immediately; she began staying out all night, coming home drunk, and not going to school. She had always been more rebellious than her sister. The other has always been the quiet one who liked to please me. She hid her alcoholism from me longer. She would come home by curfew time and sneak out after we were all asleep. She kept up with school and her extracurricular activities for a while, but eventually, she couldn't hide it anymore.

I love both of my kids and am glad we found a program that can work for individuals with different personalities. With each one of us working the Twelve Steps, our family has become much happier, healthier and more peaceful.

Today's Reminder
Each individual who works the Twelve Steps can find relief from problems. I use the Twelve Steps to guide me while I live with and parent my teenaged alcoholics.

Can Twelve Steps Work for Non-Addicts? January 8

I never expected that I would become part of a Twelve Step program myself, as I do not have an addictive personality. When my son entered one of the Enthusiastic Sobriety programs, I sought to show support for him by becoming involved in the parent meetings. After a short while attending the parent meetings, I saw that I had a unique opportunity to work on issues in *my life* that were problems. It became evident to me that these issues had affected me for many years, and the Twelve Step program might help me work on them.

I never really had much spirituality in my life, but I decided, after one of the parent meetings, that all it would take on my part was to believe there was a higher power than myself. What helped me the most was learning to *let things go*, giving them up to my higher power to work things out. It helped immensely in my relationships with my son, my wife, and my employees. I had let things overwhelm me, always trying to solve things that for the most part I didn't have control over. Now I regularly commune with my higher power asking for help to get through things over which I have no control.

It surprised me that I came to an Enthusiastic Sobriety program to help my son and ended up helping myself too! It has been almost five years and I feel an inner peace that I never felt before.

Today's Reminder
Today I remember that I have no control over other people, places, and things. I will let things go and ask my higher power to help get me through these things

Counting My Blessings — January 9

The more I practice the principles of the Twelve Steps in my life, the more I feel relaxed and serene. I see the changes and progress I am making. Every day I can find at least one instance in which I reacted differently to a life circumstance than I had in the past, and each change resulted in a better situation for me. Because I know that I am powerless over people, places, and things, I now stop and think before I react to anything someone else says or does. For example, in circumstances which used to provoke me to angry retorts, I now am able to stay calm and state my needs clearly. This usually results in a simple discussion and negotiation. Everyone feels heard. I am grateful for having a new "set of tools" that helps me in all aspects of my life.

Today's Reminder
Today I will stop and think before I react. I will speak my truth honestly and kindly, and I will be open and grateful for the chance to learn something new from each interaction.

Extended Serenity Prayer — January 10

One morning we were scheduled to meet with our son's high school administrator to determine if his many absences might result in loss of credits. I was very anxious. I read the Extended Serenity Prayer. I knew I could not change school policy; I could only argue for leniency. I also knew that it was important to be honest despite the fact that I was embarrassed by our son's behavior.

We admitted our son had "ditched" classes for no good reason. The administrator seemed impressed that neither my husband nor I made excuses for our son's behavior. We assured him that we both really cared about our son and his academic success, that he was now getting tutored at home each evening, and that we were doing everything in our power to encourage good study habits. He decided to be lenient, and we were relieved and grateful. My reading of the prayer that morning helped me to be honest and led to a successful outcome of our meeting.

Today's Reminder
I will be honest, not make excuses for my child's behavior, and remember an extended version of the Serenity Prayer.

"God, grant me the serenity to accept the things I cannot change, courage to change the things I can, and wisdom to know the difference. Grant me patience with the changes that take time, An appreciation for all that I have, tolerance for those with different struggles, and the strength to get up and try again, One day at a time."

"Parenting is a Matter of Percentages"   January 11

In *Bumper Stickers* Meehan says that parenting involves providing our children with as many good choices in life as we can. The children make a choice; we can't choose for them. If a child has twelve possible choices, eleven good and one bad, he or she has a better chance of making a good choice rather than a bad choice. We cannot make our teens choose one of the good choices.

This reminds me of the Al-Anon "Three C's": You didn't *cause* it; you can't *control* it, and you can't *cure* it. First, ordinarily parents do not introduce their children to alcohol or drugs and hope their children will become alcoholics or addicts. The kids made these choices for themselves. Second, we have no control over our teens when they are not physically home. Third, as for curing alcoholism and drug addiction, most parents tried everything to prevent our teens from abusing alcohol and drugs. To no avail. Then we sought treatment for our teens from professionals.

For my son, the only treatment program that was successful was one based on the Twelve Steps of AA. I have also known other parents whose children bailed from the same program, but later some of these teens returned. Alcoholism and drug addiction are diseases whose treatment requires the cooperation of the afflicted person. No family member can force a solution, but at least we can make our kids aware of a possible choice. We can lead a horse to water, but we can't make him drink. He'll drink when he's thirsty.

Today's Reminder
I will provide my child with as many good choices as I can; I understand that it is his choice.

Arguing with Reality   January 12

I used to compare our family with others, especially those whose children have gone to school with ours. In some cases, I felt that my husband and I, as parents, had done the same as they. Why were their teens doing well in school, sports, band, etc. while my son had become addicted to drugs? In other cases, my husband and I had provided much more for our children than other parents, but the other families' children were doing well. It didn't make sense. I argued to myself that our son shouldn't be a drug addict; we had done everything "right." Then I realized that comparison like this is a futile activity. I can't argue with reality. We got in life what we got, and the productive response is coping with it.

So how do we cope with it? "One day at a time." We look at what needs to be done that day—sometimes that moment—and do it to the best of our ability, without judging or comparing ourselves to others.

Our first step was to find treatment for our son and insist he go. When the first treatment program wasn't working for him, we decided to give him a choice of other programs he could enter. After seeing an Enthusiastic Sobriety program, he gladly chose it and has been successful and sober. He has been working the Twelve Steps, and so have we, one day at a time.

Today's Reminder
I accept my current life situation and do not compare it with others. I do what needs to be done to cope with situations each day.

Comparison   January 13

Why did my child become an alcoholic and drug addict? I started to compare his schooling and extracurricular activities with all our neighbors and friends. Why were those kids still actively involved in sports or band, getting good grades and making college plans while my son had to drop out to enter treatment?

After a while I realized that comparison made me feel worse. Someone advised me, "identify, don't compare." When in a meeting with other parents of addicts and alcoholics, we all shared from our hearts and identified with the same feelings and similar situations. I also heard that it is foolish to "compare other people's outsides with my insides." Just because other families appeared to be totally confident and successful, didn't mean that they were. More importantly, I realized that I felt sick when I compared myself with others.

In this program, I have learned that I have the power of choice. At any moment I can choose what to think. If my thoughts are making me miserable, I can change them!

Looking for the good in myself, another person, or the present circumstances makes me feel better and opens my mind to possible solutions to my problems.

Today's Reminder

Today I choose to focus my thoughts on what I have in common with others. I can choose to see the good in all people and situations and to open my mind to solutions.

Teens and Anger   January 14

I learned that the term for a sober alcoholic who is acting very irritably is known as a "dry drunk." I have found that all the teens in my family (even the ones who never abused alcohol or drugs) express anger poorly at times, often when unable to accept things that don't go their way. This "dry drunkenness" may start with complaining about how unfair things are, followed by statements of victimhood and self-pity. If it goes further, the person may yell, doors may get slammed, or walls are punched. I always felt scared when this happened, and I would try to soothe and placate the angry person. Now I realize that this is as futile as "reasoning" with a drunk. A better way to handle a "dry drunk" is to leave. Without an audience, the person may terminate this destructive line of thought and speech. Even if he doesn't, at least, I'm no longer subjected to distressful behavior.

Today's Reminder
I do not have to spend time with drunks—wet or dry ones. If I find myself with a drunk, I will leave.

Ask Your Mother or Father   January 15

When our son asked for something, my husband and I often told him, "Go ask your father" or "Go ask your mother." We each hoped the other would be responsible for answering his request. Our reacting this way enabled our son to play us against each other. He would respond, "Well, Mom (or Dad) said it was okay." Upon hearing this response, I would let him do what he wanted and then be angry or resentful toward my husband for giving him permission to do whatever "it" was that I didn't agree with. We'd argue about who was right or wrong in allowing him to do it. We never thought to bring the initial request to each other's attention when it was made. This was a form of insanity. We found help with this by reaching out and attending the parent group.

After a couple of months of being in the program, one of the first things we learned was to "be a United Front." When each of us was [separately] asked by our son if he could do this or that, we learned to respond, "I need to talk with your father (or mother) before giving you our decision." He got angry at first, but he soon learned that we were going to be a united front. Not too long after that, after hearing many parents talk about their experiences with their kids, my husband and I started to rehearse certain situations that might arise, so that we were prepared when it was time to respond. This was a very helpful tool. It brought us confidence and consistency so that we could create a more stable, dependable, and safe environment for our son, and one that was also less stressful for us. What a wonderful life lesson!

Today's Reminder
If my teen makes a request today, I will say, "I need to talk with your mom [or dad] first and then get back to you on that." And if the request requires an immediate response, I'll let my teen know that the response to last-minute requests—where a parental consultation is not possible—will most likely be "no."

Trust Is a Decision   January 16

When I first heard the statement, "Trust is a decision" I thought, "No, trust is earned." I was a parent of two teens trying to get sober and I realized I was going to need to change my thinking. My resentment due to their past broken trust was becoming a barrier in our relationships. I needed to put those feelings aside and give them another chance. If they were willing to do the hard work of getting and staying sober, the least I could do was move on, too. My willingness to *decide* to trust my teens again was very freeing to us all. They knew I was not holding resentment, and they were able to put aside their guilt.

It reminded me of a time when I was 17 years old and working out of state as a camp counselor for the summer. The rule at camp was no dating unless approved by your parent. I was asked on a date by a young man who lived near the camp. He was about 5 years older than me. I called my mom, who was 1000 miles away and told her the situation. She was hesitant but said, "I trust you will make the right decisions for yourself, so I am giving permission." That put the responsibility right where it belonged, with me. That left a huge impression on me and helped me decide to trust my teenagers again.

Today's Reminder
When I decide to trust my newly-sober teens again, it frees them from guilt and me from resentment. Most importantly, this helps repair our relationships.

A Dry Drunk   January 17

I heard the expression "dry drunk" and did not know what it meant. I asked my sponsor and found out that it means an alcoholic who, though not drinking, is nevertheless exhibiting some of the behaviors an alcoholic usually exhibits while drunk: being erratic, indecisive, harsh or angry; making poor choices; not admitting feelings; and not working through problems. I asked her what to do when my son is "dry drunk" and she said to treat it the same as if he were drunk. Stay clear and do not try to reason with him because he is "under foreign management," under the influence of anger, irritability and discontent in lieu of alcohol and drugs.

Over the past couple of years now, my son has occasionally experienced "dry drunks." I stayed away at first. Sometimes he apologized later. On other occasions, he was still irritable the next day, and I let him know that I noticed he's been irritable the past couple of days. This was usually all that was needed. Once he had a dry drunk that lasted a few days. I became worried. To keep myself from dwelling in worry and fear, I decided to make it to an extra Al-Anon meeting that week. This helped me, and eventually my son apologized to me and told me about the problem that he had been struggling with the past several days.

Today's Reminder
Today I will be compassionate and understanding with my loved ones, alcoholic *and* non-alcoholic. As humans, we are *all* subject to periods of anger, irritability and discontent.

We Let Our Son Face the Consequences   January 18

I would like other parents whose kids are suffering with a substance abuse problem to benefit from my experience. You did not cause this. Give yourself a pass on this. Concentrate on doing things that can help them. For my wife and me, ultimately this meant supporting our son in his recovery, but more importantly, allowing him to face the consequences of his decision to continue doing drugs. We felt that allowing him to live in our house, sleep in a nice bed, play his video games, and drive a car we provided for him, were not rights but privileges. We would no longer provide these for our adult son if he did drugs.

We eventually told him that he could not live with us if he continued to use drugs. When he decided to continue, we told him we loved him but he had to leave. This was the toughest thing we ever had to do. We believed if we let him face all the consequences of using drugs, he would eventually decide that drugs were not worth it. By allowing him to stay in our house and providing for him, we were really helping him continue his drug use. Once he directly faced his problem, he was much more willing to choose a drug treatment program over drugs. Now he has about a month of sobriety and has told us that making him leave the comforts of home was the best thing we did to help him.

Today's Reminder
I will let my child face the consequences of his choices. I will not help him continue abusing alcohol or drugs.

My Favorite Saying: The Three C's   January 19

To get on with my life and be in a better position to help my drug and alcohol-abusing child, I remind myself regularly of the Three C's: You didn't *cause* it, you can't *contro*l it, and you can't *cure* it. This has helped me deal with my son's substance abuse problem as well as with his ADHD. After giving it some thought, I realized that there was nothing I did or failed to do during pregnancy and childbirth to cause it. My genes may have contributed to his having these conditions but I cannot blame myself for my genes. I need to accept the fact of my son's conditions and do what I can.

So what can I do? My husband and I took our son to a therapist for the ADHD. When we became suspicious that he was using drugs, the therapist told us "just test him." The test results, in addition to earlier incidents of his getting drunk plus our finding a bong, baggies, and beer cans in his car, led us to enroll in our local Enthusiastic Sobriety program.

Things have not gone smoothly. Our son relapsed. My husband and I have held fast to the "shot" that we will not support our son unless he is working his program. I have attended meetings, worked the steps with a sponsor, served on the steering committee for the parent group, and participated in

Enthusiastic Sobriety retreats. When my son does not work his program, I know it is not about me. I am working my program so that I can live my life well and be better prepared to help him should he choose later to get sober.

Today's Reminder
I did not cause my child's condition, and I cannot control or cure it. While I can lead him to a Twelve Step Program, he gets to choose to work it or not. My energy is best spent working the program myself, helping me cope with my life.

There Aren't Any Victims—Only Volunteers   January 20

As a parent of an addict, I often wallowed in self-pity and martyrdom. Why did *my* kid have to become addicted to marijuana? Other kids, I knew, had experimented and didn't like it. Now I had to watch my purse and remember exactly how much I had in it. After a while, I came to understand what the above quote means. I have a choice about how I think about my situation and how I handle it. I can choose to get stuck in the "poor me's"—which just makes me feel worse and doesn't solve any problem—or I can choose to accept any situation caused by my son's addiction and think what part *I've* played in it. How can I change *my own actions* in the present and future?

For example, it had been my habit to toss my purse anywhere on the living room floor when I came in from work each day. In addition, I was always unclear about the cash I had on me. These habits did not serve me. I often would spend several minutes looking for my purse before I left the house in the morning. Also, occasionally, when I'd want to make a cash purchase at a store, I was embarrassed because I didn't have enough cash. By changing my irresponsible financial habits which had facilitated my son's stealing cash from my purse, I not only prevented later thefts, but also did myself a favor. Having a designated place for my purse and keeping better track of my cash, I no longer have to hunt for my purse in the morning nor be embarrassed in the store. Giving up martyrdom and taking control over aspects of my life that I can – my own thoughts, attitudes, and actions – has improved the quality of my life.

Today's Reminder
If I start to feel sorry for myself, I will think of what I can do today to improve my situation.

Achieving Balance   January 21

While looking at myself during step work, I saw that my life lacked the balance I sought. I was either totally consumed with my job or totally consumed with caring for my family. I rarely took the time to care for myself, because I didn't consider that important. Only when I got sick would I take time to rest. Then, one day when I was home sick, I remembered the admonition airline passengers receive in case of an emergency: "passengers with small children please put your own oxygen mask on first before assisting your children."

Of course! I can't help anyone else, especially my kids, if I don't take care of myself first. This means a parent must take time *daily* for self-care: eating right, exercising, getting enough rest and sleep, and even having some fun!

Ever since I began taking some time each day to take care of myself, I have felt more energetic and have been more effective both at work and at home.

Today's Reminder
Today I will take care of myself so I can be a better parent, spouse, worker, and person.

"I'm Fine" January 22

How often have I said that? Often I said this to deflect any possible criticism and to discount my own feelings. They say you need three things to work a Twelve Step program: honesty, open-mindedness, and willingness. Self-honesty is a very important part of the honesty piece. I realized that I am so good at lying to others that I believe my own lies. Usually these lies are about feelings which I expertly repress.

For example, when my son had just relapsed, I was asked the next day by a co-worker how I was. I said nothing about my son, and said, "I'm fine." But I wasn't. While I need not reveal any information to someone with whom I don't feel safe, I don't have to pretend that everything's fine. I can admit that I have something on my mind or that I have a family obligation I need to attend to which may require some time off work, for example. I can express my feelings with "safe" people, such as my sponsor. I did this to the best of my ability that day, and spoke with my sponsor. Still having trouble identifying my own emotions, I did recount the events to her, and she was able to identify feelings for me. This truly helped me to admit I was indeed feeling these things—fear, anger, frustration, apprehension about the future—and that as a human being, it was natural to feel this. Once I acknowledged the feelings, I could then move to the next step of remembering that feelings are not facts; that just because I might feel the sky was falling, I could be assured it wasn't and that I could cope with this event, taking it one day at a time and just doing the next right thing for that moment.

Today's Reminder
Today I will be aware of my feelings and admit them to another human being. Then I will be able to cope better with life and have the energy to consider how to solve the day's problems.

Crazy-Making Behavior of Teens   January 23

We told our kids plainly not to drink or use drugs. Yet, my husband and I occasionally found a pipe or empty liquor bottle in their rooms. Even though our kids kept up their grades at school, I sensed that things were not right. When I voiced my feelings to my husband, he disagreed and insisted I was being a "Negative Nellie" and should trust our kids more.

Later we discovered the truth. Our oldest is old enough to purchase alcohol. His younger siblings attended a party where some kids got drunk. Someone told us that our son had bought alcohol for the party. We confronted him, and he denied it. One of his siblings pointed the finger at another person. I felt they were both lying, but once again, my husband wanted to believe the kids. Later I noticed that my daughter had left her cell phone. I found text messages between her and her older brother, indicating that he had purchased the booze. Our denial of our kids' problems began to be stripped away. I wanted to trust our kids, but when they lied, it made me feel crazy.

Reflecting on this experience, I see that it is important to strike a balance between seeing the good in our kids, nurturing and encouraging them, on the one hand, and realizing that our kids are human and make mistakes, on the other hand. I realize that I need to listen to my intuition and not ignore clues of their wrongdoing. When their mistakes are not addressed, they can worsen from my inattention.

Today's Reminder
Let me have a balanced view of my kids, seeing both their good side and bad. While I still have the opportunity to guide them, let me help them grow, develop their strengths further, and learn from their mistakes.

Responsibility   January 24

I used to think I was responsible for *everything,* and I also felt that that I had to have the solution for everything and fix it. Participating in Enthusiastic Sobriety parent meetings, I learned that I am not responsible for other people's actions and that I cannot fix others or solve their problems. As a parent, I can do my best to set a good example and hold my kids accountable for their actions.

I also used to think it was my job as a parent to have a ready answer for my children's every request. In the past, if a particular request upset me, my temper would flare and I fired an immediate response. Today when they make a request, I apply the slogan, "Think." I pause, breathe, and calmly state, "Let me think about that, discuss it with your father, and get back with you." This is much better for my sanity and maintains a better relationship with my kids.

Today's Reminder
It is my job to be a good example, think carefully through my teens' request with their other parent, and hold my teens accountable for their actions.

Playing Stupid   January 25

Before entering an Enthusiastic Sobriety program, I frequently gave my opinion and my direction to my teenage daughter. As the parent of a recovering drug addict, I have learned to "play stupid." When she tells me that she has a problem, I do not rush to lecture or advise. Instead I ask, "What's your plan?" After she answers, I ask, "How is that going to work?" or "Did your sponsor help you with your plan?" or "What do you need from me?" These questions help her clarify her thoughts and the reasons for her decision. Should she get confused or doubt herself, I may suggest she check with her sponsor. By playing stupid, I help her develop decision-making skills and self-confidence. The program teaches her to be responsible for her choices, and I want to empower her as she acquires more life skills that will help her become an independent young adult. I feel good about myself as a mother.

Today's Reminder
By placing the responsibility for my teenager's decisions back on her, I give my child an opportunity to learn valuable life lessons necessary for independent adulthood.

Living in the Present — January 26

My mind can get caught up in all the awful experiences we had when my son was drinking and drugging, and I can use those thoughts to justify my negative outlook for the future. Meanwhile, I am not living in the present. When I stay in the moment, my life goes better. Even when facing a problem, I do not feel the weight of the world—or at least my entire family—on my shoulders when I live in the present. I can stop, go outside, and appreciate the natural beauty that surrounds me. I find that when I do that, it changes my perspective, just like getting a good night's sleep can change my perspective. *By giving my brain a rest from dwelling on a problem, I am better able to solve it later.*

I used to assume that all my problems had to be solved immediately. By challenging that assumption, I see that I was deluded. Often the concern was something I could let go of that day and wait to consider another day—often a few days, a week, or even months or years away. By letting go of future problems, I found that half disappeared because circumstances erased them. What a wonderful way to have my problems solved!

Today's Reminder

I take a break from thinking of my problems and appreciate the beauty around me. When I return to problem solving, I only consider problems I must solve today.

Ownership of One's Own Behavior — January 27

We used to rescue our son at times if he got into a jam. Yet, we have learned in our Enthusiastic Sobriety program that when our child gets to "own" his own behavior and solve his own problems, he feels much better about the situation and so do we. For example, our son was to fly to Atlanta for Step 2, the Enthusiastic Sobriety sober living facility for teenagers. We dropped him off at the airport but did not wait until he boarded the plane. Unfortunately, he missed the flight and telephoned us to let us know. We got off the phone with him, forgot about ownership, and immediately took action to find a later flight. When we called to make the arrangements, we learned that our son had already taken care of it and was on a flight to Atlanta. We were pleased with his independence and resourcefulness. It was wonderful to learn that he had been able to solve his problem himself.

Today's Reminder
Today I will remember to let go and let my child solve his own problems. We will both benefit.

"Experience is the best teacher." ~Ancient Proverb

Willing to Lose Her to Keep Her   January 28

My high-school-aged daughter stood holding a small packed bag in my garage. After a night of heavy drinking and her father and I picking her up from an unknown person's apartment, she decided she was leaving our home. I said "So, you are willing to give up your car, your phone, shelter, food and your family to be able to drink?"

She answered, "Yes."

I had a friend whose son was in our local Enthusiastic Sobriety program, and I asked her if he would talk to my daughter. Then I asked my daughter if she would talk to him. She agreed. Returning two hours later, she told us that she would try the program. Relapsing twice in the first few months of the program, she lost the privilege of driving her car for thirty days both times. I believe those were the first times I'd ever fully stuck with a consequence for her behavior. My husband and I had never really been on the same page with discipline. We were now! And she knew it. I could no longer accept her drug and alcohol use. *I had to be willing to lose her to keep her.*

I am so thankful that she has been clean and sober for over a year now. It was well worth the risk; she is the light of my life.

Today's Reminder
Today I hold firm with consequences for my teenager's unacceptable behavior. I am willing to lose my child to keep her.

"Parents are supposed to do what's best for their children, which sometimes means taking action that hurts. ... We must be firmly committed to our job as the most influential people in our children's lives, and we have to risk our relationships [with our children]." ~*Beyond the Yellow Brick Road*

Trust is a Decision, Not a Feeling   January 29

When we placed our high school student in his first treatment program, the group would take a break each afternoon and walk down to a local coffee shop for coffee with the counselor. The counselor informed me that my son would need coffee money for the week; she asked if I wanted to give her the money or give it to him. Most of the teens in the program hadn't acted very trustworthily with their parents during their drug and alcohol use, so it would be understandable if I chose to give her the money.

Yet, I realized that I *wanted* to trust my son and had been able to trust him before he became addicted. I also knew that it was highly likely that the money would not be spent on coffee. I consciously decided that the risk of the $20 was worth it. Knowing what I did, I *decided* to trust him; my eyes were open and I would not play the martyr if he did end up using the money improperly. I would know it was the disease taking him over, not my son as I knew him before the disease. If he did use the money for coffee, we both would win and a new relationship of trust could slowly build.

To this day I don't know how he used that money, but he eventually became sober and five years later we now have a very beautiful, trusting relationship.

Today's Reminder
With eyes wide open, I can choose to trust. If my child does break that trust, instead of playing martyr, I will take appropriate steps to enforce household rules with appropriate consequences. If my trust is honored, my child and I will be on our way to rebuilding a trusting relationship.

No Longer a Doormat   January 30

As a parent, I have had trouble in creating rules for my teens and enforcing the rules with logical consequences. I sometimes get very angry when one of my teens oversteps a boundary even though I know that teen rebellion against rules is part of their psychological development. I have a hard time enforcing consequences, even ones that are quite reasonable and logical.

Today I am striving to be more matter-of-fact in stating a consequence that I'll enforce when one of my teens breaks a rule. I can overcome my anger by talking with my husband. Then we present a united front in enforcing a consequence. Even when I am not as graceful as I would like, I feel better about myself, and no longer feel like a doormat. Our teens also respond. They may push to be sure we will stick with our decision, yet once they realize that we will, they disengage from battle and comply. Peace comes to our family.

Today's Reminder
When I feel angry that my teen has violated a household rule, I will talk with my spouse about it and together we can reason things out and create a calm, united front to enforce consequences.

Easy Does It January 31

When I first went to Al-Anon, I was introduced to a number of slogans. These slogans, in addition to meetings, sponsorship and phone calls are tools in a "spiritual toolkit" that members use to help them. The slogan that was most difficult for me, a "type A" personality, to grasp was: "Easy does it." I also struggled to learn patience with my teenaged son who entered an Enthusiastic Sobriety program. Not surprisingly, there is a connection between patience and "Easy does it." My Enthusiastic Sobriety sponsor had urged me to relax about my son's recovery. I wanted my son to finish outpatient treatment and work all the steps in one month and return to school full-time and sports the next. This did not happen. Recovery from alcoholism and drug addiction takes time, as does recovery from being a "type A" personality!

Both my Enthusiastic Sobriety and Al-Anon sponsors were kind and empathetic. They listened to my frustrations and fears. Their empathy helped me to stop, feel, and think. I began to take things more slowly and listen to my family members the way my sponsors listened to me. While today I am still goal-driven, I am much more realistic about my goals and the time it takes to reach them. I even allow myself to change goals. Also, I do not set goals for my family members. I give them the dignity to set their own goals, or not. I show them empathy. Not rushing, taking time to be aware of my feelings, listening to others' feelings, and acting accordingly, I lead a more relaxed life.

Today's Reminder
I will take time to become aware of my own feelings and needs, and I will listen for others' feelings and needs. By giving myself the time required to focus on these, I can let go of incompatible goals, feel more at peace, and improve my relationship with my family.

FEBRUARY

Deadlines   **February 1**

For our peace of mind and to encourage our son's recovery, my wife and I have set boundaries and deadlines with our son a few times. One was when our son relapsed and we all agreed that he would re-enter the intensive outpatient program. This involved another financial commitment on our part. After a few weeks, he began missing meetings. We talked with him and explained our heartfelt belief that it was very important for him to attend all the meetings and be committed to his recovery. We set a boundary that he must not miss more than one meeting a month. The consequence of missing more would be that he would have to move out of our house.

Unfortunately, he did miss more than one. We met with him the next day and told him we loved him and didn't want to hurt him, but he had to leave now. We all cried. We told him that if he attended all the meetings for a month, he would be welcome to return home. This was hard, scary, but loving. Our son chose to move in with his sponsor and several program members. I was very impressed by that choice and felt substantial relief of my greatest worries. He attended all the meetings after that and returned home a little over a month later. I could tell he had learned some things about himself through this experience. My wife and I also learned from that experience, especially that enforcing consequences can work.

Today's Reminder
I will let go of my fear and enforce appropriate boundaries and deadlines when it is the loving thing to do for all concerned.

Transforming Expectations   February 2

Do I expect my children to live their lives according to my plans for them? I asked myself this one day when I realized a primary reason for my anger with my son for getting involved with drugs and alcohol was his failure to follow the path that I had set for him. I saw that this expectation was selfish and unfair. As Meehan said in *Bumper Stickers*, "Expectations breed disaster."

Whose life is it? I have my life. My son has his. I recall the movie, *Dead Poets Society,* in which a boy's father insisted he spend all his time in prep school studying so he could enter an Ivy League college and eventually go to medical school. The father forbids his son's acting in a school play. The son disobeys and does a wonderful job in the play. His father threatens to send him to military school, and the son commits suicide. That parent's expectations and interference with his teenager's life bred disaster.

While it is true that expecting a teen not to use drugs and alcohol is not in the same league as having his high school activities, college, and career path planned for him, where does a parent draw the line? For me, I have changed my expectations about my child's path to options which I mention to him once. As for those expectations which support my child's life—such as getting and staying sober—I have changed these into "shots," non-negotiable household rules. My teenager still has the choice of getting and staying sober or not, but there will be consequences for his failing to follow rules that my spouse and I have determined are necessary for maintaining a healthy life. His choice of clothes, school, career, and mate are solely up to him.

Today's Reminder
My spouse and I together create a few "shots" to keep our child alive and healthy. Then we let go of our specific plans for his life and allow him to choose his own path.

Drug and Alcohol Abusing Teens are Still Teens   February 3

    The Enthusiastic Sobriety drug and alcohol abuse treatment programs were specifically designed for young people. These programs help young people become sober and learn that life can be good without drugs or alcohol. As Bob Meehan said in *Beyond the Yellow Brick Road*, "You can't cure adolescence. It cures itself when people grow up."

    So I've come to see that dealing with my alcoholic teenaged son after he got sober is no different from dealing with my non-alcoholic teenager. They both want to be independent, make their own choices, and not be judged by my husband and me or other adults. By refraining from unnecessary judgment, such as criticizing their taste in music or fashion, I can improve my relationship with both.

Today's Reminder
I bite my tongue rather than state my opinion about my teens' choices in petty matters and I avoid offering them unrequested advice

Breaking the Control Habit — February 4

In the movie, *Freaky Friday*, the daughter accuses her mother of being a control freak. When I started attending our Enthusiastic Sobriety parent meetings, I discovered that I was a control freak, and more importantly—that my controlling behavior really hurt my kids, my husband, and me. How? One "controlling" behavior of mine was to clean closets throughout the house periodically. When I did this, I went into everyone's closet and gave away or threw away any items I believed they didn't need anymore. They got angry with me, and I did not understand why. Other examples of my "controlling" behavior were: to tell each of my kids—and my husband—when they "should" get some exercise, change their clothes, and return a library book that was due soon. (I'd offer to return a library book for them, too.)

I used to consider that just "mothering" behavior, but now I see that to treat adults and teens like that is to treat them like little children. It is disrespectful and demeaning. It is as if I am saying, "You don't have the intelligence, memory, or maturity to take care of these simple life tasks yourself, so *I* have to manage you." It also hurts me because it impairs my relationship with the people I love and care about the most. Plus, it takes a lot of my time and attention which I could direct toward accomplishing my own tasks and goals.

My kid has a bad habit: drugs. I have a bad habit: controlling behavior. They both are destructive and self-defeating in their own ways. Today I want to stop trying to control my loved ones. I want to begin giving more of my attention to living my own life.

Today's Reminder
Today I will only manage myself. I will let others manage themselves.

Waiting for the Other Shoe to Drop — February 5

The more parent meetings I attend, the more I notice a pattern shared by many of us. We always worry. Even when our kids are sober, we cannot relax and enjoy the fact. When things go well for a while, we feel uncomfortable and think that it can't last, that relapse must be just around the corner. It is the waiting-for-the-other-shoe-to-drop phenomenon.

Talking with my sponsor, I realize that I have become so accustomed to things going wrong in the family that I cannot believe it when all is well. Plus, I used to think that worrying helped prepare me for the worst that might happen. Yet, now I realize that worry simply wears me out. During good times, I want to let go of worry about the future and enjoy the present moment. I will replace worry with faith that my Higher Power and the members of the parent group and Al-Anon will help me in times of need.

Today's Reminder
I enjoy the good in the present, trusting that when misfortune arises, I have help from my Higher Power and the group to see me through it.

What's My Motive? February 6

My husband and I attended parent meetings for years. He would often get frustrated with me when I quoted a slogan, "Let go and let God," in situations where he believed I was misusing it to shirk parental duty. Although we both agreed that there is a time to step back and be quiet while a teen is learning how to solve his own problems, my husband would often remind me that as parents of a high school student, we had an obligation to guide and encourage him to lead a responsible, ethical life. Finding a balance between keeping "hands off" so that our kid can learn life lessons and influencing him to make responsible, ethical choices was not always easy. I had to ask myself, whenever I had an urge to "help," "What's my motive?" Whenever my motive was to look good, I realized I had to let go. One example of an action motivated by looking good was doing my son's laundry so he wouldn't look unkempt.

On the other hand, when my motive was to teach or reinforce responsible or ethical behavior, I would offer a *suggestion* without telling our teen what he should do. An example of this was when he left a note on a car he had scratched in a parking lot. He came home, told us about the dent and the note he left, and added that he hoped the owner wouldn't call. The owner did, and he asked for help. I gave him my suggestions and, at his request, stood by him and gave him moral support while he handled it.

Today's Reminder
I encourage my kid to become independent by stepping back and letting him solve his own problems. Equally important, I guide and encourage him to behave responsibly and ethically by providing support when he asks for it.

Obedience to the Unenforceable Laws February 7

The longer I have worked the Twelve Steps, the easier it is for me to understand this phrase. Each time I do something that I feel good about, even when no one is around to see it, my self-esteem is buttressed. This applies not only to obeying unenforceable laws but also doing something extra, not required. For example, if I'm in a public restroom and I see paper towels all over the floor, I will pick these up and put them into the trashcan. No one requires it, but I feel better, a contributing member of society. I suspect that my kids feel the same whenever they "obey the unenforceable" or "go that extra mile."

What happens when I don't obey "unenforceable" laws? Even if I never go to court, I may be afraid that somehow, someday, that unlawful act will come to light. Then I'll be in trouble. Yet, in truth, I am already in trouble if my mind is weighed down with guilt and fear. I cannot live life fully and happily. That is why the steps work—especially the inventory, admission to another, readiness to have our defects removed and ways of thinking changed, and making amends—these help rid me of guilt and fear and help me to live a freer, happier life. When not weighed down by regret, fear, and guilt, life is good.

Today's Reminder
I do my best to be honest in situations where others will not catch me being dishonest. Acting with integrity at all times helps me feel good about myself.

"Honesty is the first chapter in the book of wisdom." ~Thomas Jefferson

How to Use a Sponsor   February 8

How well did I handle my child's drug problem by myself? Not so well. Now I can call on my sponsor. Although I do call my sponsor periodically, there were times that it was crucial for me to call her. Those times were: when my kid relapsed and when I wasn't sure how to handle enforcing a consequence. She not only gave me moral support but also showed me how to apply the principles of the program to real life situations.

In Al-Anon, a sponsor is someone who also has a loved one with an alcohol problem; in the Enthusiastic Sobriety parent programs, a sponsor is another parent of an addicted child. In both programs, a sponsor is usually a person of the same sex who agrees to show another how to work the Twelve Steps of the program and who answers any questions. A sponsor provides understanding without pity, does not give advice, but may suggest how to apply the program's principles.

Meetings provide general support. Each person speaks briefly and generally about how he or she has applied the principles of the program. A sponsor provides one-on-one support and learns the sponsee's whole story in detail.

Sponsorship is an important part of the program. Usually a new person will ask a person who has been in the program longer and is farther along in the Twelve Steps to sponsor him. Sponsorship is a relationship of mutual support. It is uncanny that often while a sponsor discusses a principle of the program with a sponsee, it is the very principle the sponsor needs to remember.

Today's Reminder
Have I called my sponsor lately? Today I will make a point of calling my sponsor, even if it is simply to say, "Hi!" and thank her for being my sponsor

Obsessive Thoughts Can Be Eliminated   February 9

One morning I woke up filled with fear and worry about an incident at work the day before. I couldn't stop thinking about it. This destructive obsession reminded me of how I used to spend most of the hours of my days thinking about my son—what he had done, what he might be doing, what I thought he ought to be doing, and what might happen to him because of his drug addiction.

To stop my obsessive thoughts about the incident at work, I recalled what I did to stop obsessing about my son in the past. I replaced the worry and fear with pleasant, engaging thoughts, preferably about the immediate present or near future. For example, planning an upcoming vacation might require my full mental attention. When my mind returned to its unhealthy obsession, I would gently guide it to something pleasant in the present and immediate environment—such as a breeze, the sunshine, or the warm feel of a sweater. Finally, I would steer my mind toward a survey of all the blessings in my life: all the people, places, and things I was glad to know or have known.

This last subject was very engaging and provided the most long-lasting relief. It helped lift my mind from the uncomfortable, obsessive thoughts to a healthier frame of mind.

Today's Reminder
I can choose to turn my thoughts away from worry and fear and focus on the things for which I feel gratitude right now.

"Gratitude is not only the greatest of virtues, but the parent of all the others." ~Marcus Tullius Cicer

Hope   February 10

Our son was lying to us about where he was and he was verbally belligerent. We would advise him to do certain things, he would agree, and then he would do something totally different. I even remember a time that he blamed me for misplacing one of his items, which he later found where he had left it! My husband and I were suspicious. Something was wrong, and we had no control over our son.

After a while, he came to us and admitted that he had a problem with drugs. We certainly wanted to help him. Together we went to family counseling and also took him to a psychiatrist. Things did not improve, and the psychiatrist kindly admitted that he was not sure he could help our son. He suggested we try one of the Enthusiastic Sobriety programs which provide drug rehabilitation treatment for teens and young adults based on the Twelve Steps.

We went to the Enthusiastic Sobriety parent meetings even before our son decided he would give the program a try. It was as if a fog lifted from us. For the first time there was some hope.

We met other parents. We were not alone. These people knew and understood exactly what we were going through, because they had gone through it themselves. They told us how they had handled certain situations; we now had some possible solutions to our problems. Life started to get better.

Today's Reminder
Finding people who have had similar experiences and getting the benefit of their experience gives me hope.

Am I the Worst Parent in the World?   February 11

That's what I asked myself when I discovered my son had become a drug addict. I went to an Al-Anon meeting where they told me about the "3 C's": "You didn't *cause* it, you can't *control* it, and you can't *cure* it." I also read carefully Bob Meehan's book, *Beyond the Yellow Brick Road*. This recovered drug addict, who created a successful rehabilitation program for young people, said that "parents are not responsible for their children's drug abuse...." He also said that "guilt, anger, inadequacy, hurt, and non-OKness prevent effective parenting. They paralyze us."

I realized that believing that I had caused my son's problem was egotistical. How could I singlehandedly have created his addiction? Didn't he have a choice in the matter? Didn't his father, other family members, schoolmates and friends also influence him? My feeling of inadequacy only hurt me, because it prevented me from taking constructive action.

Today, I *know* that I am neither the worst nor the best parent in the world. I am simply doing my best each day to love and guide my children. I trust in a power greater than myself to help me get through both the good and rough times. I leave the judgment about my parenting to my Higher Power.

Today's Reminder
I cannot control my child. I am not responsible for what other people say or do; I am only responsible for what I say and do. With the guidance of my Higher Power, I will do my best to do the next right thing.

C.R.A.P. February 12

The kids have an acronym in their program, C.R.A.P. "Communication resolves all problems." This works well for parents, too. When I listened at meetings, I began to hear that my "martyrdom" way of "communicating" was not very effective. For example, I would get upset and angry because I felt that I was doing all the work to keep our house clean. So, rather than ask my teens (or even my spouse!) to tackle a particular household chore, such as take out the trash, I would say in an indirect (manipulative) way: "The trash is so full; it's overflowing!" I might even add a sigh for dramatic effect. This never got any results, and in short order I'd be banging pots and pans in the kitchen or slamming doors, but not saying directly what I needed.

I decided to try honest, direct communication. "Would you please take out the trash?"

"Sure, I'll do it in a minute."

Ten minutes later, as I try to stuff more trash into the trashcan: "Could you please empty the trash now?"

"Can't it wait until my TV program is over?"

"I'd prefer you do it now, because it's already full, and I'm cleaning."

"O.K." And he got up and did it!

So I've learned that while direct communication doesn't immediately "work"—that is, get me exactly what I want right away—it does help me negotiate an acceptable settlement with another human being. I don't build up toxic levels of anger and martyrdom, like I used to do.

Today's Reminder
Communication resolves all problems

Giving Advice: *Not*   February 13

Despite the poignant scenes from the old television program *Father Knows Best*, I have learned that a good parent does not give his kid any advice unless his kid actually asks him for it. Even then, keep it short.

Before getting into the program, I was constantly telling my kid what to do and how to run his life. "Shut off the TV and do your homework," "Stop playing computer games and go mow the lawn," "You should try out for the team," and "Be sure to save some of your allowance for a rainy day," were the types of things I said. I also frequently criticized: "You only got a "B" in math; you should have gotten an "A," "Don't just sit around, look for a job or volunteer," or "Your room is a mess; you've got to get more organized!"

Today I know to let my kid run his own life. Now that he is sober—one day at a time—he is able to learn again. Plus he learns so much better if I steer clear. I keep my mouth shut and don't tell him how I would handle his problem. He can decide what to do, do it, and see how it goes for him. Then he can use that information to make future decisions. Life is a great teacher. When he was little and couldn't think through things, he needed me to help him learn how to solve problems. Now, as a teenager, he needs to learn from life, not me.

Today's Reminder
The next time I want to tell my kid what he should do, I will bite my tongue. He learns better from life, not me.

Love, Hope and Perseverance   February 14

After participating in a few months of parent support meetings I have learned that the greatest commonality that we all share is our love for our addicted children, hope for them, and the drive to never give up. My son has put himself through many ups, downs, setbacks and relapses. He has put our whole family through sleepless nights and worries as well as trials and tribulations beyond our control. If I didn't love him unconditionally, I would not have been able to endure the last few years of this disease of addiction. I have learned through listening to other parents how they dealt with similar situations and came out on the other side healthy and happy, whether or not their child got sober. I have learned that at times I had to detach and accept what is. I had to let my son go. Homeless, under the influence of drugs and alcohol, barefoot, jobless and sad was my son. Yet I still loved him enough not to accept unacceptable behavior. Later, in God's time, not mine, my son decided to get sober.

Every child may or may not get sober. Regardless, I believe all our addicted children are gifts, not burdens. Never give up loving your gift!

Today's Reminder
I love my children enough to refuse to accept unacceptable behavior.

Few Hard and Fast Rules   February 15

Every time one of our kids did something unexpected which caused us to be concerned about his or her safety, we created a new rule to cover the situation. This gave us a false sense of security. Yet, experience has taught us that, when motivated, teens are very resourceful and will always find new ways to thwart parental authority. A new unexpected behavior caused us to create yet another rule, until we had so many individual rules that we couldn't keep track of them all. My spouse and I learned that it was better to decide our core values and set three to five non-negotiable rules we could agree upon. We then created a "united front" so that our teens could not successfully "divide and conquer." Our rules: no sex or drugs—including alcohol—and no crimes. (Rock'n'roll is o.k.) Everything else is open to negotiation *before* the event occurs (such as giving permission for the teen to stay out late or do something new). We learned to consider everything else together, one request at a time.

Today's Reminder
Taking into account our core values, my partner and I will create only a few rules for our teens.

Silence is Golden (It's Not About Me)   February 16

When someone—especially my teenager—is angry with me, I have to remember that it's not usually about me. Most likely, it's a personal storm s/he is going through. Even if I said or did something that triggered my teen's very vocal or demonstrative reaction, I need to let go. I have found that both my teens go through personal "storms" which are part of the hormonal reality of teen development. Now I can choose to weather the storm in the best way for me. This usually means going elsewhere to minimize my exposure to their outbursts and doing something while the storm passes. When I get out of the storm's path and seek silence, life can be good.

Today's Reminder
I do not take my teenagers' anger personally. When my teen starts to rail, I detach physically and remind myself to stay calm; it's not about me.

Parenting with Rules, "Walls," and "Shots"   February 17

Listening to Enthusiastic Sobriety parents share at meetings and reflecting on my own experience, I realized how important it is to maintain a "united front." In our family, I was the parent who could not enforce rules. I would make excuses for my son for breaking the rules and give him "another chance." My husband, on the other hand, was the disciplinarian. In some couples, the roles are reversed. Yet the result for the kids was the same: the kids were deprived of firm rules and consequences. They began to believe that the rules—both at home and the outside world—did not apply to them. This belief caused them trouble.

My husband and I had to establish a united front, examine our values, and establish walls (aka "rules" or "boundaries.") and shots (absolute, nonnegotiable rules whose violation results in serious, nonnegotiable consequences). We decided to establish the three shots used by the Enthusiastic Sobriety programs for continued participation: no drugs or alcohol "in you or on you"' no fighting, and no sex. We also included a fourth shot: no other illegal activity (because our son had previously engaged in theft to support his habit.) There was one other rule: a curfew. Violation of the curfew was not a "shot," but would result in our son's being prohibited from going out after meetings or functions or sleeping over at another kid's house the following day.
Despite the time commitment, my husband and I found that in discussing our values, and agreeing on rules, walls, and shots, we helped our son *and* helped ourselves become closer as a couple.

Today's Reminder
We will create a united front, set and enforce household rules so that our teen will learn from consequences.

Avoiding the New Technological Rescue   February 18

I have been told that some things I did intending to help my son had actually hindered him from becoming sober. (For example, I made excuses for his absences from high school classes, and I kept giving him money for "lunch" which I suspected was being used for marijuana.) He remained "stoned," emotionally immature, and dependent when I rescued him from the consequences of his behavior.

Reading a magazine article, I learned that many college students today rely more and more on advice from home. They text or call parents frequently during their day, thus nullifying the beneficial effects of being away from home. A parent who rescues his college-aged child from solving life problems will have, in the end, a college graduate who is still a child. Grateful for the lesson I've learned in our Enthusiastic Sobriety program, I will not "rescue" my adult child who is away at college. If I receive a call for advice, I will consider whether my child can solve this problem for himself before offering advice. I will remember the advice another Enthusiastic Sobriety parent gave me. Say, "I love you and have faith in you. You have a good head on your shoulders and can use it." Validation and the opportunity to act on one's own help a young person mature.

Today's Reminder
I will not do for my teen or adult child what he can do for himself. I will give him the dignity to make his own decisions.

Working Our Program   February 19
   Benefits the Entire Family

When our son was at the nadir of his addiction, he lost all interest in sports and other activities he had previously enjoyed. He failed to attend classes regularly. His grades plummeted. He was secretive and deceptive and seemingly cared about nothing except getting high. We feared he would ruin his life or end up dead. We made the difficult decision to withdraw our son from his high school and tell him his only choice was which of several drug treatment programs he would enter. With our encouragement, he reluctantly checked out one of the

Enthusiastic Sobriety programs for himself. Fortunately, he identified with the program counselors who are young adults and recovered addicts.

Our son got sober, returned to school, and learned to drive a car responsibly. Most important for the family, he works his program, which includes not only staying away from drugs and alcohol, but also being honest and doing "the next right thing." When he is wrong, he admits it.[1] Imagine having a teenager admit he is wrong and apologizing! I almost fell over the first time this happened, but now we are all "working our program."

His example has led all of us to be more straightforward and honest in our communications. For instance, I no longer expect my teen to read my mind and help around the house with chores. I request that he do specific chores, and he follows through. When I make a mistake or promise something which I later realize I can't deliver, I promptly admit it to my kids and together we work out a way to resolve the matter. When each of us consciously works at being rigorously honest and does "the next right thing," everyone in the family benefits.

Today's Reminder

I will look at my own behavior and see how I can make changes to improve my relationship with all my family members. When wrong, I will promptly admit it.

---

[1] The Enthusiastic Sobriety Programs' Step Ten reads, "We have continued to look at ourselves and when wrong, promptly admitted it."

Unearned Highs   February 20

In the book *Beyond the Yellow Brick Road*, Bob Meehan talks about teen-aged drug addicts experiencing "unearned highs" and defines *highs* as being put "in a place where you feel good about yourself." While the normal person works to achieve a goal and feels good about his accomplishment, the addict feels good about himself merely by consuming a substance. A person, who has little experience of feeling good about himself but for drug or alcohol use, has very low self-esteem.

Coming from an economically disadvantaged background, I frequently gave my kids lots of material things, to make up for all the things I didn't have as a kid. Yet this was providing them with many "unearned highs." Once sober, my son needed to experience "earned highs." I encouraged him to work for material things he wanted, especially a car. In the meantime, he could borrow the family car, so long as he paid for gas, his portion of the insurance, maintenance and repairs. Today—years later—he works, lives on his own, is well able to handle his own finances, and has a healthy dose of confidence.

Today's Reminder
I will encourage my teen to work toward goals and earn rewards through his own effort.

I am Responsible—NOT!   February 21

Today I believe that the only time it is appropriate for a parent to force a solution is to intervene and insist upon substance abuse treatment because a child's life is endangered. I have learned, though, to be careful because of my tendency to feel responsible for everything and everybody.

In fact, my problem is assuming *too much* responsibility and not letting others take care of their own responsibilities. As a mother, I have often felt I had to solve problems for everyone in my family. I thrust my proposed solutions into their faces. I have to keep in mind that it is only appropriate to help another person if that person wants help and *asks* for my help.

Also, as a parent of an alcoholic and drug addict, I have felt that it is my duty to teach my child how to handle life's problems by example. Yet, I often forget that the example I set must be of me handling my *own* problems; I must give my teen the dignity of discovering his own solutions.

Today's Reminders

As a parent I can set an example of problem solving by facing my *own* problems. I will give my teen the dignity to solve his own problems and be available for guidance only if he *asks* for it.

Finding and Maintaining the Courage to Change

February 22

Most of the parents in our group found it difficult to set and enforce boundaries. The Serenity Prayer, especially the line, "the courage to change the things I can," has helped. We realized that the only power we have is to *change our own behavior*, because we cannot *make* our teens change.

My husband and I told our son, "You can't use and live in this house. We will not support any way for you to use, buy, or sell drugs." When he was using and left home, we disconnected his cell phone. We had to wait for him to contact us, admit he had a problem, and agree to go back into treatment. We were afraid for his life, but we knew that if he wanted to, he certainly knew how to contact us.

I got through this terrible time by doing a number of things. I attended Al-Anon meetings and the weekly Enthusiastic Sobriety parent meetings. I read Al-Anon literature and other literature about teens and drug addiction (Bob Meehan's books) and about co-dependency (Melody Beattie's books.)[2] I also called many of the other parents from the group. Talking with other parents who offered moral support helped. I prayed often. All these tools: Twelve Step meetings, reading relevant literature, phoning group members, and prayer gave me the courage to change my behavior and do "the next right thing."

Today's Reminder
I will change my parenting. I will have consequences for wrong behavior in place. I will use all the tools of the program, including: meetings, literature, phone calls, prayer, and meditation to help get through rough times.

"Love means not accepting wrong behavior. Love means establishing walls [rules]." *Beyond the Yellow Brick Road* (bracketed word added for explanation)

A Disease or a Choice? February 23

One parent complained, "I don't buy this disease model of addiction. My son has a choice to use drugs or not." As parents,

---

[2] See the Appendix: For Further Reading which lists Meehan's books and some of Beattie's books.

we have all felt angry with our kids for becoming addicts and treating us so badly, and we also needed to feel like good parents whose kids made poor choices beyond our control.

I believe that addiction is both a disease *and* a choice. Once a person is addicted, he continues to engage in behavior which he knows has negative consequences. (It costs money he could use for other expenses; it takes time to find the substance of choice and acquire it; it may cause mental states in which he does something he later regrets, etc.) A rational person doesn't make such a choice more than once or twice.

My son stole to support his habit. Although my husband and I realized our high school student had been "experimenting" with marijuana and alcohol, we were not aware of the extent of his drinking and drug use. Finding out that he had been stealing woke us from our denial. I asked my son, "Why did you steal? We've taught you right from wrong. Don't you know stealing is wrong?" He answered, "I didn't care." An addict's choice to use is a "forced choice," because the addiction is so strong that he forces all the good reasons to stop using out of his mind. He doesn't care.

Regardless of what I call it, I still do not control another person's choice *or* disease. The only thing I can do is learn how to make the best parenting choices I can through working the Twelve Steps myself.

Today's Reminder
Because my child has deceived me, it is understandable that I am angry. I will feel the anger and then let it go. Today I will focus on my *own* choices and make the best ones I can, with the guidance of my Higher Power.

Shots and Walls February 24

In Bob Meehan's book, *Beyond the Yellow Brick Road*, he talks about establishing "shots" and "walls" for our kids, which translates loosely into setting boundaries or limits and creating rules with logical consequences. He advises parents to keep the number of shots under six. Shots are non-negotiable rules whose violation results in severe consequences. Walls are more flexible guidelines or boundaries. They may relate to tasks such as household chores or curfew. These work best when they include a deadline: e.g. "Clean your room before Saturday at 5 p.m." or "Get a job within a month."

Our son knew that if he drank or got high, he would not be welcome in our home. That was a shot. In contrast, in addition to chores and curfew walls, we created a wall against smoking cigarettes. He was free to smoke elsewhere, but not in our home. Later in his recovery, he noticed that he was too winded to keep up with his younger sibling at the gym. Soon, he quit smoking. We said nothing until it was clear that he had broken the habit; then we acknowledged him for his accomplishment.

Today's Reminder
I keep the number of "shots" to a minimum, saving non-negotiable household rules for behavior I find most offensive. For less offensive behavior, I will use "walls" and let my teenager know that I don't approve.

Parenting and Trust February 25

When our son was drinking and drugging, I wanted to trust him, but experience revealed the foolishness of trusting an active addict not to lie and steal. The pattern of distrust developed over time and I felt as if I couldn't trust him with anything. I became hyper vigilant, checking on him to see if he was where he said he was and doing what he was supposed to be doing. He usually wasn't. This pattern of behavior bred more suspicion and lack of confidence in our relationship. Our family situation became ugly.

We received a respite from this distrustful environment once he entered the treatment program and he was out of the house. My husband and I worked together to develop a united front and required our son follow a few household rules. We stopped hoping that everything would work out the way we wanted. We trusted that whatever happened, things would be better if we prayed for guidance and acted on that guidance. Creating a united front and enforcing household rules, we did our best to guide and nurture our son without enabling or coddling him. We began to feel good about our parenting, regardless of how our son responded. Our confidence indirectly improved our relationship with our son. He knew that we meant what we said. After a while he became more trusting, open, and honest with us.

Today's Reminder
I trust that my Higher Power is guiding me now. I listen and I follow, letting go of the outcome and trusting that I will learn something valuable from the experience.

Living in the Moment — February 26

Recently I was reminded of the value of living in the moment and the need to "let go and let God" when faced with circumstances I do not like. Our son is in recovery and lives with another boy in our local Enthusiastic Sobriety program. My son and I planned to spend some time together and see a movie. He asked if his roommate could join us, and I agreed and pre-purchased tickets online for the three of us. I enjoy movies and like to see the movie from beginning to end; I really hate arriving late.

As the time for picking up my son and his roommate approached, my son told me that his roommate was not going to be able to join us. I was not happy, because I had purchased three tickets. However, he suggested that another friend might be able to come. We contacted this friend who did join us. However, this took ten or fifteen minutes to arrange. At this point we were a half hour's drive from the theater and it was 15 minutes before show time. I was angry but tried not to show it. I didn't want to spoil the time with my son. He knew me and said, "Dad, there's nothing we can do about it. We are going to be late. Accept it and let go." I knew he was right, so I decided to accept it, live in the moment, and enjoy the time with my son.

We arrived at the theater to find only seven other people in the entire theater. We had our pick of seats, and we did not have to sit through all the previews and ads. The feature presentation did not start until we were in our seats. Was I surprised! It was a wonderful experience of letting go.

Today's Reminder
If things do not go as planned, I will remember that God has a better idea.

Substance Abuse is a Disease   **February 27**

It was very difficult for my husband and me when we realized that our teenaged daughter had a drug problem. Nothing we did to get her to stop using drugs worked. Her drug use rapidly increased, and we saw that soon she would not be healthy enough to continue school. We were afraid that she might never make it to college. When we were looking for a treatment center for her, the first thing we learned is that an addict is unlikely to be successfully treated until she wants treatment. We repeatedly asked her if she was ready for help; had she hit bottom yet? When she admitted she had a problem and said she wanted help we decided to withdraw her from high school so she could fully focus on the drug treatment program. We reasoned that her health had to come first. If she had cancer, we would not ignore it nor would we attempt to cure it ourselves. As her parents, we needed to be sure she got the proper treatment. Through our participation in the local Enthusiastic Sobriety parent group, we have learned so much that helps us understand and live with our daughter's addiction. We are fortunate that our daughter realized that she had a problem and wanted help.

Today's Reminder
Just as if my child had cancer, I will do my best to seek proper treatment for abuse of alcohol or drugs. I will not try to treat it myself. I will seek treatment for my child's condition and learn from other families of alcoholics or addicts how better to cope.

Being Thankful   February 28

The best way to get through a tough day is to keep remembering what I am thankful for. The day after my son relapsed, I went to work. Whenever I started to return to worry and fear, I "re-minded" my thoughts back to gratitude. At work I had to review several documents, but I kept re-reading the same page. I couldn't concentrate. Having learned in the Enthusiastic Sobriety program to be kind to myself, I acknowledged that it was okay that I was having a rough day.

I took a short break and called my sponsor; I couldn't reach her, so I called another parent in the program and told her that my son had relapsed. She listened for a few minutes. She understood my pain. By talking with her, my pain lessened. I felt comforted. I went back to my task at work and got it done. I was grateful I had completed the document review that day. I gave myself a mental pat on the back for getting some work done.

I knew I was tired and needed a boost. There were no Enthusiastic Sobriety parent meetings that evening, but I found an Al-Anon meeting that night. I went. I listened. I shared. By the end of the meeting, my spirits had lifted and I felt hopeful. When I put my head on my pillow that night I thanked the groups—Al-Anon and our Enthusiastic Sobriety group, all the individuals in these groups, and God for getting me through the day. I was also able to thank God that my son was still alive and had a chance to return to sobriety if he chose.

Today's Reminder
On a tough day I can remember to be kind to myself. I can call another parent in the program, go to a meeting, and be thankful that tomorrow is another day.

"This too shall pass." ~Unknown

Breathe   February 29

Whenever I catch myself going down a mental path that I don't want to go down (such as worry and fear) I redirect my mind through a simple technique in which I focus on the slogan, "Let go and let God." I breathe in slowly and deeply while I think, "Let God" and breathe out slowly and fully while I think, "Let go." The slow breathing in conjunction with remembering this slogan helps me calm down. After doing this, I can consciously change my thoughts to more productive ones. As I change my thoughts, my feelings improve, too, and my day goes better.

Today's Reminder
Should I become worried or afraid today, I will breathe in slowly and think, "Let God;" then I will breathe out slowly and think, "Let go."

MARCH

Blame   **March 1**

When I first discovered my son was frequently getting high at his high school, I was angry. I blamed the school for having an "open campus" with no supervision; I blamed the teachers and staff for turning a blind eye to the students who were smoking marijuana on the school premises; I blamed the kids who introduced my son to marijuana.

Then I turned to self-recrimination. It was all my fault my son had become addicted to marijuana. I blamed myself for not monitoring his friends well enough, for not giving him enough attention, for working long hours and not having enough quality time with him.

Much later, after starting to go to Al-Anon meetings and Enthusiastic Sobriety parent meetings, I saw that indulging in blame was an unhealthy obsession and distraction from solving the problem. When I worked the steps and did my inventory, I saw that I had no control over the school, teachers and staff, students, and even my son. While I could not control my son, I certainly had the ability to change the way I acted around him. I could set a few rules—known as "walls and shots" in the Enthusiastic Sobriety programs—and enforce them. This *did* influence my son, who decided to join our local Enthusiastic Sobriety program and become clean and sober. When the family all started working the steps, our lives improved.

Today's Reminder
Today I will turn my thoughts from blame and the past to taking responsibility for the present and making changes to influence the future.

Working My Program   March 2

When I started attending parent meetings, I was told not to focus on my child, but on myself. I was told to "work my own program" and that if I focused on my son instead of myself, I would impede his progress.

I was told that I have developed an addiction, too, as the result of living with him, an addiction to worry and fear. I knew this was true; I had spent so much time and energy worrying about him and his future that I had become sick with worry.

So I asked, "How do I work my own program?" I was told: go to meetings, read Twelve Step literature, get a sponsor, call her regularly, and work the first four Enthusiastic Sobriety steps (similar to the first three Al-Anon steps) each day.

So now when I wake up, I remind myself that drugs and alcohol made my family life unmanageable. (Step One) I am thankful for the support I have now from other families with a drug-addicted child. For the time being, I do not spend much time with parents who do not have a drug-addicted child. I especially watch myself and avoid any temptation to compare my child to others or to start thinking about my child's future. (Step Two) I thank God for a new day, tell myself that it will be a good one, and focus on what I can do today to make it so. (Step Three) I focus on what I can control, my words and actions, and ask my higher power to help me make good decisions throughout the day. (Step Four) By letting go of my fearful thoughts and turning my mind to more constructive ones, I find relief from my own addiction.

Today's Reminder
I will focus on my own program today and free myself from worry and fear.

Turning from Resentment and Self-Pity — March 3

When we were arranging to put our son into the drug treatment program that he selected, we stopped at a local coffee shop before going to write the big check for treatment. I was already miserable and filled with self-pity when I overheard a conversation between two women. One was telling the other that she just didn't know how to decide which luggage to take on her trip to Europe. The more I overheard her struggle with this decision, the more I wallowed in self-pity. I thought, "What a problem! I wish *I* were fretting over a trip to Europe and spending thousands on a good time instead of spending thousands on my kid, with no guarantee that he'll recover from his drug addiction. He could end up dead if he keeps using drugs!" That kind of thinking naturally made me feel worse.

Since our son got into the Enthusiastic Sobriety program and my husband and I started attending the parent meetings, I began to be aware of the detrimental effect of negative thoughts. Comparing myself to others and feeling like a victim hurts me and, equally important, prevents me from effectively coping with problems. When I can turn from resentment and self-pity, remember that I can make choices, and choose to look on the bright side, I gain confidence and face difficulties more effectively.

Today's Reminder
I replace thoughts of resentment and self-pity with thoughts of appreciation for the good and my ability to choose. This empowers me to face and solve my problems.

"Stress Is the Result of Trying to Control the Uncontrollable."   March 4

Beginning her senior year of high school, my daughter, who had been a member of a church youth group, started acting differently. She went to a party, did not telephone, and did not return home that night. Frantic, I called the police and had them look for her. She came home drunk the next morning. She started disappearing for two days at a time and returning home drunk and/or high. Previously a conscientious student, fall semester she failed most of her classes. Eventually, while she was drunk one night, she got into trouble and had criminal charges brought against her. The court required her to wear a bracelet to monitor her alcohol intake. She also was required to have periodic urine analyses. I was a wreck worrying about her and trying to control my "out of control" daughter. I started attending Al-Anon meetings twice a week. This really helped me. They told me, "You didn't cause it, you can't control it, and you can't cure it."

One night she disappeared again and did not return home for a week. She greeted me with gibberish, unable to carry on a coherent conversation. She was high on something, and I was terrified. I felt that if I did not act right away, she might go out again and not come back alive. One of the ladies at Al-Anon had told me about an Enthusiastic Sobriety program in our area, and I telephoned and spoke with an Enthusiastic Sobriety counselor who suggested I bring my daughter there to see him. I got her into the car, activated the child locks, and drove her there immediately. It has been a rocky ride. It took her five months to get sober, but in the meantime, I continued attending meetings and learned better tools to cope. I stopped trying to control her and started taking care of myself. My stress has been relieved.

Today's Reminder
I can get my child into an alcohol and drug rehabilitation program, but the decision to participate is hers. I do what I can, take care of myself, and let go of the rest.

With One Leg in the Past and One in the Future, What am I Doing with Today?   March 5

While my kid is addicted to drugs, I must confess that I'm addicted to regret, worry and fear (the three terrible horsemen). I used to provide lots of space in my mind to thoughts of the terrible three. I'd relive past situations and continue to scold myself for my poor behavior. I'd also consider the future and wonder, "What if he gets into a car with a drunken or stoned friend?" "What if he ditches school again?" or "What if we have to go to court?" Then I would visualize all kinds of miserable scenarios with the worst possible outcomes, even revising some to arrive at even more dire results! (Did I mention I am a drama queen?)

Through the Twelve Step program, I have learned to say "no" to my addiction. As soon as I realize where my thoughts are going, I stop. I remember what my sponsor told me, "You can't change your past." And "Why assume the worst? It *is* possible that something good might happen in the future!" By consciously changing my thoughts, I give myself a break from the cycle of regret, worry, and fear. Sometimes, when I'm really upset and can't change my thoughts but know these thoughts are making me miserable, I telephone another parent in the program who can help me think it through and get me thinking in a healthier, more realistic way. Then I can go about my daily activities with some peace of mind.

Today's Reminder
I let go of my addiction to unproductive thoughts; I do not waste today. Receiving guidance from my Higher Power, I focus on my plans for the day and do what needs to be done. Then at the end of the day, I can honestly say, "It's been a good day" and feel at peace.

Accepting Things I Cannot Change   March 6

Tabula rasa was an old theory stating that each child comes into the world as a "blank slate." Every parent soon learns that this theory doesn't fit reality. Each child has his or her own personality and while we can take advantage of a child's innate abilities and predispositions to encourage particular behavior, we have no power to change our child's basic make-up.

For example, our son, who loves physical activity, was not willing to sit quietly for an hour and do homework. When he was little, I quickly learned to work *with* his strengths, not against them. To finish his school assignments, he would read in 15 minute segments, followed by a "break" where he could get around and move. When I accepted his nature and gave him the time and space to do his assignments in a way that would work for him, he got them done. I had to give up insisting he spend uninterrupted time doing homework so that he could get it done within *my* preferred time frame (which was homework first before all other activities.)

Similarly, when we learned of his drug and alcohol addiction, we had to accept this and get our high school student into treatment. Once again I had to let go of *my* schedule. I wanted him to be out of treatment in six weeks, back in school, and involved in sports and other extracurricular activities. I had to let go and accept that drug and alcohol addiction is serious and life-threatening; it requires more than six weeks of treatment before a more "normal" life can be resumed. I am glad I learned to be more patient with my son, because although it took longer than I wished, we now have a more "normal" life today.

Today's Reminder
I will let go of my schedule for my child and be patient with his own internal schedule. I see him as a flower, slowly unfolding into his unique beauty.

"Working the Steps"   March 7

One day I decided to apply the steps to all the stressful situations in my life. The first challenge that morning was my teen-aged daughter was not up in time to get a ride from me to school. I started to feel pressure, because if I waited for her to be ready, I would be late for work. This was definitely unmanageable! (Step One: "We admitted...that our lives had become unmanageable.")

To release the pressure building from trying to do two mutually exclusive things at once, I decided to take care of myself. The counselors and the other parents had told me to let my child "own" her behavior, so I followed their advice and told my daughter that I had to leave and she would have to find another way to get to school. I went to work.

Part of me felt guilty for not taking my daughter to school, and I prayed, "God, please help this come out alright!" (Al-Anon's Step Two: "Came to believe that a power greater than ourselves could restore us to sanity." and Step Three: "Made a decision to turn our will and our lives over to the care of God *as we understood Him*.") Things did work out that day. She found another ride and got to school a few minutes late, and I got to work on time. With more practice working the steps, I now know that even when things don't work out the way I'd like them to, God gives me the ability to cope with whatever circumstances arise.

Today's Reminder
I will use the steps to help me discern new ways of coping with frustrating situations.

Changing My Mindset　　　　　　　　　　March 8

Once I started going to Enthusiastic Sobriety parent meetings and Al-Anon meetings, reading the literature, and talking with other parents, I began to feel less stressed about our family situation. I saw that I was not alone, and that there was hope. Many teens had become sober and were staying sober. After awhile, I began to stop myself from mentally cataloguing every conceivable bleak "What if" scenario involving my son. However, one evening, I forgot to turn my mind away from the negative. My son hadn't returned home at the time I expected him, and he failed to call. I tried to call his cell phone, only to have it go directly to voice mail. I immediately began thinking of car accidents, hospitals, morgues, and then called my sponsor in a panic. She reminded me that it was also possible that my son was having sober fun with his friends and had lost track of the time, or had turned off his cell phone. I needed that reminder. Ironically, after my call to my sponsor, my son called from his friend's cell phone. He apologized for being late, said that his cell phone battery was dead, and that he had lost track of time. He was fine and returned home within the hour. I learned that it's just as possible that something neutral or good has happened as something bad. Changing my mind from the negative to neutral or positive saves me from useless worry.

Today's Reminder
When I start to think, "What if…[something bad happens to my kid]," I'll remember that good things can happen, too.

Gratitude   March 9

How am I grateful? Let me count the ways. Counting my blessings quickly works to adjust my attitude. This little trick is especially helpful when I start to see my life as a "half-empty glass" instead of "half-full."

In the past I felt justified—because of my child's s drug addiction—to have feelings of self-pity, martyrdom, victimization, jealousy, resentment and fear. Thinking about the good in my life dissolves those negative feelings. By focusing on what is good in my life, I start to balance my thinking. Gratitude does not make life's problems disappear, but it does enable me to appraise them more realistically and bolsters my courage in tackling them. I have been told by an AA friend that we each have a "magic magnifying mind;" whatever we choose to focus on magnifies. Because I want good things in my life, I will try, one day at a time—sometimes one minute at a time—to focus on the good I have.

Today's Reminder
Today when I see I need an attitude adjustment, I will count my blessings.

"Life is good." ~*Bumper Stickers*

Grateful for Hindsight   March 10

I really feel grateful as I look back over the years. I watched other parents whose kids were sober for awhile, and I wondered, "Will I ever be able to say that my son is sober and doing well?" I decided that I had to have faith that if I stayed in the program I could get to a better place. I did. "One day at a time."

I know that our family's journey is not over. With baby steps, I'm in a better place. My son has his ups and downs. He has had relapses. So have I.

I use many of the slogans to get me through rough times. The Serenity Prayer is my favorite. At times, I needed to say it once every 10 minutes. But I've used many slogans, such as: "One day at a time," "Fake it until you make it," and "FEAR stands for 'False events appearing real,' or 'Face everything and recover.'"

Sometimes saying the slogans like mantras was all that got me through the week until the next parent meeting. Staying in the program has helped my worries subside and my attitude become more hopeful.

Today's Reminder
Should I fall into worry or fear, I will use a slogan or the Serenity Prayer to help me regain hope.

## The Three C's													March 11

I had heard about the "three C's": "You didn't cause it; you can't control it, and you can't cure it." At first, it was really hard to believe that as a mother, I was not responsible for my child's alcoholism and drug addiction. Yet, someone asked me, "Would you blame yourself if your child had tuberculosis?" I realized that blaming myself was counterproductive. I needed to focus on my parental job of seeing that my child got the treatment for his illness that he needed. I realized it was *not* my place to try to "cure" him—which I can't do. My role was to get him to a treatment program, and I personally believe the programs based on the Twelve Steps of Alcoholics Anonymous are the most effective.

So my husband and I told our son that he had to be in a treatment program if he wanted to live with us, but that we would take him to different programs and let him choose the program. We did this because we can't control what he does, we can only tell him what *we* are going to do, and follow through with what we say. Of course, I was afraid he would run away from home. (He was underage at the time.) We were lucky—and I am so grateful—that he decided that he would stay home and go into treatment. We then learned to let the counselors work with him and to stay out of his treatment. So long as he continues the program, *how* he works his Twelve Step program is not our business. Since that time, our home life has gone much more smoothly.

Today's Reminder
If my child has a substance abuse problem, I can't cure it. I will do my parental duty by seeking appropriate treatment and encouraging him to accept treatment.

Overcoming Shame — March 12

Discovering that my son had a problem with marijuana and alcohol, I thought that he was throwing his life away. I also felt guilty and ashamed, because I believed that I had done something to cause his addiction. While my husband and I were looking over our health insurance plans and trying to find a treatment program for our son, I remembered there was a support group that existed for the family of problem drinkers, Al-Anon, and I went. I heard that it was best to go to 90 meetings in 90 days, and I found a local meeting which met every week day. What a relief! I learned that alcoholism is medically recognized as a disease, and that I need not blame myself for my son's condition—no more so than I would if he had tuberculosis. As I continued to go to meetings, I began to feel better. My son was not sober, but *I* felt more like I could cope with the situation. I did not have to be stuck in feelings of guilt or shame. (I heard that S.H.A.M.E. is the belief that I "should have already mastered everything.") I felt okay about learning more about alcoholism, how alcoholics and addicts act, and obtaining tools for coping.

Once the guilt and shame were lifted from my shoulders, I could share responsibility with my husband for finding a treatment program for our son who eventually entered our local Enthusiastic Sobriety program. Soon my husband and I began attending the weekly parent meetings and our whole family began recovering from the effects of alcohol and other mind-changing chemicals.

Today's Reminder
I am not alone. When I find others at a Twelve Step meeting who are coping with similar struggles, I can draw on their experience, strength, and hope to cope with my child and our family's problem.

"Hope deferred maketh the heart sick: but when the desire cometh, it is a tree of life." Proverbs 13:12

Tough Love with Compassion   March 13

I remember being very angry that my son was smoking marijuana and perhaps getting prescription drugs from classmates at his local high school. The school has an "open campus"; there is no monitoring of the school halls or grounds, and students can come and go as they please. I was angry that the school had facilitated an environment where teens could engage in such activities. I felt as though society and the courts were blaming me for my son's drug use; yet I was not even at the school where it occurred! However, I began attending Al-Anon meetings daily, got a sponsor, and started working the steps. I realized that my focus on "blame and shame" was getting me nowhere. No one can control a teen-aged drug addict!

Because I love my son, I had to intervene and find help. I insisted that my son receive drug rehabilitation and took him out of school for treatment. He got to choose the treatment program, but he had to go. Tough love, in the form of intervention, combined with compassion for the difficulty of breaking an addictive habit, moved us forward. When I focused my thoughts on possible solutions and did not dwell on the problem, I began to find answers.

Today's Reminder
I move my thoughts from blame and shame about the problem toward compassion with a firm insistence on working toward a solution.

Think   March 14

I have often done things for my children when I didn't feel like it or when a nagging part of me felt that they were clearly old enough to do these things for themselves. Later, I felt angry and I would add the item to a mental list of "all I've done for you" to lash out at them whenever they really irritated me. One day I was struck by the idea that I really hated having this mental list. It tied me down to a feeling of resentment for my children. I wanted to avoid future resentments. The first thing I decided I could do whenever I felt I "ought" to "help" my teenager was to stop and *think* before I acted. Did I really need to bring that assignment to school that was left on the kitchen counter? Wouldn't he learn more by experiencing the consequence of not having brought it? Wouldn't I feel better if I didn't interrupt my own plans to bring it to the school? It felt strange, and at first I felt a pang of guilt, but I soon realized that a brief pang of guilt was worth saving myself from days of resentment.

Today's Reminder
Today I will pause before I rush to do something for my children. In doing this, would I be assuming their rightful

responsibilities? What will they learn if I do this? And will I feel angry and resentful after doing it?

"An ounce of prevention is worth a pound of cure." ~Benjamin Franklin

Being Quiet   March 15

My child had gotten into the bad habit of pestering me for things he wanted, even though my default response was usually, "No." He would go on to badger me, sometimes to the point of yelling at me, until finally I would succumb and he got what he wanted. This left me frustrated and angry. He would badger me for things as trivial as $5.00 as well as more significant requests such as permission to extend his curfew a few hours for a "worthy" cause. For whatever reason, I felt it was my obligation to give him an immediate answer.

Early in our recovery, a parent mentioned the simple technique of being quiet. She suggested I just listen when my child makes a request. Then I could calmly reply, "Let me get together with your dad about this, and we'll get back to you."

Wow! What power those words had! I no longer felt like I owed him an immediate response to every request, and when we did get back with him, whether it was affirmative or negative, he accepted the response with minimal to no arguing. This technique gave my husband and me the power of a united front. Our child would no longer go behind the back of one of us to get something he wanted from the other. He knew we were talking to each other, and he could no longer manipulate us.

Today's Reminder
A teenager's request need not be answered immediately. Today, when my teen asks me something I wish to consider, I will consult with his other parent. When a parental agreement is reached, I will respond to my teen's request.

"Whatever you decide, stick with your principles and remain both logical and loving—and always remain united and consistent." ~*Beyond the Yellow Brick Road*

Divorce and Different Household Rules March 16

Before program I was not as firm with my kids as I knew I should be. Then my husband and I separated and eventually divorced. Hearing from the Enthusiastic Sobriety parents that I needed to have "shots" (non-negotiable rules and consequences) and "walls" (negotiable rules) and to present a "united front" with my kids' father upset me. My ex-husband felt uncomfortable with a Twelve Step program. He did his best to attend parent meetings until our oldest child finished the outpatient treatment program. After that, he did not participate. I knew that my getting angry and frustrated would not help our kids. I also knew from the program that I can't control other people.

What I did control was my words, actions, and home. I set up walls and shots for my home and enforced these, with the help of my sponsor, other parents, and the counselors. My kids learned that Mom "means what she says and says what she means." Also, when my kids were visiting their father, I consciously chose to avoid self-pity; I made sure to do something positive for myself

At this time my relationship with my kids is good. As we all continue working our own Twelve Step programs, life gets better and better.

Today's Reminder
I cannot control others, but I can take control of my own life. I will create walls and shots for my home and enforce them so that my children know I mean what I say.

Better Bipolar than a Drunk or Drug Abuser   March 17

When my son was in middle school, he began experimenting with pot but I didn't worry. It was just pot, not a big deal. By high school he started skipping school and tried to impress a girl who liked "bad boys." He ended up in truancy court.

Now worried, I took him to a therapist who diagnosed him as bipolar. My son accepted the diagnosis and the prescription pills that came with it. Meanwhile, I felt relieved. Unknown to me, my son was happy to take prescription pills along with the marijuana and alcohol he continued to smoke and drink.

Later he broke up with his girlfriend. He drank so much alcohol that he blacked out, was picked up by the police, and was hospitalized. Two weeks later the same thing happened. Not long after that, it happened again. He also got into more legal trouble. The fog of denial lifted from my eyes. *I had wanted to believe that my son had a mental health challenge, but that he could quit smoking marijuana and drinking alcohol whenever he chose.* I finally realized that alcohol and/or pot, taken in addition to prescription drugs, might kill him. He himself began to be afraid that he couldn't stop. I sought and found treatment for him at our local Enthusiastic Sobriety program.

From my experience I would suggest that parents, who are afraid their teen has a mental health challenge and/or is experimenting with alcohol or pot, not ignore it and not keep it a secret. No secret is worth keeping when a child's life may be at stake. At the Enthusiastic Sobriety parent meetings I found other parents with similar experiences. I didn't have to be ashamed of our family situation. When I faced it and got help, our lives began to improve.

Today's Reminder
Don't put off till tomorrow what can be dealt with today.

Father Knows Best March 18

I was a master rescuer of my drug-addicted child. Whenever my teen-aged son mentioned he was facing a potential problem, I worked hard to circumvent it for him. I made excuses for his missed classes, stayed up half the night to "help" him finish school projects, and drove an hour to a library to check out a copy of a book he needed to do his homework. Now that he's older and sober I still find myself wanting to rescue him. Luckily for my son and me, his dad is much better at avoiding rescuing behavior.

A couple of weeks ago our son, now an adult, mentioned that he had holes in his shoes and did not have enough money to buy new ones. I had enough sense to say nothing and wait until later when my husband and I were alone. I asked him if we could give our son some money to buy shoes. My husband reminded me that our son had just recently bought new sporting equipment; he concluded that our son had apparently not managed his money well. The next time I saw our son, I casually asked him how much he spent on the sporting equipment. The equipment cost much more than a pair of shoes! I am grateful to my husband who prevented a "rescue." Our son will learn a good lesson about money management.

Today's Reminder
Today I will squelch my maternal instinct to "take care of my baby." As a young adult, he can and should do most things for himself. As a mother of an adult child, I can and should spend my time taking care of myself.

Get Out of Their Way March 19

How can a Twelve Step program help parents of young drug addicts/alcoholics? The most important thing I learned was to get out of my teenager's way and let her feel the consequences of her own actions. As a parent I had previously spent time trying to prevent my child from making mistakes, and if she made one, fixing" it so she wouldn't be "hurt." Now, I am clear that such behavior actually hurts my teenager. She cannot learn from her own actions if I'm there to rescue her. Today, I make it clear to her that whatever she does, it's *her* choice. She is not a little child anymore, and *I cannot control her*. I can help her most by staying out of the way and letting her face the results of her choices. I can support her and encourage her when she makes good choices, but I cannot intervene when she makes poor choices. For me, the only intervention that I felt was necessary for my teenager was to help her get into a drug abuse treatment program. Once there, she had to make her own choices. And once I started working the Twelve Steps, too, I learned not only that I can't make choices for her, but that I *can* make choices for myself.

Today's Reminder
As a parent I am morally responsible to teach my minor children right from wrong and how to take care of themselves. By providing them with love and boundaries which I consistently enforce, I do my job.

"Take Care of Yourself"   **March 20**

When I first came to an Enthusiastic Sobriety parent meeting, other parents said, "Take care of yourself." I thought they must be crazy. *My kid* was the one with the problem; he was addicted to drugs, failing in school, and in trouble with the law. I had to take care of him first! Except for him, my life was fine.

Then one year later, having done my best to follow the advice, I had an experience which convinced me of the wisdom of taking care of myself. My son has been sober for almost a year and has gotten his GED. I have been supporting him by letting him live at my home and giving him gas and spending money. Yet, lately I have felt uncomfortable paying for his expenses while he stays home part of the day and plays computer games while I work. I decided to take the initiative—although a bit uncertain and afraid—and told him that he could continue to live at home and I will feed him, but I am going to stop giving him money two weeks from now. He agreed with me that it was time for him to do something! I felt great about taking care of myself. The resentment I had begun to nurse immediately lifted. Moreover, I believe that my son actually feels good about my encouraging his independence, something he wants, too. By stating clearly and calmly what I am willing and not willing to do, I am improving my relationship with my son.

Today's Reminder
If I start to feel a twinge of resentment for my actions toward my child, I will look at the situation. What do I need to take care of myself? Once I have a clear answer, I will take steps to see that my needs are met.

Gratitude Lists   March 21

When I am going through a difficult time, I write lists of whatever I'm grateful for in my life. During especially trying times, I have written lists hourly. This helps me to focus on the good things in my life and prevents my mind from returning to a catalogue of woes. Dwelling on fears, worries, resentments, and self-pity merely intensifies my pain. It is best to focus on solutions and not stay in the problem. Many things are out of my control, but I can control my actions, so I focus on them.

For example, once our area experienced a debilitating blizzard. Most businesses and all schools were closed. I began feeling frustrated about all the work I could not do that day. Finally, I remembered to be grateful. We were all home, safe and sound. My daughter suggested we bake yeast bread. So we began the time-consuming process, which we otherwise would not have been able to do. We took turns kneading. When we both got tired, I asked my husband and son to take turns. We made a game of how fast or how flamboyantly we could knead; we shared a few good laughs. Later the entire family shoveled our lengthy driveway. When we returned inside, we enjoyed piping hot bread out of the oven. What began as a frustrating day turned into a very happy family experience.

Today's Reminder
I will write a gratitude list today. Should I be going through a rough time, I will write as many as needed to prevent my mind from dwelling on fear, worry, resentment, or self-pity.

How Important Is It? March 22

The first holiday we were in the Enthusiastic Sobriety program was Easter. We had always held an extended family dinner at our house, but this year we invited only the children's grandmother. Easter morning I learned that my son would be returning home from his overnight visit at 4 p.m., two hours after dinner was scheduled. I was very upset and called a parent in the program.

She was very kind and listened to me. She validated my feelings and told me how she, too, had felt the same way when her son first got sober. After awhile, I began to feel better. Feeling heard by her, I was then able to listen. She encouraged my efforts to simplify the holiday celebration. She said that she and her husband had done that, too. Also, they had learned over time to take into account their son's schedule when planning. They negotiated in advance with him and planned the family holiday celebrations together. I liked what she said. I realized that it was not so important what time our family ate Easter dinner. After this phone call, I called our children's grandmother. She was quite accommodating and gracious about the last minute change. Easter dinner turned out okay with our son participating and sober.

Not only did I apply the slogan, "How important is it," but I also learned about sponsorship. Feeling comfortable with the parent I had called, I asked her to be my sponsor and she said, "Yes." Her kindness and understanding approach helped me look at situations from a new perspective.

Today's Reminder
I will give up control of family holiday celebrations. I will negotiate with my family members to create holiday plans with which we all feel comfortable. I will remember that family harmony is more important than doing things the way we always have done them.

Honesty and Trust Take Time   March 23

Before entering an Enthusiastic Sobriety program, the hardest idea for me to grasp was how easy it is for an addict to lie to loved ones. During my son's early days of recovery I soon realized that an addict easily lies to himself and others to justify getting what he wants. I felt angry and confused when I caught him in his first lie while sober. But as the weeks went on, I listened to other parents and realized it was all part of the addictive experience in which lying becomes second nature. It would take time to break this habit.

Nowadays if I catch my son in a lie, I remind him that his answer can have one of two effects: one is to build trust between us; the other is to tear it down. It's his choice. We've discovered that if he discusses the fear behind his lie, trust is established.

After having focused on my son's dishonesty and its destructive effect on our relationship, my *own* aha moment came one day when I realized I had been lying to him. At times, I would snoop in his room. He would usually notice something out of place and ask me about it, and I'd lie. How ironic! Now I, too, will tell him what he did or what I was thinking that triggered my fear to snoop. Rebuilding trust in our relationship is taking awareness, honesty, and time.

Today's Reminder
While the addict's behavior is sometimes hard to understand, I will remember that we are all capable of doing things out of fear. Today I will not let fear control me. I will do my best to model honesty and build a trusting relationship with my child.

Self-Forgiveness — March 24

At my first Al-Anon meeting I heard the "three C's:" You didn't *cause* it, you can't *control* it, and you can't *cure* it. I thought that might be true for spouses of alcoholics, but it couldn't be true for parents of alcoholics or drug addicts. After all, don't parents shape their children's environment *and* provide their children's genetic make-up? When I questioned another person after the Al-Anon meeting, she reminded me that a child has two parents, so one parent only provides half the genetic make-up for a child. Also, there are many other factors in a child's environment besides parents: extended family, friends, day care, school, teachers, neighbors, television, etc. I realized I was not *all-powerful* over my child. He had other influences in his life. Further, my teenager was quite capable of exercising his own choices in life, and he had.

Later in program I did an inventory and saw how some of my less desirable behaviors had negatively influenced my child. On the other hand, I had done many things which had positively influenced him, too. Most importantly, my sponsor helped me to see that I needed to forgive myself. I had to accept myself as a human being who is not perfect and who dearly loves my child. While I can't undo the past, I can strive today and every day to show my love for my teen in ways which will more positively influence him now.

Today's Reminder
I am neither a perfect parent nor the *only* influence on my child. Today I choose to learn from the past, let go of it, and work to improve my parenting skills.

Trusting an Active Addict is Denial — March 25

When my husband and I entered the room of our first Enthusiastic Sobriety parent meeting, our trust had been depleted. Our son had manipulated, lied, and stolen from us. Yet, we wanted to trust him. For months we had engaged in a family pattern of his lying to us, our believing him, our discovering that he had lied, and our choosing to believe his subsequent lies, despite the mounting evidence of untrustworthiness. Trust under such circumstances is foolhardy. It is denial. We could not accept the fact that our son truly had a substance abuse problem, so we continued to act as if he didn't and as if everything was fine.

In working the steps, we found that we could choose to rebuild trust in small increments. At first our trust was simply in believing him when he called after a meeting to tell us that he was staying overnight at one of the homes of another boy in the Enthusiastic Sobriety program. The next morning, having not heard from him by ten o'clock, I telephoned the parents of the boy to ask if my son was still there. Indeed he was. After awhile, we chose to trust by giving him small amounts of cash for coffee or dinner out with the other Enthusiastic Sobriety teens. As time went on and he continued to stay sober, we continued to choose to trust him with larger responsibilities and he continued to show his trustworthiness. Beginning with a small item in which we could choose to trust but verify, in due course we rebuilt a trusting relationship with our son.

Today's Reminder
If my child is not sober or trying to get sober, I will not deny his problem. Yet I realize that once he and the family are in recovery, we can rebuild trust slowly, one day at a time.

"Right Here Right Now" and Acceptance   March 26

As a parent of a young drug addict, I have found using the slogan, "Right Here Right Now", together with the full version of the Serenity Prayer, valuable. I often think of the book *Bumper Stickers* in which Bob Meehan mentions a day he returned from work feeling sorry for himself. Then he realized that he wanted to be home with the people he loved, so he made a decision to act like it. Instead of stewing in self-pity, he was "Right Here Right Now" and appreciated his family and home. These days when I have had a hard day's work, I remember to be "Right Here Right Now," avoid self-pity, and appreciate my family. This includes my son whose drug addiction helped me find the Twelve Steps which have deepened my faith and given me a better way of life.

By being "Right Here Right Now," I also let go of worries. I can decide "Right Here Right Now" if there is anything I can do about a problem today. If so, I do it, and then let go of the outcome.

I trust that God is in everything and all will work out according to His will. Accepting what I cannot change in the world is the key. While the outer circumstances may not change, my attitude adjustment vastly improves my ability to cope with them.

Today's Reminder
I appreciate the good in my life, and when faced with a problem I apply the Serenity Prayer. I take courage to change things that I can and accept what I cannot.

When the Worst Thing Becomes the Best Thing   March 27

Our son began smoking pot in junior high. In the summer before he began high school, we removed the pipes we found in his room and started drug testing him. He clearly knew we did not want him using illegal drugs.

When he was in high school, he said that he was depressed and wanted to see a psychiatrist. The doctor put him on antidepressants. Fearful that he might abuse the pills, yet concerned that he needed them, I dutifully doled them out one at a time as prescribed. Early in the morning one week later, my husband and I received a telephone call from the sheriff. We thought our son had received a ticket for a curfew violation. After arriving at the police station, however, I learned that the boys had done much more than violate curfew; they had drunk alcohol, smoked dope and snorted my son's stockpiled pills. Under the influence, they had destroyed property, ransacked cars, and gone joy riding. Although our son was facing felony charges, my husband and I signed a waiver so the police could speak with him. He was scared; we told him to be honest. Subsequently, he was placed in a diversion program to avoid criminal charges and a record. Nevertheless, he could not stop using drugs and alcohol even though he really wanted to. This frightened him even more. Fortunately, we found a Twelve Step program for young people, our local Enthusiastic Sobriety program. I felt hope for the first time. The worst thing in our family now became the best thing. Our son had reached his bottom and was ready for help.

Today's Reminder
If something I am inclined to judge as "bad" happens today, I will remember that good can come out of even the worst situation.

Deciding on and Using "Shots" March 28

I was told by the Enthusiastic Sobriety counselors that I needed to create three to five shots[3], the violation of which would result in serious consequences. I thought about what I needed for my sanity, i.e. not become sick with worry and fear. I needed my daughter to be sober, working (a job or in school), and working her Twelve Step program. I also needed her not to wear provocative clothes. I set up these rules to maintain my sanity.

At one point when my daughter relapsed and was missing a few days, I worked my own program. I called my sponsor and consulted with him. I enforced my "shot" by locking the house so she could not get inside. Eventually she agreed to get sober,

---

[3] Shots are strict household rules reflecting my values.

meet with her sponsor, and start working the steps again. As long as she follows through on her agreement, she is welcome in my home.

Today's Reminder
I have a right to have peace in my home. After careful reflection, I will tell my teen what I need from her so that she can remain living in my home.

"As parents, we must offer our children the gift of choice."
~*Beyond the Yellow Brick Road*

Being Proactive with Trust   March 29

In the year before he entered the Enthusiastic Sobriety program, our son he had received failing grades at school and disrupted our home. I had many reasons not to trust him. Yet, after he had just successfully completed three months of outpatient treatment and I had been faithfully going to weekly parent meetings, we both had changed. My anger and embarrassment was slowly being replaced with understanding and forgiveness, but I was still nervous. During outpatient, the counselors had encouraged my wife and me to "back off" or detach; now we knew it was time for our re-entry as parents.

I went to an Enthusiastic Sobriety men's retreat and mentioned that I was nervous about teaching my son to drive, but the other fathers thought that it was a *great* idea. They said it could be a very positive father-son interaction. I would be devoting my time to give him an important life skill and showing that I trust him with a real responsibility. I didn't fully understand, but I trusted them and decided to follow their advice.

I was awed by how well this worked. It turned out to be the most positive interaction we had had in years! I was patient with him, and he seriously listened to my advice about driving. His self-confidence grew. In a short time, he was driving 30 miles to the shop on highways in a large city.

This worked because we were both ready. He had given us positive signals by improving his relationship with us and finishing his outpatient program. By taking a leap of faith and trusting him to learn to drive, I was telling him, "I still love you, want the best for you, and am willing to trust you again."

Today's Reminder
Today I will remember that trust is not a feeling; it is a decision.
~Bumper Stickers

Taking Care of Our Kids   March 30

Parents who attend the weekly Enthusiastic Sobriety parent meetings spend time working their programs. Besides going to meetings, we meet with our sponsors, telephone other parents between meetings, and discuss values, "walls," and "shots" with our spouses.

My husband and I have two kids; the older is in the program, the younger is not. The child who is not in an Enthusiastic Sobriety program may feel neglected. When our daughter was too young to stay at home alone, our children's grandmother was able and willing to spend time with her. This worked out well, because our daughter bonded more deeply with her grandmother who gave her much love and attention. Although young when we entered the program, our daughter came to understand that her brother needed special help. We did our best to make it up to her. We took her on a family trip and arranged for our son to stay with another Enthusiastic Sobriety family so he could participate in program meetings and functions. She enjoyed the individual attention.

Because my husband and I have spent a lot of time discussing values, establishing household rules, and being sure to be on the same page in dealing with requests from our kids—both have benefited by our calmer and better-reasoned parenting.

Most importantly, in attending so many Twelve Step meetings, I have learned the value of listening without interruption and really hearing what someone has to say without criticism or judgment. As time has passed and I listen more to both of my kids, I realize how much they both share with me, including things that I doubt they would have told me had I not become a better listener.

Today's Reminder
I reflect on what I can do today to meet the unique needs of each of my children. If necessary, I find others who can help me to meet a child's needs.

Unconditional Love and Recovery — March 31

Unconditional love means love without conditions, loving the person regardless of that person's actions. When my kids were born, I felt a great wave of unconditional love toward them. Later, I remember getting frustrated when my kids wrote on the wall with their crayons. I had to take a deep breath, cool down, and remember that I love my kids; they were excited that they were learning to write their letters. I did not stop loving my kids.

I had to show my love for them and, at the same time, teach them socially acceptable behavior.

Teenagers are *very* sensitive to criticism. Whenever I ask my kids anything, they tend to take it as criticism. Questions such as, "Is your room clean?" "Do you have any homework?" and "Why don't you get a job?" can cause them to react negatively. "Easy does it" is a slogan which helps. I remember to stop and consider my motives for all these questions. Am I trying to control my kids? They have their own lives. I need to focus on my own life and remember to practice the slogan, "Live and let live."

Today's Reminder
I let go of using questions to try to control my kids. I express my love for them, let them live their own lives, and avoid criticism.

APRIL

Enthusiastic Sobriety Programs' Step One April 1
"We admitted that mind-changing chemicals have caused at least part of our lives to become unmanageable."

When my son was on drugs, it was clear to me that at least part of my own life was unmanageable. I was always trying to arrange things so my son would get to school (yet he often left after I dropped him off). At home, I would not tell him about phone calls from his "friends" who I suspected were a bad influence on him. If he found out later about a call, I would claim to have "forgotten." When my son failed to do his household chores, I would plead and beg him to do them. He would make excuses, promise to do them later, and leave the house as quickly as possible. I would be afraid of the wrath of my husband, who would yell at me for not getting our son to do his chores. Also, I would hear all the things my husband wanted to say to my son but said to me instead, because I was home. Sometimes we would yell at each other, blaming the other for our son's poor behavior. To avoid conflict, I would sometimes do my son's chores without telling my husband. I thought I was making things easier, but I was just perpetuating a dysfunctional merry-go-round.

Today, all three of us do our best to follow the Twelve Steps, with an emphasis on honesty, open-mindedness, and willingness to change our behavior. With everyone doing his or her best to be honest and meet his or her obligations, life has become much more pleasant. The element of trust—which had vanished from our family—has been restored.

Today's Reminder
Lying, begging, pleading, yelling, and blaming are all unhealthy behaviors which make family life unmanageable. Today I will openly and honestly communicate with my family.

"To overcome any problem, the first step is to admit that it exists." ~*Beyond the Yellow Brick Road*

Enthusiastic Sobriety Programs' Step Two April 2
"We have found it necessary to stick with winners in order to grow."

I understood what the Enthusiastic Sobriety Programs' Step Two, "Stick with winners" meant for my teenager. The teens stick with sober teens and leave behind their drinking and drugging friends to stay sober. But what does "stick with winners" mean for parents? At first, I wasn't sure. Then I began to see that I needed to spend time with parents in the program. Some other parents who knew my kid was in treatment avoided me. Other parents gave me a pitying look. I felt like an outcast from my former PTA friends.

"Stick with winners" means that we stick with other parents who are working a Twelve Step program and apply it to all aspects of our lives, including parenting. We don't pity; we understand each other. We don't judge; we empathize. We work hard to look at situations with our kids, see our own part in it, and admit our mistakes to ourselves and other parents. We work on changing our behavior. As similar situations arise in the future with our kids, we try out new and different behavior to see if we can get more positive results. We strive toward balance, being neither authoritarian nor permissive. We set appropriate rules for our kids with fitting consequences. We muster up the courage to follow through, no matter how uncomfortable it feels. The support of other parents makes us feel like "winners" for having the courage to change.

Today's Reminder
Today I will stick with winners: other parents who do not judge me and who support me and my family in our recovery from the effects of mind-changing chemicals.

Enthusiastic Sobriety Programs' Step Three — April 3
"We realize that a Higher Power, expressed through our love for each other, can help restore us to sanity."

For those parents who are familiar with other Twelve Step programs, this is similar to the second step, "Came to believe that a Power greater than ourselves could restore us to sanity." Being a scientist at heart, my husband really doesn't believe anything unless he sees evidence of it. When we first got to an Enthusiastic Sobriety program, I had been in a Twelve Step program myself, and had seen the miracles. My husband had not. Each week, after parent meetings, we met with teens and young adults in the program who had years of sobriety, who were happy, friendly, got along reasonably well with their parents and siblings, and were in school and/or holding jobs. We also met parents who had been coming to parent meetings for years. They described the dramatic change for the better that had taken place in their children and their relationship with their children as the family worked the steps. My husband saw the evidence that the program worked. We both witnessed the gradual positive changes that were taking place in our family and other families. Seeing is definitely believing!

Today's Reminder
Many families have experienced gradual, positive changes after one or more members began working the steps. Today I will work the steps and trust that my family situation will gradually improve also.

Enthusiastic Sobriety Programs' Step Four — April 4
"We made a decision to turn our will and our lives over to the care of God as we understand Him."

How many times have I become frantic over the misbehavior of my teenagers? My husband and I would discuss our concerns for hours on Saturday mornings and try to force solutions. We did not achieve our goals for the day and usually ended up frustrated with each other because his solution and mine were at odds. Step Four was the turning point. As soon as I was able to let a power greater than myself guide my thinking and my life, I was on the road to recovery. That Higher Power can be God, but not necessarily. Many of the kids use the concept "Good Orderly Direction" or their group for God. For many parents, the collective wisdom of the parent group can serve as a higher power.

Sometimes I think of God as the wind, always there, a gentle yet powerful source of strength rustling the leaves and rippling the water.

How do I "let go and let God?" I give one problem at a time to my Higher Power. Sometimes I write the problem on a slip of paper and put it in my "God bag." I set aside my belief about how the problem should be solved or my belief that it is unsolvable. Each time I ask for help, my belief in my Higher Power is strengthened and my hope is renewed.

Today's Reminder
Today I will do the next right thing, trust in God, as I understand God, and let go of the outcome.

Enthusiastic Sobriety Programs' Step Five   April 5
"We made a searching and fearless moral inventory of ourselves."

After I did my inventory, I realized that I had good qualities that had gone awry. I deeply love my children, but I had channeled much of my loving energy into "rescuing" them from the consequences of their behavior because I didn't want them to "suffer." Sometimes, too, I didn't follow through with consequences for their misbehavior because to ground them on a weekend would mean giving up the tickets or other costly plans for the family that we had been looking forward to. So, long before my son became an addict, I had been engaging in behavior that was harmful to my kids. I had been violating one of the most important rules of parenting: "Say what you mean; mean what you say, and don't say it mean." I also saw that in the past, I had had to get *very* angry with my kids before I could enforce consequences. Why? Because I wanted to feel loved by my children and didn't want to risk their anger and disapproval. Without a doubt no parent ever hears from his or her child, "Thanks, I'm so glad you grounded me!"

This inventory step, followed by giving it away to my sponsor, prayer and meditation, and daily reflection have improved the quality of my life.

Today's Reminder
Today I will let go of my desire to please everyone and avoid conflict. I will enforce consequences for my child's violation of household rules.

"Parents are supposed to do what's best for [our] children, which sometimes means taking action which hurts...We must be firmly committed to our job as the most influential people in our children's lives, and we have to risk our relationships. We have to *do* – not just say." ~*Beyond the Yellow Brick Road*

Enthusiastic Sobriety Programs' Step Six   April 6
"We admit to God, to ourselves, and to another human being the exact nature of our wrongs."

The first time I read my inventory to my sponsor, I was tremendously relieved. Many of the things that I had done which I had felt were so terrible were things that she admitted that she had done, too. I really liked my sponsor, and her sharing helped me see that we were both okay. All human beings make mistakes. I don't have to fear sharing my "secrets" because I now know that people in a Twelve Step program are understanding and keep things confidential. Also when I share troubling things with another, my stress subsides.

My sponsor suggested that I write my character assets, too. When I shared these, I felt much better and saw how many of my defects were simply my strengths gone haywire.

Today's Reminder
Today I will take a few minutes to reflect on my actions. If there is something that I did which really bothers me, I will share it with another parent in program and learn from my mistake. I will reflect on how to correct my wrong and how to handle future situations in a better way.

"Shared joy is double joy, and shared sorrow is half-sorrow."
~Swedish proverb

Enthusiastic Sobriety Programs' Step Seven — April 7

"We became willing to allow our Higher Power, through the love of the group, to help change our way of thinking and humbly ask Him to help us change."

Many Enthusiastic Sobriety parents feel jealous when friends and neighbors speak about their children's college applications, great jobs, and other awards and accomplishments. We also can wallow in self-pity when our kids are spending all their time working on getting and keeping sober. Every time I feel jealousy, resentment or self-pity, I remember that these thought patterns are counterproductive. My awareness of these patterns is necessary before I can change, but I realize that I cannot change them by myself. Just as my son needs the group and his Higher Power to help him change his way of thinking to get and stay sober, I need the help of the parent group and my Higher Power to change my negative, counterproductive thoughts. The parent group has helped me to appreciate my family's progress without expecting perfection.

Today's Reminder

The Twelve Step group has helped many parents. By reaching out to my group, I receive support in thinking more positively.

"The whole is greater than the sum of its parts." ~Aristotle

Enthusiastic Sobriety Programs' Step Eight — April 8

"We made a list of all persons we have harmed and became willing to make amends to such people, whenever possible, except when to do so would injure them, others, or ourselves."

My sponsor told me that we don't have to make amends immediately to everyone. We can make three lists: a list of "those I am willing to make amends to right away," "those I want to make amends to, but don't feel ready to," and "those I can't ever imagine wanting to make amends to." Starting with the "easy" ones first, I spoke with my sponsor and decided how I could repair the harm.

Afterwards I prayed for the willingness to become ready to make amends to the second group of people. When I felt ready, I again consulted my sponsor to get feedback on how best to repair the harm.

Others in the program told me that after working through the first two lists, they felt a shift and were more willing to start looking at how to make amends to the last group.

Today's Reminder

Step Eight is making a list of persons I have harmed. It does not require I make amends to everyone immediately. I need only pray for the willingness to face each person when the time is right.

"Before I did Step Eight, I would lie in bed at night thinking about all the things I'd done to people, and it kept me from falling asleep. But when I made a list of everyone I'd wronged and expressed my 'willingness' to make amends to them, I found I could sleep again. So I call this "The Sleeping Step." ~*Beyond the Yellow Brick Road*

Enthusiastic Sobriety Programs' Step Nine   April 9
"We made direct amends to such people, whenever possible, except when to do so would injure them, others, or ourselves."

Working with a sponsor on Step Nine, I learned that no matter how much I wish I could, I can't rewrite the past. I can't turn back the clock and parent my children differently. But I can make "living amends" to my husband and kids and act differently today. Now I am more conscious of my thoughts and actions, especially as it affects my family. I look for the good in every person, place and situation and avoid a negative outlook. I bite my tongue before criticizing anyone but do not hesitate to give a sincere compliment. I express my gratitude to my family and others for the many little things they do that make my life easier. Perhaps most important, I no longer obsess about all the household tasks I have to do when someone in my family wants to talk. I listen, don't interrupt, and give my loved one the time and attention he or she deserves. The housework will always be there, and my family needs me now.

As I have practiced my "living amends" these past few years, the quality of our lives has become better. My kids stop and talk with me more often, perhaps because they know I will listen. They more readily assume small household tasks, such as folding laundry, without even being asked. Everyone more quickly expresses gratitude. Our home has become a happier place.

Today's Reminder
Today I can give each person sincere compliments. I can say, "Thank you," for the little things they do for me. I can stop and listen to each family member, thus letting them know I value hearing from them.

Enthusiastic Sobriety Programs' Step Ten   April 10
"We have continued to look at ourselves and when wrong, promptly admitted it."

Step Ten is the perfect barometer of my current mental and emotional health. This step reminds me to continue to watch for selfishness, dishonesty, resentment and fear, which are parts of my personality that are at the root of my problems. By practicing Step Ten regularly, I remain humble and remind myself of the slogan, "progress not perfection." The miracle of Step Ten is that as I continue to be honest with another person about my character defects, these stumbling blocks to success have begun to lessen and in some instances disappear. So, it turns out that Step Ten is not the act of self-flagellation I originally believed, but a path to the removal of those characteristics in my personality which keep me separated from my Higher Power.

Today's Reminder
Today I will be diligent in practicing my Tenth Step and removing stumbling blocks to improvement.

Enthusiastic Sobriety Programs' Step Eleven — April 11

"We have sought through prayer and meditation to improve our conscious contact with our Higher Power, that which we have chosen to call God, praying only for knowledge of His will for us and the courage to carry that out."

The Enthusiastic Sobriety Programs' Step Eleven is very similar to the AA & Al-Anon Step Eleven which reads: "Sought through prayer and meditation to improve our conscious contact with God *as we understood Him,* praying only for knowledge of His will for us and the power to carry that out."

One difference between the two is the use of the word "courage" rather than "power." For me, the word "courage" reminds me that I need to have *courage to change* negative behavior patterns which I discovered when I did my inventory. Today I recognize situations which trigger my negative coping mechanisms and muster the courage to change. The use of the word "power" reminds me that it's a partnership between me and my Higher Power. I need my Higher Power's help to overcome the inertia that has set in from negative habits. I need to take the time to pray and meditate so I can be open to new ideas. My Higher Power helps me get "unstuck" and find new, healthier ways to handle recurring situations with my teens.

Today's Reminder
It takes courage to acknowledge and change negative habits. With help from a power greater than myself I *can* do this.

Enthusiastic Sobriety Programs' Step Twelve   April 12

"We, having had a spiritual awakening as a result of these steps, tried to carry our love and understanding to others, and to practice these principles in our daily lives."

Every time I see a parent suffering because of self-destructive actions of his child, my heart goes out to him. Even if the teen or young adult's behavior does not involve alcohol or drugs, I can identify with the parent's anger, hurt, sense of despair, and self-recriminating thoughts. When a teen shoplifts, cuts himself, or has an eating disorder, I may not share the same experience as the parent, but I do share the same feelings.

With the parent of a drug addict or alcoholic, my personal experiences may be quite similar. My kid has: been evasive, been verbally abusive, had his grades in school drop, lied to me, stolen money from me, avoided his old friends and activities, developed new "friends" (fellow drug abusers or alcoholics), lost a job, and gotten into legal trouble. I can share with this parent my similar experiences. This parent may ask me how I handled the situation. I can share how applying the Twelve Steps and slogans of the program have helped me.

As for parents with different painful experiences with their teens, I can listen and empathize. I can avoid judgment, criticism, advice, or gossip. This is how I can "carry ...love and understanding to others."

Today's Reminder

Twelve Step Programs are for those who want it, not for those who need it. Today I will listen and empathize with others going through difficult times. I will not judge or criticize anyone, nor will I give unsolicited advice.

Use Your Resources — April 13

I was dumbfounded by my teenager's use and addiction to drugs and alcohol. I did not know where to turn. Luckily, my son's therapist referred us to our local Enthusiastic Sobriety drug treatment program. My son related to the young counselors, recovering alcoholics and drug addicts themselves. He was drawn to the fun activities the teens did on Friday and Saturday nights. He found good friends in this group of sober teens.

Meanwhile, I found an unexpected huge benefit for myself. The parent group's meetings are a source of support. The parents have experienced things similar to me and they have a wealth of experience and knowledge from which I can draw. This is so different from other friends who have no idea what I have gone through. The sponsor relationship, too, has been of enormous help. Having someone's shoulder to cry on when needed and someone to help me see my part in our family patterns has been both a comfort and an eye-opener. For all these helpful resources, I am grateful.

Today's Reminder
I will use my resources today. I will go to a parent or Al-Anon meeting and talk with my sponsor or another parent in a Twelve Step program.

Church Alone Was Not the Answer — April 14

My son had a drug problem and was out of control. He had overdosed and been rushed to the emergency room more than once. He had been in fights and returned home with black eyes and broken teeth. He was arrested for shoplifting. I was at my wit's end and did not know what to do. I heard about one of the Enthusiastic Sobriety programs, and I talked with one of the counselors. At the time I knew that my son did not want help and that I would be unable to convince him to go into treatment.

I tried getting him involved in a church youth group. He did participate, but this did not stop his drug use. He simply used drugs after attending youth group meetings and socials. Eventually, my son reached his own "bottom;" he wanted to become drug free but could not stop. At just the right moment, I told him about the young person (an Enthusiastic Sobriety program counselor) I had spoken with who was a drug addict and was now clean and sober. I told him what I knew about the treatment program and he agreed to go.

He was greeted warmly by the other young people in the group; they welcomed him and really reached out to help him. This was in sharp contrast to his former drug-using "friends" who seemed to use each other. Early in the program he suffered relapses, but he stuck with it, renewed his commitment to the program and has now been sober for three and a half years.

The Twelve Steps require faith and trust in God (or a power greater than oneself) as well as prayer and meditation. Yet, part of the success for our family has been the power of the support groups, both the young persons' group and the parents' group. Without the moral support of his group, I don't believe my son could have gotten sober. And with the support of the parent group, I have been able to not only survive but deepen my faith and enjoy life more.

Today's Reminder
Today I will be grateful for the continuing support of the parent group.

Getting Rid of Guilt April 15

My husband had been working long hours and had some medical challenges, so I had been doing the lion's share of parenting. I recall drug screening one son and taking him to psychologists for help. Not only did I find drugs and paraphernalia in his room, but I found he had a pitcher of urine hidden (to use for the drug screening tests). Luckily a psychologist told us to stop the drug testing and check out our local Enthusiastic Sobriety program.

When I first came to the parent meetings, I began to see that my life had been consumed by worry and fear for my kids. Gradually I changed. At first I detached by leaving my son's care in the hands of the counselors and group. Later I let my son solve his own problems. I stopped spending so much time thinking about him. This was a great relief.

Now I can set boundaries with my kids and not feel guilty about enforcing them. For example, when our older son became an adult and wanted to continue living in our home, my husband and I first discussed it alone. As a united front we let him know that he could live with us as long as he paid rent. He agreed to this, but by the second month he told us that he had used his rent money to bail out some friends busted for drugs. Presenting a united front, we told him that that was his choice and that he had to leave our home. Years before, we would not have been able to do that. Now we knew it was the right thing to do and we did it without guilt.

Today's Reminder
Because guilt does not help my children mature, I turn away from it. Instead, I set boundaries and enforce consequences so that my children will learn and mature.

My Worth as a Person is Not Dependent on My Child

April 16

God made me. God does not make junk. God loves me. I have my own identity. I will not allow my child's success or failure in her recovery to control me. Failure does hurt at times. I do not need to deny my feelings. However, my child's life is not my life. Her decisions are not my decisions. It is good to want the best for my child even when she does not want the best or maybe cannot see the best for her life. However, God gives us choices, and I must give my child choices as well.

I will develop myself as a person who loves God and people. I will strive to be healthy mentally, spiritually, and physically. I will make an effort to have relationships and activities apart from my child so as not to become overly concerned about her recovery. I will acknowledge that there are always people who have a worse situation than mine. I will count my blessings every day. I will pray for my child and myself. I will ask God to use my child's recovery or lack of recovery to help other people.

Today's Reminder

I am a separate person from my child. I will not allow my child's success or failure to dictate my feelings. Today I will pray for my child, let her make her own choices, and then live and enjoy my own life.

Needs Communicated

April 17

Before our son got sober, he would be vague about where and with whom he was going out in the evening. We would tell him to be home by a certain time, and he either would ignore us or come home by curfew and sneak out later. This resulted in much anger and frustration.

Once we all began working a Twelve Step program, things changed dramatically. We all learned that we had to be honest, open-minded, and willing to change our behavior patterns. We told our son that for our peace of mind, we needed him to be safe at home at midnight, or he could call us and tell us at whose home he was spending the night. Of course, it needed to be with one of his sober friends. He respected our need for peace of mind, and we respected his need to spend time with his peers. With respect and open communication, our relationship with our son improved.

Today's Reminder
Honest and open communication about needs leads to improved relationships.

Patience and Progress — April 18

I have always thought of myself as relatively patient. However, waiting for my son's full recovery has proven to be a far more difficult task than I anticipated. Discovering the extent of my son's addiction was heart wrenching. His drug and alcohol use "protected" him from feeling and dealing with difficult adolescent situations, which in turn resulted in him being behind in the game of growing up. My dreams of raising a responsible, dependable, moral, independent, loving young man were totally destroyed. I grieved. In spite of my best efforts, the dreams and plans I had for my son were dead. Or so it seemed.

"Progress not perfection" makes perfectly good sense. When our child strayed from the orderly path we had mapped out for him, we found ourselves in a strange no-man's land. Around us, the children of friends, family, and neighbors seemed to be on the "right" path. Initially, I believed that in four to six weeks, our son could work through the Twelve Steps and get back on track. Not so for us, nor for most who join an Enthusiastic Sobriety program. It is a long journey. Yet, when I get discouraged, it helps to look back at where we were a year ago. Many small steps add up to great strides.

A spiritual life that includes prayer and meditation has been my most valuable tool in finding and keeping patience and hope. It fends off F.E.A.R (false events appearing real). It also helps to tap into my higher power when I need wisdom on what to say and do—and when to keep my mouth firmly shut and do nothing. Fellowship with kindred spirits from the parent group helps to keep me relatively sane and centered when the seas of life are wildly churning. What a gift to have those same friends to laugh and celebrate with when the waters are blessedly calm.

Today's Reminder
With patience, prayer, meditation, and the support of the parent group, I stay sane and centered in the seas of life.

How I Began Working My Program — April 19

When my daughter entered an Enthusiastic Sobriety program, I eagerly started working the steps—for myself. I knew that my child definitely needed help with her addiction to drugs. However, I realized that I, too, needed help. I was sick with anxiety for my child and had a hard time thinking about anything else. Before getting into the program, I tried to do something more constructive for my daughter. My family members and I prayed for her. Once we got into the program, I got a sponsor and joined a weekly prayer meeting. Each week we parents turned our worries and nervous energy over into faith and prayer. We prayed that our kids would eventually recover. I worked the steps with my sponsor. In addition to the Enthusiastic Sobriety parent meetings, I began attending Al-Anon meetings. Although not everyone in Al-Anon is a parent of an alcoholic, members do understand. Giving my time and energy to positive thoughts and actions, I find my anxiety lifted. Despite the fact that my daughter's journey has been long and difficult, since working my program I feel more at peace.

Today's Reminder
Faith, prayer, meetings, talking with my sponsor, and working the steps bring serenity to my life.

"Through the love and support of other parents who share their problem, they learn to like themselves and become better parents and better people." ~*Beyond the Yellow Brick Road*

P.O.P.P. April 20

This stands for the "Powers of Positive Parenting, a phrase in Bob Meehan's book, *Bumper Stickers.* Meehan suggests that a parent can manage himself by thinking, "What is it that I want to say to me that makes me feel good?" For parenting, he suggests we can be "looking at what we are saying or doing with our child or ourselves and asking what is it going to bring about in the future."

I was unable to follow this advice for a year until I had gone to enough Enthusiastic Sobriety parent and Al-Anon meetings and worked with a sponsor. Despite my best intentions, something prevented me from stopping my automatic, sarcastic responses to my children's misbehavior.

What changed after a year? *I* did. I softened. Attending many Al-Anon and Enthusiastic Sobriety parent meetings, I watched people and heard them share in a caring and loving way. I talked often with my sponsor who offered a compassionate ear, had faith in my ability to apply the Twelve Steps to my life, and offered suggestions only when I asked for them. Over time I began to see that I had lived all my life with constant criticism and perfectionism (self-imposed after I left home as a young adult). I knew no other way to think and self-talk. This had also spilled over to my children. As I slowly became more aware of gentler ways to self-talk, I spoke more gently to my kids. Today I am much more capable of following the sage advice mentioned in the first paragraph above.

Today's Reminder
I will speak both honestly and kindly to myself as well as to everyone else.

"As a man thinks in his heart, so is he." Proverbs 23:7

Setting Boundaries: I'd Rather Feel   April 21
Uncomfortable for a Few Minutes than a Few Months!

Changing the way we parent is a slow process of two steps forward and one step back. When I did my inventory, I realized that I was a grand people-pleaser, unconsciously seeking my children's approval for any discipline I asserted. While I was able to set rules, I rarely was able to enforce them, because that made me too unpopular with my kids. I wanted them to love me. The result of not following through with consequences was that my kids did not respect me; they knew every way to manipulate me.

Today I realize that it is a parent's job not only to *set* boundaries but to *enforce* them. My husband and I discussed and agreed upon the rules so we could present a united front. This prevented our teens from dividing and conquering. Our next step was being sure they knew the rules and consequences for violation. Now, when one of the kids asks permission to do anything, my answer is, "I have to talk with your dad and I will get back to you on that."

Another important lesson I learned about consequences was that they have to be *solely* within our control, such as withdrawal of privileges. When necessary, I have needed my husband's back-up to enforce consequences; I am stronger when we act in concert. I have even telephoned another Enthusiastic Sobriety parent for moral support before and after enforcement of consequences. As we all became more diligent in working our programs, things have gone more smoothly. Today our son accepts the consequences of any rules he breaks. I also feel more competent as a parent.

Today's Reminder
I have set boundaries with my kids and use tools—such as a united front, enforceable consequences, and telephone calls to other parents—to help me enforce consequences when necessary.

Enforcing Consequences   April 22

One problem I had with my teen was enforcing consequences for misbehavior. This problem had existed for years with all of my kids, not just with my drug-addicted son. After careful thought, I realized my problem was twofold: I chose unenforceable consequences and I was afraid to enforce any consequences.

An unenforceable consequence is one over which I have little or no control. For example, "If you stay out past curfew, you will have to clean the garage." This consequence is hard to enforce; even if I stand duty in the garage and watch my kid, he may still stand there defiantly and not clean. I have little control over another person's actions. In contrast, an enforceable consequence is one over which I do have control. For example, "If you stay out past curfew, I will not give you the keys to the family car the following evening." This consequence is simple to implement.

In reviewing the household rules I had created for my kids, I had to examine the corresponding consequences for infraction. Why had I chosen so many unenforceable consequences? Maybe I wanted to achieve too much with the consequences—not only "teach them a lesson" but get some housework done by my kids, too. Or maybe I wanted to exert power over them by having them do an unsavory job. I was "showing them who's boss." Regardless, if the consequence involved my kids' doing something that I wanted them to do, I couldn't be sure I could enforce it. I started creating new consequences that I could enforce.

Today's Reminder
I choose a consequence for my teen's misbehavior that is within *my* control, something that *I* can do or refrain from doing.

"Although parents cannot control their children or their environment outside of the home, they can control themselves and their domestic circle." ~*Beyond the Yellow Brick Road*

Enforcing Consequences Revisited   April 23

After creating enforceable consequences, I had to face my fear of enforcing them. In the past I would give my kids a warning. Sometimes I would start to implement a consequence and then let my kids talk me out of it. At other times, the consequence was not immediate and I would conveniently "forget" when the time came.

Why was I so wimpy? I was afraid of my children's disapproval and of conflict. Another parent told me, "No kid says, 'Thank you,' when you give him a consequence!" I needed to have the ego strength to enforce a rule because *I knew it was the right thing to do*, despite the inevitable conflict.

Conflict has always been uncomfortable for me. As a child I avoided it by being very obedient. As a parent I really did not feel calm when my kids would balk at my attempts to enforce rules. To change my own behavior, I began by simply walking into another room when my kids would argue with me about a consequence. Sometimes, I called another parent who encouraged me and reinforced my desire to carry out the consequence. Then I stood firm and refused to listen to their pleas. I used enforceable consequences within my personal control such as not giving them money or a ride or the use of the family car. Slowly I became successful at enforcing consequences. My kids began to see that I meant what I said. They began following my household rules. After an initial rocky start, conflict lessened.

Today's Reminder
As I stand firm and follow through with a consequence despite my teen's displeasure, he receives a consistent, logical message about my household rules.

"Kids will not always follow the rules…They will experiment with all kinds of navigational tools of which you don't approve. But although they may drift out of your sight from time to time, they will always see the land out the corner of their eye…[B]e the land, firm, immovable, reassuring." ~*Beyond the Yellow Brick Road*

Chaos Void   April 24

A few months into the Enthusiastic Sobriety parent group, I became aware of a feeling of unease. Things seemed to be going well for my son in his recovery, for the rest of my family, and for myself. I was changing, and I also knew that I needed to change more. But something was still nagging me. It felt like the calm before the storm or waiting for the second shoe to drop.

At one of Bob Meehan's visits to our Enthusiastic Sobriety Program I spoke with him about my ill-defined, uneasy feeling. "What you're suffering from," he said, "I call 'chaos void'. You've been living in the chaotic world of your substance-abusing child for so long that it has become a way of life. Now that your child is in recovery and the chaos has subsided, you need to change your 'normal' way of life, which was actually an abnormal way of life."

In an instant, it made so much sense. The uneasy feeling did not instantly evaporate. With any mysterious ailment, once there is a label for it, work can begin to address it. So it was with this new label of what I was feeling. There was a path to follow to make appropriate changes. I recognized that it would be folly to slip back into the chaos-reaction mode again. When the world around us is in chaos, we have a choice as to whether to join the fray.

Today's Reminder
There is often chaos and drama when living with an active addict or alcoholic. Once that person is in recovery, I can enjoy the quiet and choose to stay in peace.

Self-Care is More Important Than My "To Do" List
April 25

When I heard a friend say this, I felt like a thunderbolt had struck me. Most of the items of my "to do list" related to my teenagers. Truly, many of these things didn't need to be on my "to do" list, anyway! For example, "make breakfast for the kids" and "fill the family car with gas before the kids leave for school" were two things that my teens are perfectly capable of doing themselves. Instead of feeling I have to take care of everyone else's needs in the family first – which may have been appropriate for me as a mother when my children were toddlers – I can actually take care of myself first.

Although unlearning old behavior which served the family well when the kids were little takes time, I have noticed that when I start my day out with some time for myself to pray, meditate, work out, or sit quietly with a cup of coffee, I feel so much better during the entire day. I usually get many things done, and I find that the items that don't get done either are wholly unnecessary or can wait until tomorrow. Somehow I have learned better how to prioritize. My life is becoming more relaxed and serene today as I remember to take care of myself first.

Today's Reminder
I will take care of myself first, then check my "to do" list and delete any item which is not really my responsibility.

Unmanageability: Step One April 26
The Enthusiastic Sobriety Programs' Step One is: "We admitted that mind-changing chemicals have caused at least part of our lives to become unmanageable."

My kid has caused me all kinds of grief I never anticipated. His lying, sneaking, stealing, and brushes with the law have sent me reeling. Hadn't I taught him better than that? Yes, I taught him right from wrong, but he didn't care because he was "under foreign management"—the influence of drugs! I have spent nights awake, wondering if he was really home or had sneaked out; I cried and prayed to God to help my baby. Even though our family was not yet in the program, I was turning to a Higher Power. Except I thought that only my son needed help!

The more I realized what a wreck I was—without sleep, worrying, and fearing the worst in the future—the more I saw that *I* needed relief, that *I* needed a change in *my* life. Just as much as I wanted my son to become sober, I also wanted to experience a good night's sleep and feel confident in setting and enforcing consequences. I needed a map for parenting in these uncharted waters. I became open to the idea of participating in parent meetings and a Twelve Step program where I could get some help, too. And now I thank God that I did.

Today's Reminder
Dealing with a dishonest youth who is abusing alcohol and drugs makes *my* life unmanageable. To get respite from this stress, I will turn to a Higher Power and a Twelve Step program, such as Al-Anon or one of the Enthusiastic Sobriety programs.

Unexpected Benefits April 27

When my son entered an Enthusiastic Sobriety treatment program, I sought to show support for him by becoming involved in the parent meetings. Soon I saw that I had a unique opportunity to work on problems in *my life* that could be solved through the Twelve Steps. These issues had affected me for many years, so I decided to use this opportunity to work on them. I came to the Enthusiastic Sobriety parent group to help my son and, unexpectedly ended up helping myself too.

What really helped me was to learn to *let things go*, giving them up to my higher power to work things out. I never had much spirituality in my life and decided that all it would take was to believe there was a power greater than myself, (not intellectualizing about who, what or how). I started to give things up to him (her, or it). I found that it helped in my relationships with my son, my wife, and at my work. I had let things overwhelm me, trying to solve things that I didn't have control over. I regularly commune with my higher power asking help to get through these things that I have no control over. It has made an incredible change in my life. It has been almost five years and I feel an inner peace that I have never felt before.

Today's Reminder
I let go of other people, places, and things that I have no control over. I relax, knowing that things will work out as they were meant to.

Don't Major in Minor Things   April 28

When our family was first introduced to a sobriety program, our only objective was to get help for our daughter. We were willing to buy her cigarettes (a habit which we detested), participate in the parent program, and let her hang out until all hours of the morning. When her out-patient treatment ended, we expected her to start cleaning her room, go back to school, and become a respectful young adult. That was our first lesson in expectations breeding disaster. Several years have passed. We now understand that dirty socks, messy rooms, and trashy cars don't really matter in life. What does matter is accepting our kids for who they are and remembering where we were at 15, 16 and 17 years of age. We work on the major issues in life: loving and respecting each member of our family, giving them hope, enjoying even the stupid stuff they do, and letting minor things go. There will come a day when our child will discover that she likes clean socks!

Today's Reminder
Dear Lord, help me discover what is really important in my life.

Life is More Than Good Grades — April 29

For a long time we did not know that our son had a drug problem. We suspected that he had experimented with marijuana, but we considered it "just pot," nothing to raise concern. Plus, his grades were always good.

In time, he went to college. He continued to have good grades. Later, though, we noticed that a significant sum of money was missing from our son's bank account. He came to us and admitted he had a problem with drugs. He told us that he knew if he maintained good grades, we would not suspect he was abusing drugs. We asked him if he wanted help, and he said, "Yes." We took him to see a counselor who strongly urged us to look at a local Enthusiastic Sobriety drug treatment program. It was the beginning of the family's road to recovery. He went to Step Two, the Enthusiastic Sobriety sober living facility, and he relapsed afterward. Nevertheless, he stuck with the local Enthusiastic Sobriety intensive out-patient program, and we continued going to parent meetings. He has some sobriety now, and we all work our own program one day at a time.

Today's Reminder
Today I strive for balance. As a parent, I will be aware of different aspects of my kid's life. I will also show him love and understanding, one day at a time.

My Gift to My Son Was a Gift to Myself — April 30

A co-worker kindly told me about her son's experience with drugs and alcohol and about an Enthusiastic Sobriety program for young people which had helped her family. When I finally realized that my son was both an alcoholic and drug addict, I took action. I wasn't sure that I could afford the program, but with a few sacrifices, I found a way. He entered our local program, and I began going faithfully to the parent meetings. I also did service for the group, got a sponsor, and began working Step One.

After a few months I discovered that my self-sacrificing gift to my son turned out to be a gift to myself as well. I had been a Love and Logic parent gone bad. That is, I had given up on any logical consequences for my son's poor behavior and had hoped that natural consequences would suffice. While I told myself that I didn't want to stifle his creativity, the truth is that I was afraid to enforce logical consequences. With the help of the Twelve Step program as well as the legal consequences of my son's poor choices, I have been taking back my role as a parent. I now see that truly loving my child means that I cannot support his unhealthy and unproductive behavior. In the past I exhausted my strength by rescuing and enabling him after he made poor choices. With the help of our Enthusiastic Sobriety program, I now use my strength to guide him toward healthy choices by using logical consequences. The other parents in the program have been my "winners" with whom I stick; they help me navigate the challenging waters of raising an alcoholic and drug-abusing teenager.

Today's Reminder
I find the courage to enforce consequences for my teenager's poor choices; I no longer leave consequences to the outside world.

"Love means not accepting wrong behavior." ~*Beyond the Yellow Brick Road*

MAY

International Help   **May 1**

I have family in another country and have felt sad that they do not have available to them the same kind of teen and young adult drug and alcohol treatment program that we have in the United States. Yet, I have been reminded that the programs of Alcoholic's Anonymous (for alcoholics) and Al-Anon (for families of alcoholics) are in many countries today. A 2008 survey from the A.A. website states that there is A.A. activity in 180 countries; the book, *Alcoholics Anonymous*, has been translated into 50 languages and other AA pamphlets have been translated into 80 languages.[4] Plus the Al-Anon website in 2009 reported Al-Anon in 115 countries. Al-Anon literature has been translated into 30 languages and more translations are expected.[5] There are meetings in many places.

Reading of Al-Anon and Alcoholics Anonymous literature can help answer many questions about the programs. Also, the Internet is a great communication tool. Electronic meetings are available by request on the Al-Anon website.[6] There are also on-line meetings for A.A.[7] It is comforting to know that no matter where a family is, some form of help is available for those who seek it.

---

[4] From AA Guidelines Literature Committees, p. 4, found at: http://www.aa.org/en_pdfs/mg-09_literaturecommittees.pdf
[5] From Ten Questions About Conference Approved Literature, pp. 1 &2, found at: http://siafg.org/Literature/TenLiteratureQuestions.pdf
[6] See http://www.al-anon.alateen.org/grpsrvreqform.html
[7] See http://aa-intergroup.org/

Today's Reminder
If a parent wants to find help for himself and his alcoholic child, he can find it.

Bullets and Walls May 2

We Enthusiastic Sobriety parents have all heard the importance of establishing bullets (or shots) and walls with our children. I prefer to think of bullets as "What hills are you prepared to die for?" My wife and I thought long and hard over this. We decided we had just two.

The first was that he had to truly want to get and stay sober. His actions had to match his words. Then we would do everything in our power to help him.

The second was that we would not in any way enable or support his use of drugs. If he chose to continue doing drugs, he would not be able to: live in our home, play his video games, have a car and all the other things that came with being part of our family. We would wish him the best of luck, but we loved him too much to watch him continue his self-destructive behavior.

We had our discussion on a Sunday morning. He went out that night, returned later, and told us that he had used drugs. We defended our hill and informed him he had to move out. The first few weeks were the hardest, but I believe that we did the right thing. That was seven weeks ago. We are not out of the woods yet, but I truly believe he is doing well and really working the program. He has said that this was the best thing that we could have done. He is working on earning the right to move back in with us and be part of our family.

Today's Reminder
A parent's job includes setting boundaries and letting a child know what acceptable and unacceptable behavior is. Today I will not shirk my parental responsibility; I will have boundaries in place and enforce consequences when necessary.

"The school of hard knocks is an accelerated curriculum."
~Menander of Athens

How I Successfully Used the Program to Help with Other Life Challenges   May 3

Coping with a drug-addicted son was a significant life challenge for my husband, and me and we attended many parent meetings. After some time I incorporated a number of slogans into my life as ways of coping with daily occurrences.

I did not know that the Twelve Step program would help me with yet another significant life challenge. My husband contracted a rare disease which was difficult for the doctors to diagnose. He was in a coma for many days while I stayed by his bedside at the hospital. I could not accept it when the hospital suggested placing him in a nursing home. Amazingly, he came out of the coma and started on the slow road to recovery. I used all the tools I had learned from the program. I had to keep calm for him as well as myself. Although I was quite sad when he didn't know my name, I remembered what I had heard from the program: "Don't take it personally; it's the disease." I wrote in my gratitude journal daily. Each day I found things to be grateful for. He continued to make progress. While he is not fully recovered today, I am grateful for the life we have together now. I use the slogans often. For example when he forgets something,

I can get upset, or ask myself, "How important is it?" I had no idea that the Twelve Step way of life would help me so much, and I am glad today that I found it.

Today's Reminder
I will remember that the Twelve Step program is a way of life and can help me handle *all* situations.

Making My Children Happy — May 4

Whenever my kids suffered one of life's little disappointments, I always rushed to do something to "make them happy." While I was obliged to see that their basic needs were met, I really had no *control* over their happiness. The story of the two boys who wake up on Christmas morning and find a room full of manure is illustrative. One is dejected; the other excitedly asks, "Where's the pony?" While I can control *my* actions, I cannot control external circumstances or the response of others.

Today, I recognize that I am *not* responsible for my teenagers' happiness. I will not manipulate situations to "make them happy." I will let my teens experience their feelings, and I will experience mine. I accept what is.

Today's Reminder
I am not responsible for others' happiness. In lieu of trying to shut off feelings of discomfort, I experience a range of feelings and accept life as it is.

"People are disturbed not by things, but by the view they take of them." ~Epictetus

Beyond Blame   May 5

When my kid was getting high, he was unbearable to live with. He avoided me except to ask for money. I suspected he was taking money from my wallet. He would stay out past curfew or come home only to sneak out again. He was neither civil nor respectful in his brief conversations with me, which often ended in yelling. At first, I saw everything he was doing wrong and blamed him. I believed that the unhappiness in the family was entirely his fault.

Later, as I started attending both Enthusiastic Sobriety parent and Al-Anon meetings, I was able to see things differently. I started to look at how I caused some unhappiness, too. I did not say what I meant and stick to it. I did not have the gumption to enforce rules. Since my son saw that he could get away with breaking the rules, he did.

Eventually, I stopped blaming and being resentful. My son and I both had our problems. My son's problem was drinking alcohol and using drugs; mine was not being a confident, assertive parent who could state rules clearly and enforce consequences. The blaming and shaming did nothing to help change the situation.

Gradually, I moved from blame to acceptance. The past cannot be changed, but I can take action in the present. I talked with other parents who were more skilled at setting rules and enforcing consequences. I learned to respond more appropriately to different situations and improve my parenting skills as my son got sober. Recovery meant progress for both of us.

Today's Reminder
When setting rules and consequences today, if in doubt, I conduct a reality check with other parents in program. Are my

rules and consequences logical and reasonable? If so, I am confident and do not back down. My kids see that I mean what I say.

Detachment Means No Tears   May 6

Detachment means no tears in front of your kids. You may be upset and afraid but you cannot show it in front of them. Talk with your spouse and members of the parent group before you talk with your kids. Cry with the other parents but then be firm with your kids.

We faced a "tough love" situation with our younger son—the one *not* in an Enthusiastic Sobriety program. My husband and I told both of our kids that there could be "no drugs in them or on them" and that we expected *everyone* in our house to be sober. Because our younger son violated this rule, we told him he had to leave our home. He did and moved in with a drug-using friend whose parent did not appear to mind their using drugs. Later when our son was arrested for possession of marijuana, I wrote the judge on the case. I explained about our older son being in a drug rehab program and the family household rules. Believing that "tough love" would help our younger son make better choices, I asked the judge to impose the heaviest sentence possible. The judge obliged by taking away my son's driver's license and ordering a fine, community service, and one year's probation. He also had to give periodic urine samples. If he violated probation, he would have to return to court and most likely serve a jail sentence. This worked out quite well for our second son. Although he was furious at the time, he now admits that this helped him steer clear of trouble.

Today's Reminder
Enforcing consequences can be difficult and require moral support. If I am faced with a "tough love" situation, I can "bookend" enforcement of a consequence with a phone call to a parent in program both before and after.

The Value of Step Meetings and Other Parents   May 7

As part of working my Twelve Step program, I went to the weekly parent meetings and also attended the parent step meetings (meetings devoted to working the Twelve Steps.) I worked the steps to the best of my ability and got to know the other parents.

It was a cold and snowy December night that my daughter told me she intended to leave her group and use illegal drugs again. The parent group encouraged me to hold fast to the rule of only sober people can live in our home. I met her at home and I handed her coat to her and said, "You know the walls in our house. You cannot live here when you are using drugs. See you when you are willing to be sober." It was a very hard thing to do, but it was also a relief for me and a turning point in both of our lives. Two weeks later she called me from a gas station and said she was willing to talk with an Enthusiastic Sobriety counselor and return to treatment.

Talking one-on-one with other parents, outside of formal meetings, I gained so much knowledge of how to handle life with a teenaged-drug addict. I am so grateful for the parents who have shared their experience with me. I no longer pride myself on my self-sufficiency. I know now that there are problems I cannot solve alone, and it is wise to use my resources, including the Twelve Steps and the parent group.

Today's Reminder
Garnering help when needed is not a sign of weakness but a sign of wisdom and strength.

From a Deer in the Headlights to a Person Who Enjoys Life   May 8

I walked into an Enthusiastic Sobriety parent meeting and felt like a deer in the headlights. I was so lost. This was my last resort; I had tried everything else and nothing worked. As I entered, I felt a peace come over me. I sunk into a chair to observe, hoping to find some answers. I heard others tell *my* story. How did they know? They knew, and they had compassion in their hearts and knowledge that I was seeking. I asked thousands of questions and left with hope. That was two years ago. I am now a person who lives my own life and is not running around trying to live everyone else's. I am at peace and the sickly fear that overtook my life for many years has passed. I am filled with hope. The road for a parent of an addict is never easy. Yet, who said that life was easy? I find that the way I handle things now is very different from that day when I first walked in.

The answer for me was the parent *support* group. I asked and gleaned information from so many people. I also found a sponsor who helped me cope by being there for me as I worked the Twelve Steps. I can now smile, laugh and enjoy.

Today's Reminder
The fellowship of the program helps me cope with my child's addiction. I will attend meetings, talk with other parents, get a sponsor and be a sponsor to others.

"To some parents, the program is a mixed blessing...to other parents, the program...has gotten their child off drugs and healed wounds in family relationships that they thought were terminal. Such parents have used their child's experience with drugs as a catalyst for change." ~*Beyond the Yellow Brick Road*

Ode to the Cornerstone[8] Counselors   May 9

Dear Counselors,

You are God's hands on this earth
And I am eternally grateful for the work you have done
On behalf of my two favorite people.
You make your chosen profession as personal as breathing
And the impact on my kids has been just as profound.
Just as I still love to peek into my grown-up kids' rooms
And see their sleeping faces,
I love to chance peeking into their souls,
Because that door is now open.
A great gift to this mother!

Thank you, Counselors,
For encouraging my kids
To trust that open door in themselves
And to seek that door in others.

---

[8] Cornerstone is the Enthusiastic Sobriety program located in Denver, Colorado.

Today's Reminder

I am grateful today for the recovery opportunities available to me and my family through Twelve Step programs.

Keeping Faith   May 10

My son reluctantly went through an Enthusiastic Sobriety outpatient program and also went on to Step 2, the sober living facility. I think he was sober and working the program for about 100 days before he started drinking again. Because of his return to drinking, he dropped out of the program and left home.

He has continued to go to school and get good grades. He holds down a part-time job and for the most part, looks normal to the outside world and to himself. However, he continues to drink and the drinking continues to have disastrous consequences. He has totaled two cars while drunk. Fortunately, no one was hurt, but he is now on probation. Because of his disease, he doesn't see how the DUI's on his record could hurt him or how close he came to death, so he continues to believe he is just like everyone else and can drink and party.

There is currently a ray of hope. He is seeing a counselor, and after a significant time in therapy he is starting to perceive there is a problem.

Throughout this process, I have cried and pleaded with God and prayed for my son, only to come to the realization that my son's path will be what it will be and that God's plan for him is not my plan. It has been a long road of letting go for me. I know I can't change him. I know that all I can do is let go and let God. I have to do that every single day.

Today's Reminder:
Dear God, I know that it is "Your will" and on "Your time". Please give me faith to believe that Your plan is the right plan and continue to guide me to do Your will.

The 4th "C" — May 11

There is an Al-Anon saying, the "three 'C's: I didn't cause it (alcoholism), I can't control it, and I can't cure it." We parents can remember a 4th C, too, "don't complicate." That is, if we try to get into our kid's business, we can really complicate things. Even though I know I should stay out of my son's way and let him live his own life in recovery, I am especially fond of giving him unsolicited advice. He, luckily, is very good about reminding me when I am overstepping my parental role. In the early days, he would get very angry with me, but now we are both gentler with each other as we make mistakes. He is a young adult, in recovery, and can handle most situations for himself. Yet I have tried to "advise" him on such things as: what outfit to wear, how to ask for time off from his boss, and what social clubs he should join. Giving such advice creates two problems. On the one hand, it is insulting. On the other hand, should he actually decide to take my advice, he might blame me if things don't go well. It is so much better to steer clear of his business and let him make his own decisions.

Today's Reminder
I will avoid complicating matters for my child and keep it simple. I will keep my mouth closed and breathe deeply (through my nose!) the next time I am tempted to give unsolicited advice.

Parenting and Unproductive Thoughts   May 12

When we took our son in for treatment, I felt miserable and could certainly believe that my life was unmanageable. I felt like a failure as a parent, and I was angry with my son for experimenting with drugs in the first place which led to his addiction.

The longer I kept going to parent meetings and reading Twelve Step literature, the wider my eyes opened. When I was a child, I did my best to be a good little girl who followed all the rules. As an adult, I wanted to have children who would strive for perfection. When my kids rebelled, I was angry with them and afraid that I was not being the perfect parent. I wondered, "What's wrong with me? Why has my son turned out like this?"

My problem was my longstanding false and unproductive thoughts. First, I was under the delusion that children should act like perfect little adults with minimal need for correction. On the contrary, it is *normal* for kids to test the rules. They learn by doing and discovering what consequences follow—not by having an intellectual discussion. So my anger with my kids for misbehaving was unproductive. Second, I didn't realize the magnitude of a parent's job in teaching a child appropriate social behavior. I was afraid I couldn't learn to do this well. (No problem: there are many opportunities for "on the job training.") And third, I was being very self-centered. My thoughts revolved around me: what *I* was doing wrong, how *I* had failed as a parent, what my son was doing *to me* by failing to follow the path *I* had for him, etc. Since this realization, I have worked on catching myself in false and unproductive thoughts. As I change my thoughts, I change my behavior, and my life changes for the better.

Today's Reminder
When I begin to feel disturbed, I look at my thoughts. Are they grounded in reality or filled with unrealistic expectations of myself and others? If necessary, I will call my sponsor or another parent in the program to help me sort things out.

The Guilt Game   May 13

In Bob Meehan's book, *Beyond the Yellow Brick Road,* he writes about the "guilt game:" a parent assuming responsibility for his child's actions and blaming himself whenever his child doesn't meet his expectations.

As parents, we do the best we can with the information and skills we have at any given time. We can always look back and see how we could have done something differently or "better," but what purpose does this serve? I've heard that it is alright to look at the past, but it is impolite to stare.

I want my life and family to be happier now. I have to relinquish my hold on the past and think about what I can do today to meet my goal. I can focus on my own emotional sobriety and notice my own fears and resentments when they crop up. I can talk with another parent about these and/or pray and meditate, and then take any actions necessary. It is amazing to me that the process of getting a second opinion from another parent helps me sort out things. Then I often take no action or a very limited action with confidence. When I do this, I no longer feel guilty about my parenting decisions.

Today's Reminder
I release guilt about my past parenting, and I use the tools of the program to help with parenting decisions over which I am struggling today.

Little Red Hen No More — May 14

As a mom, I acted like the little red hen, except that I did the hen one better. Instead of asking people for help, getting none, and doing it all myself, I assumed no one in my family would help. After all, hadn't each one of them refused in the past? So I did everything and unwittingly fueled my self-righteousness, martyrdom, and resentments. As for my kids, they developed a dependence and lack of faith in their ability to do anything. Reflecting on statements by other parents in program helped me recognize this. What I had thought was a virtue—doing everything—was actually a vice. It embittered me and dwarfed my children's growth and self-confidence.

Now I am more conscious of my actions and let go of the desire to do it all. I ask for help and delegate household tasks. This keeps me more connected with my children and increases their experience and self-confidence.

Today's Reminder
Today I ask for help with specific tasks from my children. I rely on them, avoid isolation, and receive the rewards of seeing my children develop into mature, confident persons.

"Give a man a fish and you feed him for a day. Teach a man to fish and you feed him for a lifetime." ~Chinese Proverb

Help is a Four Letter Word   May 15

I used to "help" my teenager get up in the morning by waking him. I used to "help" him get to school by chauffeuring him the mile and a half to school. I used to "help" him keep track of his homework by e-mailing his teachers or checking their websites to find out the current homework. I used to "help" him get schoolwork done by buying all materials he needed for projects, staying up late with him to edit his papers, and "helping" him put together posters. I used to "help" him by paying his fines for overdue library books—because, after all, it was really *my fault* for not "helping" him remember when they were due. I used to "help" him if he did something wrong by giving him a warning, forgiving him, and giving him another chance.

At meetings I listened to other parents; I was not alone. We had all hindered our children from learning and maturing. Now I see that my energy is better spent creating and enforcing boundaries (aka "walls" and "shots") to encourage my child to make good choices.

Today's Reminder
Today I will not interfere with my child's learning.

"Instead of placing ourselves between our children and the consequences of their actions, we should spend our energy building walls between our children and actions that lead to negative consequences. If we build good, strong walls, we as parents will feel good about ourselves." ~*Beyond the Yellow Brick Road,*

How My Sponsor Helped   May 16

After having been in the program for a while, my son became critical of the group and started calling it a "cult." He "graduated" from his Enthusiastic Sobriety program and went to Alcoholics Anonymous for a short time, another "cult" in his mind. His attitude became cocky, he landed in jail for dishonest, drug-related behavior, and when he was released he talked like he was a victim of the system. He wasn't taking responsibility for his own part in causing his problems.

It was clear to me that I had to be strong. My husband and I needed to stand fast to our resolve and refuse to "rescue" our son or do for him what he ought to do for himself. Feeling weak, I knew my husband and I had to present a "united front" or else our son would manipulate us to get what he wanted. When faced with a request, I made *no* decision. First I called my sponsor; I did not make a move without consulting her. She helped me clarify my thoughts so I could see which responses would truly help and which were just repeating our old pattern of "rescuing" him. I then discussed it with my husband, and we decided which response was best for us. My sponsor was a great help and comfort during this difficult time. I recommend both having and being a sponsor.

Today's Reminder
When in doubt about how to handle my child's request, I will not give an immediate answer. I will consult my sponsor or another parent in the program to reason things out, and I will discuss it with my spouse so we can create a united front.

"People become better parents when they get together and share their mistakes and successes – when they educate one another.

This is particularly true when parents confront a drug-abusing teenager. They have no precedent to act upon...and their best resource is someone who has faced it." ~*Beyond the Yellow Brick Road*

It's Only Halftime   May 17

My kid's life was spinning out of control with drugs; I felt like a failure as a mother. I was consumed with thoughts about what I did wrong, what I should have done instead of what I did, and what horrible things might happen to him if he continued on the same trajectory. My constant, futile mental efforts to re-write the past and predict the future were driving me crazy. I had to STOP! I remembered what Bob Meehan said in *Beyond the Yellow Brick Road*, "It's only halftime."

Right now I can decide to change how I interact with my teen. I can take it one day—and if necessary, one minute—at a time. When I feel myself getting into a mental frenzy about the past or future, I can stop, take a deep breath, and look at my life this very minute. Is *my* life okay? Do I have everything I need to make it through this day? If so, I take a deep breath and relax. If not, I do the next right thing to get my own needs met. Often I am not even with my kid, so I need to keep my thoughts on *my own life*. By relieving the self-made pressure, I become tranquil and better able to handle any situation concerning my teen as it arises.

Today's Reminder
Because interacting with my teen has become so emotionally charged for me, I can do myself a favor by simply turning my

thoughts away from my child and turning them toward what I need to do for myself right now and get busy doing it.

I Made a Decision Not to Live in Fear — May 18

When my underage daughter was newly sober, she had to pay court-ordered restitution for a harm she had caused. At first, I would make a payment when she was unable to do so. She would say things like, "My sobriety's more important. I can't work and stay sober."

Eventually, I realized that she was manipulating me. I resolved that I did not want to "walk on eggshells" around her. *Nothing I said or did was going to keep her sober! She and her Higher Power had to do that!* So, I made a decision right then to risk my relationship with my daughter and stop living in fear. Then I acted upon my decision. I made it clear that I would not be making any more payments for her and that she would have to find a way to pay, such as getting a job. I let the natural consequences flow. She knew she could go to jail if she did not pay by the deadline. I stopped doing for her what she could and needed to do for herself. Also I stopped worrying and engaging in "What if" thoughts that led to fear. Instead, today if I become aware of a thought of worry or fear, I turn my thoughts to my many blessings and feel grateful.

Today's Reminder
Today I do not allow my child to manipulate me into taking ownership of her responsibilities. She knows that she must take care of her responsibilities and I will take care of mine.

Willing to Go to Any Lengths   May 19

When my wife and I married, it became clear to us that her daughter was angry at the world and out of control. We would drop her off at school by the front door only to have her leave school immediately out the back door. She would not come home for a couple of days. She was found once at a known drug user's home. We tried to monitor her by putting a tracker on her cell phone and using cyber alert. To no avail. She was still getting high. At the rate she was going with drugs, I thought, "We may only have one shot at this. If we don't get it right the first time, there may not be a second chance."

We confronted her and insisted that she get treatment. We were familiar with an Enthusiastic Sobriety drug rehabilitation program based on the Twelve Steps. The program was located several hours' from our home, so we arranged to drop her off so she could stay for a long weekend, spend time with the teens in the program, and attend some of the young people's functions. She decided she was interested in the program and sobriety, so we picked her up and brought her home to pack and get ready. We planned to drive her back to the program in a few days. At this point she had three or four days' sobriety. Once back home she was afraid she might get high, so she called some of her newly-made Enthusiastic Sobriety friends to help her to stay sober. These kids drove several hours to pick her up and encourage her to stay sober! My wife and I were sold on the program. We moved to the area to support our child. Attending the parent meetings and working the Twelve Steps, I have been impressed with the change for the better in our family life.

Today's Reminder
I do everything I can to encourage my teenager to get treatment. I also attend meetings and work the Twelve Steps myself.

Getting Support from Other Parents — May 20

My daughters, both sober and in program for a year, are working and over eighteen. I decided it was time for them, as adults, to take more responsibility for their lives and told them that they will have to pay me $100 rent each month to continue living in my home, beginning the first of next month – about two weeks from now. They were very angry with me and let me know it. They called me selfish, among other things, but I held fast, and did not take their remarks personally. After all, who likes having more bills to pay? Immediately after this I went to an Enthusiastic Sobriety parent meeting and shared about my experience. Parents approached me after the meeting and supported me. I know that my kids will have to live entirely on their own and be financially independent soon. I want them to be prepared and start budgeting for necessities, not using all of their income for luxuries. My job as a parent is to help them become independent. Despite their reaction, I know I am doing the right thing for them. The support of the parent group makes it easier to carry on with my job.

Today's Reminder
My kids do not always like it when I set limits, but I will do it anyway and let their objections go by the wayside.

"Don't Just Do Something, Sit There" — May 21

I was told at a newcomers' Al-Anon meeting that this is not an official Al-Anon slogan, but many people find it useful. I soon took the slogan to heart. It reminds me to keep my "hands off" my teen whenever there is something that is her responsibility. I have to let her take ownership of the chores and tasks that are hers. If she chooses not to do them, she can learn from life what happens.

I have added to this slogan, "Don't just do something, sit there, or do something for yourself." So whenever I get the urge to "fix" something for my daughter or another, I stop. Instead, I sit and relax, or I think of something to do for myself. This reminds me to take the focus off my teen and others. If I don't feel I can sit and relax, I can do something for me, such as read a good book or take a bubble bath.

Today's Reminder
Instead of trying to solve my teen's problems, I choose to "back off." I will take it easy and relax, or focus on what I can do to take care of myself.

Getting Better After Getting Started — May 22

When our son first entered the Enthusiastic Sobriety program, my husband and I went out for coffee with other parents after meetings every week. This really helped us get a "jump start" on a more effective approach to parenting. Another benefit of treatment was that our son was so busy working his program that he was rarely home! This was a welcome relief from all the negative interactions we had had with him before he got into treatment. He was getting immersed in the ideas needed for sobriety while we were getting immersed in ideas which would help us parent a troubled teen.

As we continued to go to weekly meetings, we learned about situations that other parents faced and how they handled these. We all had similar situations to face as our children grew into adulthood: our child's returning to school, getting (or getting back) a driver's license, getting a job, living at home or on his own, receiving financial support (or not) while transitioning to sobriety and adulthood. We shared how we faced our individual situations and used the principles of the Twelve Steps to guide us. Hearing how other parents had managed really helped. It gave us the courage to face these issues head-on and communicate clearly and directly with our son, who did the same with us.

We do our best each day to apply the principles of the program. Some days we forget and return to old patterns. Yet, the more we practice the principles, the better our parenting gets.

Today's Reminder
Parenting a troubled teen takes energy and commitment. Today I commit to doing what I can to help my child, including going to meetings, listening and sharing with other parents, and applying the Twelve Steps in my daily life.

"A journey of a thousand miles must begin with a single step."
~Lao-tzu

A Parent's Dreams of Success   May 23

Soon after our family started coming to an Enthusiastic Sobriety program, I was advised by one of the counselors to get a sponsor, a parent who could answer my questions and help me apply the Twelve Steps to my own life. She also advised me to list the ways that I had been manipulated by my kids. When they did something they shouldn't, they often asked me to negotiate with their father for a softer penalty. Many times my daughter told me that she was going to the library, going to a friend's house to do homework, or staying up late to study for a test when she was actually drinking or doing coke. Many times she whined and pleaded for something and said things such as, "If you loved me, you'd do this," or "All the other kids can do this, why can't I?" All these manipulative techniques worked on me.

I needed to learn a new way of coping. I needed to risk my children's disapproval. I needed to gain confidence in my parenting skills and the courage to confront my children with their wrongdoing and enforce consequences. I also needed to recognize when my kids were lying by using worthy excuses to leave the house. In the past whenever they mentioned anything that I believed would further their academic success, I wanted so much for them to be successful that I believed them.

With the help of my sponsor and other parents in the group, I learned to recognize manipulative techniques. Now I have firm limits in place with enforceable consequences, and my husband and I stay on the same page. Together we are able to calmly and lovingly implement tough love when necessary. Now that my children know there will be consequences for poor choices, I contribute much more to their success in life than I did in the past.

Today's Reminder
By becoming aware of manipulative techniques my children use, I can stay firm and enforce consequences for their wrongdoings.

Why Do *I* Have to Change? — May 24

This was my question as a parent new to an Enthusiastic Sobriety program. I felt that my husband and I had been kind and loving parents and that our son had gone astray for reasons we could not fathom. Our son, who has a problem with mind-changing chemicals, needed to change; we didn't. At this stage we could not see how our own thinking had become distorted, and at times unreasonable, by living with our wayward son.

I soon learned that we didn't have to change, unless we wanted our relationship with our son to change. Before entering a Twelve Step program, all that we had done to change him –and I felt that we had tried *everything* imaginable to "cure" him—had not worked. The definition of insanity is doing the same thing over and over again and expecting a different result. Our relationship with our son had deteriorated so much that we realized that to get him back again, we needed to change our own behavior.

My husband and I have chosen to change our behavior, each of us at our own pace, as we learn more about the Twelve Steps through attending meetings, reading literature, and working with a sponsor. Meanwhile, so has our son. Today, we have our son back and a much improved relationship with him.

Today's Reminder
I have to change myself because I cannot change any one else.

Receiving the Benefit of the Steps — May 25

My son was shy and suffered from social anxiety. When he went away to college, he struggled. He began using drugs and told me. Initially I was not alarmed, thinking that drinking and smoking pot were merely his social lubricants. However, soon drugs marred his college career. He dropped out and was allowed back in three times. The last time he had a bad experience requiring emergency medical attention and had to leave college permanently. The following summer when he asked to return to his college town to see his friends, I would not agree because I knew that they all used drugs. He locked himself in his room and drank, smoked, and played computer games. He needed help.

I heard that my niece, who lived in another city, was in a drug treatment program located there and doing well, so I suggested we go visit. He agreed. He accompanied her to a weekend social function of the local Enthusiastic Sobriety program. When they arrived, the kids immediately surrounded him and made him feel welcome. He had fun with them and decided to stay with a host family (another family in the program willing to take our son into their home.)

My son has been sober since he began the program two years ago. I have seen him change into a confident young man. He has become a living example of how the steps work. He sponsors a number of other kids and is very happy. I, too, have changed and regularly remind myself to let go and accept that some things are beyond my control.

I am grateful to the Enthusiastic Sobriety program and the Twelve Steps for bringing out the best in my son and me.

Today's Reminder
Once I know that my adult child has a problem with alcohol and/or drugs, I will let him know what options are available for his recovery. It is up to my child to choose; I accept that his choice is beyond my control. Should he choose recovery, I will do what I can to support and encourage him.

Worry is a Poor Use of Imagination — May 26

Early in this program the parent comment that helped me the most was, "I like to be efficient. I only worry about something once." For the next few months, I did my best to remember that idea when I started feeling anxious. If I had already thought through the problem and done my worrying, then I let it go, and recited the Serenity Prayer instead of worrying. It relieved my anxiety and freed my time.

Today's Reminder
Worry is a poor use of imagination. I worry once, let it go, and recite the Serenity Prayer.

Parental Jedi Mind Trick — May 27

Prior to his going to an Enthusiastic Sobriety program, our son refused to do *anything* we asked him to do, even something minor that clearly would benefit him. After he went to the sober living facility, my husband and I spoke with the counselors who taught us to adopt a "Jedi Mind Trick" to *influence* (note: *not* control) our son. We learned that whatever we want our son to do, we have to let go of our emotions, make a request or suggestion, and accept that he may not do it. He has to feel that he has choices in his life and that we respect his decisions. If our request is emotionally charged, it may trigger rebellion. So now we make any suggestion in a very neutral tone. By doing this "Jedi Mind Trick" we avoid power struggles, keep communication open, and influence him on occasion to do what we suggest.

For example, one night our son got home from an Enthusiastic Sobriety function at midnight. My husband and I were very tired and ready for bed. Our son wanted to go out again for coffee with some of his friends. Although we really didn't want him to go out again, I said in a neutral, quiet voice, "You could stay home." He accepted this suggestion, and we retired and got a good night's sleep.

Today's Reminder
I will let go of my desire to have my teen do everything I want. When I want to make a suggestion, I will use the Jedi Mind Trick and let go of the outcome. My teen will have the dignity to make choices.

Dealing with Relapse   May 28

During the years that I've gone to parent meetings, I have heard parents share about their kids who have relapsed. My daughter has relapsed. It is sad, but I have learned that relapse is often part of the recovery path for addicts and alcoholics. I have also learned that I need to take care of myself and do what's healthy for me, no matter where my child is in her sobriety.

I have told my kids that I now know two things for certain: 1) I love them unconditionally. No matter what they do, I will always love them. 2) My children's sobriety is their business; it's their lives and their choices. I will support each of them so long as it's healthy for me. When I begin to feel that my support might be enabling or rescuing, I back off. I consider my motives for wanting to do things for them, and I speak with my sponsor to help me decide on the next right thing. Then I can do it and let go of the outcome.

Today's Reminder
My child's sobriety is her business, and I need to keep healthy myself. That means I will not do for my child what she needs to do for herself. Nor will I shield her from the consequences of poor choices.

Trust but Verify   May 29

Holding my daughter accountable is an important part of recovery for both her and me. As a teenager, she needs structure and an opportunity to be honest. As a parent, I need to set walls and hold her to them. Usually I believe I can trust my child, but I need to verify her statements when I suspect that something is amiss. Verification may result in finding out she told me the truth, so I can rejoice in that. Or, I can find that my parental lie detector was working accurately and it's time to stand fast to my walls and hold her accountable.

For example, once when my daughter's sobriety was fragile, she told me that she wanted to go to the movies with a 'friend" (fellow drug addict, not in recovery) and then stay over at the friend's house. I gave her permission, but I added the condition that she telephone me from the friend's home phone (land line) when they arrived at her house. She decided not to go and willingly entered an intensive inpatient program a couple of days later.

Today's Reminder
I decide to trust my child, but if my gut tells me something is not right, I verify.

No Victims, Only Volunteers May 30

What does this saying have to do with parenting a child with an alcohol problem? After spending some time in the parent group, I realized that I have felt like a victim all my life. Whenever my daughter and anyone else criticized me, I assumed that they were right and I was wrong. I internalized their criticism.

I now see that I can choose. When someone criticizes me, I can choose whether to accept their criticism or not. I can decide that their criticism is not valid and not let it bother me. Occasionally, I may decide a criticism has some merit. In that case, I can accept myself as a human being who, like everyone else, is not perfect. I haven't got my angel wings yet, so I'll simply resolve to do better in the future.

I also no longer "volunteering" to be treated disrespectfully. If anyone does not treat me with respect, I tell that person how I want to be treated. By speaking up for myself, I let go of the "victim" role and am empowered to have happier, healthier relationships.

Today's Reminder
I have a choice to accept or reject criticism or disrespectful behavior. Today I choose to assert my need to be treated respectfully and I treat others with respect.

Expectations Breed Disaster   May 31

Drug addiction and alcoholism are not like other diseases. One can be treated for tuberculosis today and fully recover, but addictions are trickier. Addicts can receive the treatment—the most effective being a Twelve Step program—and reject it; or they can accept it for a while and then relapse. My husband and I placed our son in an Enthusiastic Sobriety out-patient treatment program. He did very well and was a "model" of recovery: sober for five years, doing lots of Twelve Step work and sponsoring a number of other teens and young adults. Once he "graduated" from the young adult program and was to enter AA, though, he lost his resolve and stopped working the program. He started spending time with former friends who had done drugs and eventually started using again. I was devastated. I had expected him to be "cured" after five years of recovery.

I have to remember that drug addiction is a disease. I didn't cause it, I can't control it, and I can't cure it. My son is on his own path. As a mother, I did my best by providing him with a program that worked when he chose to work it. The rest is up to him and his Higher Power. I have to let go and let God. This is easier said than done, of course. I do this one day at a time. I use the tools of the Al-Anon program. I read literature, not only Al-Anon, but the books, *Beyond the Yellow Brick Road* by Bob Meehan and *Co-Dependent No More* by Melody Beattie. I go to as many meetings as I can. I speak with other parents in the program and keep in close contact with my sponsor. I work the steps myself. With the help of the group I get through difficult times.

Today's Reminder
I am realistic about the nature of this disease. I am grateful for every day of sobriety my child has, but I do not expect a "cure." I do my best to live one day at a time, detaching from my child's illness and maintaining my own *emotional* sobriety by letting go of worry and unhealthy fear.

JUNE

Family Celebrations   **June 1**

    Family celebrations can be a challenge for anyone in a Twelve Step recovery program. We parents have found that we have to let go of our idea of how a family gathering should look. We may set boundaries with other family members. Some parents have held a family dinner at *our* homes so we can set the tone. We explain we will not have any alcohol, ask that no one bring any alcohol, and ask that family members arrive at our homes sober if they want to participate in our celebration. If an extended family member wants to drink, we ask them to do so *after* leaving our home. Where such requests are not likely to be honored, some parents choose to have a quiet holiday celebration with our kids. This was my family's choice the first year we were in the program. My husband and I did not yet feel comfortable setting boundaries in our home with extended family members.

    As for travel to weddings or funerals, we keep the visit short. We stay in a hotel and drive our car or a rental car so we can leave whenever a situation threatens our child's or our well-being.

    The cell phone is another great tool. Whenever I have felt uncomfortable with a family situation, I have telephoned another parent in the program for moral support and suggestions. Also, I got an Al-Anon meeting list for the area where we would be and called the contact numbers before I left. That way, I was sure that a meeting was still going on at the time and place indicated on the list.

With a bit of planning and preparation, family gatherings can be good experiences.

Today's Reminders
I accept that a new kind of planning is needed for family celebrations, plan, and choose to enjoy them.

Being Creative with "Shots" June 2

Enthusiastic Sobriety Programs' parent meetings and Bob Meehan's book, *Beyond the Yellow Brick Road*, introduce parents to the concepts of what Meehan calls "walls" and "shots." (See the Preface) To me, "walls" are the rules I have in my home for my teenager. They reflect our family values. "Shots" are the consequences for violation of a basic rule to live in society. One of the basic rules is not to steal. My son had attempted to shoplift with one of his drug-using friends, but once in the store he was unable to complete the act. His friend, though, did indeed lift some items. My son walked out of the store without anything. His friend attempted to leave but was detained by a store security person. My son came home and told me about this. I was distraught and met with my sponsor. She pointed out that it was good that he was being honest with me. I wanted to be on my child's side, but I could not condone stealing. My husband and I discussed it at length and finally decided on a "shot" we could both live with. We arranged for our family to tour the local juvenile detention hall and showed him where he might have gone and what it would have been like for him. Not long after this tour our son chose to return to sobriety and drug treatment.

Today's Reminder
I will take the time to talk with my spouse and set up walls and shots so that we provide parental guidance to our teen about what we value.

"The purpose of walls is not to barricade your children in, but to show them where you stand, to show them what you define as right and wrong. ...Use shots as sparingly as possible. Save them for wrong behavior and for actions that have damaging consequences for your children or others." ~*Beyond the Yellow Brick Road*

Just the Facts   June 3

When dealing with a difficult teenager-alcoholic, I have discovered that my emotions need to be held in check. It is fine for me to express my feelings with my sponsor, another parent, or my spouse, but once a decision is made, I need to stay calm, state my boundaries, and let my daughter learn life's lessons from the world around her.

For example, our young adult daughter had accumulated some credit card debt at a high interest rate. To help her, my husband and I agreed to co-sign a consolidated loan at a lower rate. We had already spent money on her treatment program and had assisted her financially in the past. Because we are getting older now and looking toward our own retirement, we know we won't be able to help her financially again. So, we told her that this would be the last time we could help her financially. Although not happy, she understood. By being clear with our daughter about our financial boundaries, we avoided hurt feelings or surprises in the future.

Today's Reminder
I clearly state my boundaries with my child and am ready to enforce them if necessary.

"When your kids do things you don't like, they are bucking; they are tapping against what they perceive to be a wall. Let them know the wall is there!" ~*Beyond the Yellow Brick Road*

What are Friends For? June 4

In the Enthusiastic Sobriety programs, parents are encouraged to get a sponsor. At one of my first parent meetings, some parents shared how they really liked their sponsor and felt they could talk with him or her about anything stressful going on with their kid. I thought, "What are friends for?" Surely I didn't need a sponsor; I could talk to my closest friends.

Soon, I learned the difference between friends and a sponsor. Even sympathetic friends did not really know what I was going through, because their children hadn't had a problem with drugs and alcohol. Their well-meaning advice was worse than not helpful; it conflicted with the advice of the counselors in the treatment program! At first, I called the counselors, but it soon became apparent that the counselors expected each parent to get a sponsor—a more experienced parent in the parent group who was working the steps. The counselors were there for the teens. We parents needed to help each other.

Once I got a sponsor, I was very pleased. She listened, encouraged me, never gave outright advice, but always shared with me her experiences with her son and how she and her husband had handled similar issues with their kids, such as curfew, giving their kids money, and rules about driving. It became clear that each family had unique circumstances and that there are really no hard-and-fast rules for all. Working the steps also helped me to detach with love from my kids' problems. They get to experience consequences and learn naturally. My husband and I got to spend more time together—sometimes talking about parenting issues to get on the same page and other times just having fun together.

Today's Reminder
I will call my sponsor today, just to check in and let her know how my day is going.

A Letter to God June 5

Dear God,

    Help me to remember the love I have in my heart for the addicts in my life. Guide my words and actions so that I nurture and support. Help me to resist feeding my own ego by saying things that are hurtful and destructive. Remind me that there is more good in people than bad and that failure is a part of growing up for all of us.

Gratefully yours,
A Parent of a Drug Addict

Today's Reminder
Throughout the day, when interacting with my kids I will remember that the best way to teach is by example.

The Common Thread   June 6

We were as traditional and middle-of-the-road as they come—one mom, one dad, both college-educated, two kids (one boy and one girl), one dog, same home for 20 years, solid work history. How could this happen? How could our son be in trouble? This isn't how the story is supposed to go. What happened to just finishing high school and going off to the college dorm? Why us? Where did we take the wrong turn?

Life is what happens. Some questions have no definitive answers. Some things have no rhyme or reason. Sometimes a reason may be revealed years or decades later. The common thread is that the parents or grandparents, aunts or uncles came to the program to help a loved one. They came because they were at the end of their rope. Through listening and sharing, a common bond developed. What I discovered after being buried as deep as my child in denial, non-acceptance, and complete despair, was that a burden was lifted from my shoulders when I came to the program. The common thread of addicted kids connected me to this room of parents. They were the only ones who really knew where I was coming from.

Today's Reminder
Today I know that I am not unique, that I have no reason to feel shame, and that when I share with another parent, the family disease of drug addiction loosens its grip on both of us.

Live and Let Live   June 7

One important part of the slogan, "Live and let live," is to "let live"—detach from my addicted child. I do not have to obsess and worry about everything he is doing each day. In fact, worry doesn't help him and only hurts me. I have focused on the "let live" part of the slogan quite a lot since coming to meetings and working the steps.

Yet, I also need to remember the first part, "live." When I remember not to worry about my child, I *am* focusing on my child! I want to spend more time living my own life. Over the past few years that I have known my son is an alcoholic and addict, I have spent *so* many hours thinking and worrying about him, that I have had little or no time for the things in life I used to enjoy. I want to spend some time today pursuing my own life goals and having fun.

Today's Reminder
Life is too short to fritter it away on useless worry. Today I find time to follow my own dreams and have fun.

Listen and Learn   June 8

As a mom, I want the best for my teenager. So I am not shy about getting all the help available for her and me. I have benefitted from the weekly parent meetings held in conjunction with my teen's Enthusiastic Sobriety treatment program. I also find it very helpful to attend Al-Anon meetings at other times during the week. What is wonderful about meetings is that there are many people who have been through what I have gone through. No matter what I am experiencing that day, there is someone else who has gone through it, too. At meetings, when I share insights I have gained from applying the Twelve Steps to my life, I help others. When I listen to others, I learn.

Today's Reminder
I go to meetings, hear how others apply the principles of the program, and learn.

"We have two ears and one mouth so that we can listen twice as much as we speak." ~Epictetus

Walls Versus Shots   June 9

In the lingo of the Enthusiastic Sobriety programs, a "wall" is a household rule which is flexible. A typical example might be a teen's curfew, which might be one time for most occasions but later for a special occasion, such as prom night. A "shot" is an inflexible rule which, if broken by a young person, will result in severe consequences, such as the parents telling their child to leave their home. For most of us parents, any use of drugs or alcohol by our child is a shot. Some parents used a shot and their kid did not respond by getting sober immediately. (See: "Preface," "Detachment Means No Tears," "Do You Really Want to Shoot?," "Finding and Maintaining the Courage to Change," "Trust in God's Will, Not Mine," "We Let Our Son Face the Consequences," and "Willing to Lose Her to Keep Her.")

However, when my son honestly wanted to get and stay sober, I found my use of walls and shots helped guide him toward healthy and socially desirable behavior. I used the support of the Enthusiastic Sobriety group's parents, kids and counselors to influence my son to follow my rules. Life at home became much less stressful for us all.

Today's Reminder
By having and enforcing household rules, I steer my children toward the behavior I believe is in their best interests.

"The Loving Thing to Do Does Not Always Feel Loving" — June 10

That statement became my mantra as I started to apply the principles I learned in the Enthusiastic Sobriety parent meetings.

I decided to take care of myself, so I set rules to feel safe in my own home and good about myself. These were: 1) no drugs or alcohol in you or on you 2) no stealing 3) no verbal or physical abuse in the house 4) no lying and 5) everyone keeps the common areas of the house clean and picked up.

I created a plan for confronting my kids with unacceptable behavior. I focused on handling conflict while maintaining self-respect. In the past, I had always caved in. For example, an original consequence of no cell phone for 30 days inevitably was reduced to no cell phone for one day, because the kid had apologized to me. Setting boundaries and sticking to them was not easy, but I used every resource available: calling my sponsor, other parents, and the Enthusiastic Sobriety counselors; reading *Codependents' Guide to the Twelve Steps* by Melody Beattie, *Beyond the Yellow Brick Road* and *Bumper Stickers* by Bob Meehan, and Al-Anon's *One Day at a Time*; and going to parent meetings.

It did not feel loving to tell my daughter that if she couldn't live with my rules, she could go live with her father, yet it *was.* She moved out, and I set boundaries around phone calls. If she phoned, I would be happy to talk with her but not listen to complaints about her father. If she called and started to complain about him, I told her I couldn't listen to this and said, "I'm sure you two can work it out." Then I got off the phone. Eventually, she did come back to live with me and followed my household rules. We are both happier now and love and respect each other.

Today's Reminder
I set boundaries and stick with them, knowing that the loving thing to do does not always feel loving.

Benefits of Moral Inventory — June 11

I had a revelation the first time I did an inventory, namely, the traits that bother me most in other people are those I have also struggled with. For example, I am not as organized as I would like to be and have spent years working on becoming more organized. I find it especially disconcerting when my daughter leaves her school books and papers scattered throughout the common areas of the house and later cannot find something she needs for school. My husband, who has always had a battle with the clock, is especially frustrated with our son when he is late for school. Now we are both more aware of our sore spots and that each one of us may overreact to a particular problem of our children. This helps us keep each other in check, especially when we are considering what consequences are appropriate to help drive home the lessons we want our children to learn while they are still young.

Today's Reminder
Today I will not lash out with criticism when I see my child exhibiting behavior that I do not like in myself. Instead, I will remain calm, think of how I want to correct my own behavior,

and consult with my spouse to determine what, if any, consequences we should have for our child's behavior.

Strength, Hope and Understanding in the Parent Group June 12

I wanted to fast-forward through the hard times. Other parents told me that it gets better with time. I wasn't sure I had the willingness to wait. They told me to "work my program". How could I "work" anything when I was so exhausted I could barely lift my hands to my computer keyboard? Yet the seasoned parents had something that I knew I didn't. They had a peace and a calmness that I found not only enviable but incredible. The stories about their kids were similar. Their stories about coming to the Enthusiastic Sobriety program shared a common theme of despair and hopelessness, but yet they smiled and seemed to be able to get through the day in a way that I certainly wasn't. I listened. I attended meetings. I shared when I was ready. I slowly came to rely on the strength, hope, and understanding that the other parents offered.

Today's Reminder
Coping with an alcoholic or drug-addicted kid is not easy. I will seek out other parents working a Twelve Step program to learn from their experience and gain strength.

Confessions of a Compulsive "Hoverer" June 13

Despite my best efforts to mind my own business and let my teenager solve her own problems, I got into her business yesterday. I made phone calls—just to get information for her, you understand—that she did not even ask me to do. It's amazing how I rationalize my compulsive behavior, especially being a "helicopter parent"—hovering over my child and not letting her take care of her own life.

I am glad I am now more self-aware and can "catch" myself in hovering behavior. With awareness, I can stop and let my teenager take control of her own life. I know that she prefers to take care of herself, on her own terms, in her own time and in her own way. When I get out of the way, she learns so much more. She builds self-confidence from all the tasks she completes independently and learns from any errors she makes. Also, when I am not spending my time trying to solve her problems, I have more time and energy to put into my own life. I can face my own problems that I have been avoiding by hovering over her.

Today's Reminder
Today I will stay out of my teen's business and attend to mine. If at any time I am unclear about whether something is my parental responsibility or my child's responsibility, I will check with my sponsor or another parent in the program to get a detached view.

Resentment, Fear, and Self-Pity   June 14

As a parent of a drug addict, I know there are three types of thoughts that are signs of trouble unless I nip them in the bud. These are resentment, fear and self-pity. Before beginning the Twelve Step program, I often pondered thoughts of "Why me? What did I do to deserve this? Why are other kids planning for college while my kid is flunking out of high school and refuses to get help for his drug problem? What will happen to him if he doesn't even get a high school diploma?"

I learned in program that there are three wonderful antidotes to these types of thoughts. For resentment, I can change my thoughts by making a list of things for which I am grateful, which will bring my heart to an "attitude of gratitude." For fear, I can "let go and let God." Half my fears are of things that will probably never happen; the others are usually things I cannot control. So I stop worrying and trust things will work out. For self-pity, I remind myself of the slogan "How important is it?" Many things—such as whether my kid hands in his homework today—are not that important in the larger scheme of things. For things that are important, I can look at what is going on today. If today, my family has all our basic needs met, I can talk with my sponsor and think through how I can plan for tomorrow without distressing myself with anxious, useless thoughts of "what if's." So long as I remember the antidotes to the three poisonous types of thought, I can achieve some peace of mind.

Today's Reminder
I am grateful that I have tools to get past negative thoughts and I will remember to use them today.

A Family Disease   June 15

When we first come to an Enthusiastic Sobriety program we do so because our children are suffering. They are afflicted with the disease of addiction. It is easy to think that this is their issue, their problem. However, addiction is a family disease. It affects everyone who is close to the addict. We who are in a relationship with the suffering addict have made adaptations to the insanity of addiction. We adapt behaviors and attitudes that are very unhealthy and can even enable the addict to continue using. At some point we must ask ourselves the question; "What is my role in all of this?" Having an addict in our life has caused at least part of our lives to become unmanageable. We have a process of recovery to go through as well. As we recover, our relationships become strong and healthy. We enhance the process that our children are going through.

Working the steps does not mean that every tiny element of our lives is to be examined by someone else. Working the steps does not require us to make radical personality changes. Yet, working the steps is enlightening. There is an exciting and extremely fulfilling outcome when we work the steps. Old, non-beneficial elements of our lives fade away. Our old fears dissipate and we are empowered with a strong sense of "centeredness." We find peace.

Today's Reminder
Just for today I will not focus my thoughts on my child's recovery. Instead, I will focus on how *I* can apply the steps in *my* life, so that I find peace.

Avoidance of Conflict Got Us Here   June 16

When the kids were in elementary school, I would ask them to clean up, and they wouldn't. I would then tell them they couldn't watch television or play video games until they did. Then I'd cook dinner or do laundry. When I checked on them, I'd find them either watching television or playing video games in the family room. I was often too tired to enforce the consequence I had threatened. Or I wanted everything to be pleasant. Sometimes I might say, "Wait until your Dad gets home," but often I was too tired and/or forgot to tell him. When I did remember to tell him, sometimes my husband was too tired to enforce the consequence or disagreed with it.

There were times that we had special family plans—e.g. to take the kids on a special outing on a Saturday such as the zoo, a ball game, or the science museum. If one or both misbehaved, I felt that I couldn't take away the special outing because it would be "punishing" us adults, too. After all, I reasoned, my husband and I looked forward after a hard week's work to an enjoyable family outing.

Looking back on it, I see that my kids got the frequent message from my actions, "Mom doesn't mean what she says." Also, I wasn't doing my job as a parent well, which *does* require unpleasant conflict, disappointment, and personal sacrifice. Now I remember, "Say what you mean, mean what you say, and don't say it mean." This is one way I can make amends to myself and my family. Better late than never, my husband and I are enforcing any rules we do set for them. Because we know that it's hard for us to enforce rules, we keep them to a minimum and the consequences to those we will enforce.

Today's Reminder
Today I will find the courage to face and carry out the consequences for my kid's misbehavior. I will say what I mean, mean what I say, and not say it mean.

An Act of Faith   June 17

Just as I handed my children over to their first teachers at school and had to have faith that all would go well, I had to hand my child over to a substance abuse treatment program when it was clear that he had a problem. In each case I had to let go of my worries and fears and trust the other people involved: the teachers, the school personnel, the counselors, and others in the treatment program. My sponsor pointed out that there are many things we do each day that require an act of faith: trusting that the traffic lights will be in working order, trusting that other drivers will act predictably, trusting that we will still have our jobs when we arrive at our workplaces, etc. It is ironic how many things in the world I trust will go well. Should something go amiss, I can usually take it in stride and deal with it calmly.

When it comes to my kids, however, I suddenly lose trust and become fearful. I need to broaden my trust, let go, and know that whatever happens, I have no control over other people, places, and things. I am one human being, doing the best that I can. Worrying and constantly watching do not expedite my child's healing. When I rid my mind of worry, I free myself to become a much happier person.

Today's Reminder
Today I decide to trust that all is well. Should I learn that something has gone amiss, I trust that my Higher Power will give me the ability to handle it.

Celebrating Milestones   June 18

When my child reached one year of sobriety, I acknowledged her "birthday" and offered her a choice of going on a shopping spree or eating at a favorite restaurant. By celebrating with her, I let her know that I was pleased with her accomplishment. Just as the Enthusiastic Sobriety programs give kids a thirty-day fist[9] and parents a thirty-day heart[10] I believe celebration and acknowledgment of our effort in the Twelve Step program keeps us coming back. Kids and parents alike appreciate acknowledgement of their effort and achievement.

Today's Reminder
I will encourage and support my child as well as everyone else in our Twelve Step program.

Step One: First Step   June 19
Enthusiastic Sobriety Programs' Step One reads: "We admitted that mind-changing chemicals have caused at least part of our lives to become unmanageable."

Before getting sober, my teenager thought that his life getting stoned all the time was just fine, except for all the adults who "bugged him" about getting high. In fact, if marijuana were legalized, he would have been quite happy. I, on the other hand, was a nervous wreck. I tried to prevent his access and use of drugs by spending as much time as possible with him. I became so preoccupied with his life that I neglected my own. My job started to suffer. Moreover, while my son received an inordinate amount of my (ineffective) attention, his sister was emotionally orphaned. The only topic of conversation between my husband and me was our son and how to get him "back on the right track." We were obsessed. We introduced him to new activities

---

[9] After a young person has thirty days of sobriety, he or she is awarded a thirty-day monkey fist necklace by an Enthusiastic Sobriety program.
[10] After a parent has been participating in one of the Enthusiastic Sobriety programs, including attending parent meetings, he or she is awarded a thirty-day heart necklace.

and hoped he would find one sufficiently appealing to steer him away from drugs. We tutored him in his schoolwork, we encouraged the activities he had engaged in before drugs—scouts, sports, music. We consulted our physician and a couple of therapists. Nothing worked.

Finally, we looked at drug rehabilitation programs. Our local Enthusiastic Sobriety program has worked for us. A crucial step for me, as a parent, was to realize that *my* life had become unmanageable. I was so focused on doing things for my son that I let most of my other responsibilities lapse. I also took on my son's responsibilities. As his parent, I could intervene and make sure he had an opportunity to enter a drug rehabilitation program, but *he* had to be the one who was willing to stop using drugs. *He* had to find other things in his life to fill the void once he stopped using drugs. I could not know what activities would appeal to him. *He* had to decide that graduating from school was important *to him* so that *he* was motivated to study. These were all his jobs which I had usurped during his drug use. Once he got into an Enthusiastic Sobriety program, I relinquished his responsibilities and began resuming my own. My work and my relationship with my husband and daughter improved. I started living my own life again.

Today's Reminder
My first step is to let go of my children's responsibilities and to resume my own. Today I take care of my responsibilities and leave my children's to them.

Step Two: Parents Need a Support Group Too   June 20
Enthusiastic Sobriety Programs' Step Two reads: "We have found it necessary to stick with winners in order to grow."

This step is as important for the parents as the young people. Our kids disengage from their drug-using "friends" and delete those names from their cell phone contact lists; they choose to spend all their social time with sober peers. We, too, have to discover who our true friends are. As in any situation of adversity, we parents learn who we can count on to be there for us and support us through both good and rough times.

I personally learned that the length of time of a friendship is not necessarily proportionate to the quality of the friendship. For example, I have a circle of friends that have enjoyed getting together periodically for well over a decade. Sometimes we meet outdoors and other times we meet at a person's home. Recently we had a meeting planned outdoors. As the date approached, we were experiencing inclement weather, so I offered my home as an alternative meeting place. One of my "friends" told the rest of the group that she did not want to meet at my home because I do not serve alcohol. I was sorely disappointed to discover that this "friend," who could not go without a glass of wine for two hours while in my home, vetoed the group's meeting at my home. I was also disappointed that the rest of my "friends" permitted this veto.

In contrast, when I spend time with other parents whose kids are alcoholics or drug addicts, I feel accepted. They do not judge me. They offer me understanding and moral support. I offer them the same, and we can do together what we cannot do alone.

Today's Reminder
I make a conscious choice of the persons with whom I associate. I choose people who are understanding and nonjudgmental.

Step Three: A Higher Power Expressed Through Love

June 21

Enthusiastic Sobriety Programs' Step Three reads: "We realized that a Higher Power, expressed through our love for each other, can help restore us to sanity."

After a slow start and a stay in Phoenix for Step 2[11], my son embraced the Twelve Steps and has remained enthusiastic in his sobriety for 14 months now. I resisted doing the steps myself, because it was my son who had the drug problem, not me. For four months I attended parent meetings and assumed that reading and agreeing with the steps was enough for my "program."

Strongly encouraged by the Enthusiastic Sobriety counselors, I asked someone to be my sponsor. She agreed and we've been meeting almost weekly ever since. As I approach Step Four on my second time around, I am finding a lot that I missed the first time through. I feel blessed to have a sponsor who meets regularly with me, because that pushes me to do a little something of my step work each time we see each other—even if it is only one or two questions in our step book, *Paths to Recovery Al-Anon's Steps, Traditions, and Concepts.* Our meetings bring me a feeling of peace and love which I treasure. I still struggle with feelings of anger and resentment, often towards myself, but I realize that it will take time and effort to replace them with more positive ways of viewing things. My step work, the love of the group, and my sponsor has made me stronger. I also feel more resilient in the face of life's daily challenges. I am not glad my son has a drug addiction, but I believe both he and I are better people for being a part of an Enthusiastic Sobriety program and embracing the Twelve Steps.

---

[11] Step 2 is a sober living facility for young persons who are not successful at first in the outpatient program.

Today's Reminder
I will find a sponsor I can trust and work regularly with her on the steps.

Step Four: My Story June 22
Enthusiastic Sobriety Programs' Step Four reads: "We made a decision to turn our will and our lives over to the care of God as we understand him."

I was not happy about going to the parent meetings; I didn't understand why *I* had to go to meetings and work some steps for alcoholics. To me, the meetings were a reminder that our son had tortured us for a year with his meth addiction, and here was something else I didn't want to face. But I kept going. Soon I realized that although I didn't have control over whether or not my son used drugs, I did have control over my own actions and thoughts. I began to see the meetings and the parent group as an opportunity to relieve myself of the burden of needing to control situations. Just before I went on a hunting trip, I picked up a book entitled, *The Greatest Miracle in the World,* recommended by the Enthusiastic Sobriety group.

Camped that night in a tent at the top of a mountain, we read. The other guys had brought books such as Zane Gray western books or "Harlequin" type men's books. I took out the book and started to read. Blown away, I started to cry with every page. Totally embarrassed, I walked out of the tent to compose myself and keep the others guys from seeing me weep. That night at 10,000 ft in that tent I had a "burning bush" experience. I realized that most of the issues in my life that I had struggled with—and which usually preceded the way they would despite my efforts—could be just given up to my higher power. Things would still go as per his will. I didn't have to fight that which I couldn't change anymore!

I have regularly prayed to my higher power *every morning and evening ever since...* It has been over five years now.

Today's Reminder
I will let go of a futile struggle to control the uncontrollable. I will surrender those things to a higher power and give myself a break.

Steps Five and Six: Sharing My Inventory — June 23
Enthusiastic Sobriety Programs' Steps Five and Six are:
5. "We made a searching and fearless moral inventory of ourselves.
6. We admit to God, to ourselves, and to another human being the exact nature of our wrongs."

The sharing of my inventory with my sponsor was very liberating. In admitting my wrongdoing to my sponsor, I got immediate feedback. In some instances, she told me that she had done similar things. By letting go of my secrets, I no longer felt like the worst person in the world. Plus, I was surprised when she told me some things that I did had not hurt anyone but me. I didn't owe anyone an apology; I needed to simply forgive myself for being less than perfect. Experiencing is believing. Doing Step Six helped me believe: Confession (to a trustworthy person) is good for the soul.

Today's Reminder
Sharing an inventory is a freeing experience.

"There is no pillow so soft as a clear conscience." ~French proverb

Step Seven: Cooperation, Not Self-Sufficiency June 24
Enthusiastic Sobriety Programs' Step Seven reads: "We became willing to allow our Higher Power, through the love of the group, to help change our way of thinking and humbly ask Him to help us change."

I always prided myself on being self-sufficient and never wanted to ask for help. However, in dealing with my son's alcoholism, self-sufficiency did not work. I see, now, that there is a time for both doing things on my own and a time for working with others. The burden of having an out-of-control teenager who was binge drinking and doing drugs was too much for me to carry alone. I had to reach out for help from others who had the same problem. With the help and support of the group, I was able to handle upsetting situations with calm and grace.

Today's Reminder
I will not go it alone today. When I need help, I will call someone from my Twelve Step group.

Step Eight: Letting Go of Resentment June 25
Enthusiastic Sobriety Programs' Step Eight is: "We made a list of all persons we have harmed and became willing to make amends to such people, whenever possible, except when to do so would injure them, others, or ourselves."

I was inhibited from working Step Eight because of the thought of Step Nine, making amends. However, I knew that Step Eight is a private one, more of contemplation than action. So thinking first things first, I determined what was weighing on my heart and mind that was preventing me from moving on, the people I had harmed and the actions or interactions I regretted.

Step Eight is about recognition and willingness: recognition of what is needed to clear the air and willingness to take action. In some cases, willingness is all that is possible because the other person involved is not around anymore or is in a place where interaction would cause more harm than good. But it was the *willingness* to let go of my resentments that was the key. I recalled hearing that resentment is like taking poison and expecting someone else to die. I realized that hanging onto resentment was leading to a slow death of my soul. So I made my list and checked it twice, with my sponsor. I was pleasantly surprised that simply making the list was a big first step toward lifting my burdens.

Today's Reminder
I will make a list of all persons I have harmed, discuss my list with my sponsor, and use prayer, meditation, and reflection to become willing to make amends to them all.

Step Nine: Amends   June 26
Enthusiastic Sobriety Programs' Step Nine reads: "We made direct amends to such people, whenever possible, except when to do so would injure them, others, or ourselves."

The transition from Step Eight to Step Nine became for me one of catharsis and relief, rather than the embarrassment and shame I had feared. What I found surprising was that sometimes, during the process of making an amend, the other person was clueless about what I thought was a major transgression, or even a major rift in our relationship. I have heard similar reports from others about amends: at the outset of the discussion, the other person's response was often, "Huh?"

Probably the most important thing to remember in making amends is that it is really *not about* the other person, nor is it about receiving forgiveness from the other person. For me, it was more about *self-forgiveness* and dropping the remorse, regret, guilt, and/or resentment. The presence of the other person was more like a catalyst in a chemical reaction: it helped to trigger the change and speed it to completion. I made amends with everyone possible on my list. I did not approach someone with whom an amends discussion would bring pain to that person. I knew it would be selfish to use another person's pain to relieve my own guilt or remorse. My sponsor suggested another way to make amends. Write a letter as if it were to be sent to the other person, being as specific and clear about the event or interaction as possible. This is also effective if the other person is no longer around. The amends letter can serve the same cathartic purpose as a discussion. Either way, completing this process helped relieve me of the dead weight burdens of the past.

Today's Reminder
I will face each person I can on my list and make amends, not to obtain that person's forgiveness, but to forgive myself and let go of remorse, regret, guilt, or resentment.

Step Ten: Continued Reflection June 27

Enthusiastic Sobriety Programs' Step Ten reads: "We have continued to look at ourselves and when wrong, promptly admitted it."

After experiencing the relief from doing an inventory and reading it to a sponsor, I felt very comfortable with on the spot inventories." In fact, it has become a habit.

Whenever I feel angry or afraid, I stop and look at the person or situation. Why do I feel angry or afraid? How is this person or situation "making me" feel this? Then, after letting out those thoughts and feelings—and it helps to jot this down, if possible—I go back to see how this person or situation adversely affects me: my self-esteem, my security, ambitions, or relationships. Next, I look at it from a different perspective. What was my part in this? Where have I been selfish, dishonest, or lacked the courage to speak my truth? Sometimes I can't see my part in it; sometimes I can. In either case, if something or someone is really bothering me it helps to call my sponsor and discuss this. My sponsor helps me to identify and express my feelings. Letting out anger, frustration, and fear with a "safe" person really helps me to see my part in a situation. It then becomes very simple, although not always easy, to take the necessary action.

Today's Reminder

I will look at each situation today and stop focusing on any other person's part in it. I will focus on my own.

"Why do you look at the speck of sawdust in your brother's eye and pay no attention to the plank in your own eye?" Matthew 7:3

Step Eleven: Thoughts on Prayer and Meditation — June 28

Enthusiastic Sobriety Programs' Step Eleven is: "We have sought through prayer and meditation to improve our conscious contact with our Higher Power, that which we have chosen to call God, praying only for knowledge of His will for us and the courage to carry that out."

Practicing the Eleventh Step requires prayer and meditation. It has been suggested that prayer is speaking to God and meditation is listening to God. I like this idea. As an inveterate talker, I need to be reminded to spend a lot more time in the listening mode than in the speaking mode – whether it's conversations with God or anyone else!

Today's Reminder

I will take some quiet time to meditate today, and for the remainder of the day, I will listen to others and do very little talking.

Step Twelve: Carry the Message — June 29

Enthusiastic Sobriety Programs' Step Twelve is: "We, having had a spiritual awakening as a result of these steps, tried to carry our love and understanding to others, and to practice these principles in our daily lives."

We are so happy to find help that we often want to share the program with other parents whose kids are troubled by drugs and/or alcohol. Yet Twelve Step programs are programs of attraction, not promotion. That is why we need to back off and let people mention the subject first. If a parent—not in the program—confides in us that his child is having trouble with drugs and/or alcohol, it is fine to say that our child is in a program and to ask if the parent would like to hear about it. If he says yes, we can share our experience. It is also okay to admit to others, with whom we feel safe, that our child is in a drug/alcohol rehab program. People who may have a child, nephew, niece, or grandchild they are concerned about may then ask us about the program. Otherwise, we just do our best to work the Twelve Steps and trust that people who want the program will be led to it.

I have found the message of "love and understanding" specifically mentioned in the Enthusiastic Sobriety programs' version of Step Twelve to be particularly helpful. I have become much more understanding and compassionate with all other parents of troubled teens, regardless of their particular trouble. I do not jump to the conclusion that the parent is a "bad parent" who has "caused" the child's difficulties. I listen with compassion, knowing that "there but for the grace of God go I." Just by the act of listening without judgment to another parent's difficulties, both of us feel better.

Step Twelve: Practice the Principles   June 30
Enthusiastic Sobriety Programs' Step Twelve is: "We, having had a spiritual awakening as a result of these steps, tried to carry our love and understanding to others, and to practice these principles in our daily lives."

The more I work the Steps, the more I am changing old habits. I used to: rush in to give my kids advice, try to prevent bad outcomes because of their poor behavior, react to someone's criticism defensively, judge others constantly, and keep on doing things for my family until I dropped from exhaustion. (This is not a complete list!)

Today I keep my mouth shut and do not tell my kids how to solve their problems. I do not jump in to erase or diminish consequences my kids may suffer because of their actions. If someone criticizes me, I do my best not to react with anger but with curiosity. What prompted that criticism? Is there some truth to it? If not, I don't let the criticism bother me. If so, how can I improve? I am less quick to judge others. When I do judge, I recognize it more quickly and do my best to see the situation from the other person's perspective. I only do a realistic amount of chores a day, delegate tasks to other family members, and take care of myself by getting proper rest. On a bad day, I recognize that I'm having a bad day and say, "This too shall pass." This helps me get through the bad day, and usually I wake up the next day feeling better.

Practicing the principles is simply that: *practicing*. I don't have to get it perfectly. I feel better as I continue, day by day, to take small steps to improve the quality of my life.

Today's Reminder
"If at first you don't succeed, try, try again." ~William Hickson

JULY

Do You Really Want to Shoot? July 1

Shots and walls[12] used in the Enthusiastic Sobriety programs are not violent; they are a lifeline. They are metaphors for consistent and clear directions which parents must have to restore peace in our home. Before our daughter became an addict, she was a three-sport varsity athlete and honors student upon whom we had little need to place restrictions. Thus, she found it difficult to accept shots and walls and the program restrictions.

She was 21 when she entered the program, so our family had only one shot. She had to stay sober to live in our house. One night we had to put her out of the house when she came home high. As we sat on the couch I was thinking of all the reasons why I did not want this to happen. She knew the shot; she knew the consequence and chose the behavior anyway. We sent her out into the night with the clothes on her back. It was the best thing we have done. The hardest, but the best.

Our Enthusiastic Sobriety parent group came to the rescue and allowed her to stay with one of the families as long as she stayed in the program, which she did. We felt gratitude that she was safe and with a sober family.

---

[12] A "wall" is a negotiable household rule, such as curfew, which might be extended for special circumstances, such as prom night. A "shot" is a non-negotiable household rule whose consequence is the child must leave the family home.

Our daughter did not believe that we would use our shot and we did. It was a turning point in her recovery. It was a turning point in our lives as well. We are all in a much better place today because we were willing to take a shot.

Today's Reminder
Today I will make my home a sanctuary for our family and enforce shots and walls with my children as necessary.

"[L]ogical consequences that create real feelings make people change; that's what forces teenagers to grow up." ~*Beyond the Yellow Brick Road*

Is My Kid Safe?   July 2

Sometimes it gets really annoying to hear about friends' kids who are the same age as my daughter. She should have finished college last spring. However, during her freshman year she started seeing a boy who was a drug addict and shortly thereafter got addicted to drugs and him. She flunked out of college. After a stormy relationship with her boyfriend, she is finally home with us and considering getting help. Meanwhile her childhood friends have recently launched careers and are getting married. One is even entering medical school this fall. They are living on their own as happy, successful, productive adults. When I think about my kid, I get upset. She had all the same advantages of a good home and the good schools that her friends had. Why is my daughter not on the same path as her friends?

When I start to feel this way, I know I have to change my thoughts. The "what if's?" and "why me's" only lead to more pain and suffering. As the parent of a drug addict, I've had enough pain and suffering already. There's no sense in me voluntarily and willingly heaping more on myself. I will look at the present. Instead of moaning over the past or fearing for her future, I will consider, "What's most important now? Is my kid safe right now?" (Yes, she's at home.) We have offered to pay for her treatment, to keep a roof over her head, and to provide her food and clothing while she gets help. Right now, my kid is safe and that's the most important thing to me. For today, I will let go of comparisons, jealousies, and self-pity. These lead to resentment, which is a poison. Today I choose to focus on what's good in my life now. My daughter is home and safe, and for this I am truly grateful.

Today's Reminder
I will not compare my kid with others nor will I ask, 'Why me?' I will accept what I cannot change and change what I can, my attitude, and focus on gratitude.

Life is Good   **July 3**

I used to get bogged down with negative thoughts about circumstances in my life. Some things were serious and life threatening, such as my child taking drugs. Other things were minor, such as burnt toast; yet I amassed all as evidence that my life was miserable.

One of the slogans on the wall of our Enthusiastic Sobriety location reads, "Life is Good." When we first arrived, I didn't believe it. Yet I kept coming back to the parent meetings. I received love and understanding from other parents facing similar problems with their kids. I shared my concerns with them. I heard their stories, learned from their personal experiences, and began to capture their hope and strength. After awhile, I started to appreciate simple pleasures: the sunrise over the mountains, the smell of freshly cut grass, the feel of a light breeze against my face, a friend's smile. By coming back each week to the parent meetings, listening, and sharing, I came to believe that life is good.

Today's Reminder
I keep coming back to meetings and experience love and understanding. Receiving hope and strength, I believe that life is good.

Faith Without Works Is Dead   July 4

Some parents who came to our Enthusiastic Sobriety parent meetings did not believe in God or a Higher Power. Yet, like them, I came to the parent meetings to help my child. I wondered why my belief in God hadn't already saved our family and gotten my son off drugs. Hadn't I been praying to God for months to cure my son of his addiction?

As I continued to attend Enthusiastic Sobriety parent meetings and Al-Anon meetings and work the steps with a sponsor, I soon realized the difference. Before entering a Twelve Step program, I had simply believed that God existed and prayed for a Divine cure. Meanwhile I was rescuing my son from the consequences of his addictive behavior and unconsciously enabling him to continue his life as an active addict and alcoholic.

Working the steps meant I had to take action consistent with my prayers. I had to have enough trust in God that I could stop rescuing my son and let him feel the consequences of his addictive behavior. I needed faith in the process of the Twelve Step program so I could "back off" and not try to micromanage his life. Once I truly believed that God was looking after my child, I could let go of my attempts to control or cure my son's addiction. I could work my own program. With an active faith, I found hope and comfort.

Today's Reminder
My actions match my belief today. God has my family in His Loving Hands. I back off my efforts to control and cure my child. Instead, I watch God's plan unfold. Meanwhile, I work the steps myself.

"Faith without works is dead." James 2:20

How I Rested My Mind and Got Relief   July 5

Making excuses for my teen's missing school, nagging and pleading with him, failing to deliver phone messages from his friends with whom I suspected he was doing drugs, eavesdropping on his phone calls, taking him from one therapist to another, and following him are some of the crazy things I did when my kid was doing drugs. My son's actions were certainly crazy: lying about his whereabouts and friends, stealing, and making short, furtive late-night phone calls. He did his crazy things while under the influence of drugs and alcohol. What was *my* excuse? Sick with worry, I decided. I had become addicted to worry and fear, my two constant companions before we took steps to put him into treatment.

I realized I had to use my mind more productively. I was told I was at Step One[13]; I realized my life had become unmanageable. I needed help to be delivered from my insanity. I was told I needed to believe in a power greater than (or other than) myself. At first, my higher power was the counselors of the program, but it quickly became the other parents in the group. These parents had gone through similar problems with their kids and were able to offer suggestions about what had worked for them and what hadn't. It really didn't matter what the power was, so long as it was not one person, because no one person can be available 24/7. Any group working the Twelve Steps was fine. Turning to this power when feeling helpless and in a difficult situation, I received relief. My rattled brain and my life became less stressed, more relaxed. What a relief! What a God send!

Today's Reminder
I will turn to a power outside myself to find relief from worry and fear.

Does It Need to Be Said? Now? By Me?   July 6

I have learned that while my daughter has the problem of being a drug addict, I have the problem of wanting to control and fix her. My sponsor has helped me see that the things I say to "help" my kids are really my attempts to solve their problems and control their behavior. My kids are capable of solving their own problems. Recently, my rather shy, people-pleasing

---

[13] The Enthusiastic Sobriety Programs' Step One reads: "We admitted that mind-changing chemicals have caused at least part of our lives to become unmanageable.

teenaged daughter, who has been in an Enthusiastic Sobriety program and sober several months, began a new science class at school. Two girls, her acquaintances for several years, who are not especially interested in science, enrolled in the same class. My "mother's antenna" rose, and I was concerned that the girls were going to try to use my daughter to do their work for them. I wanted to warn my daughter, but I remembered my sponsor's words: "Does it need to be said? Now? By me?" So I said nothing.

I was happy to hear my daughter tell me one day that when those girls asked if they could copy her worksheet, she told them, "No, you need to do your own work so you can learn something." I was so proud of her for developing assertiveness, which she has learned since becoming sober and participating in her Enthusiastic Sobriety support group.

Today's Reminder
I will think before I open my mouth today, "Does it need to be said? Now? By me?"

"Remember not only to say the right thing in the right place, but far more difficult still, to leave unsaid the wrong thing at the tempting moment." ~Benjamin Franklin

How Do You Plan to Do That? July 7
The Enthusiastic Sobriety Programs' Step Four is: "We made a decision to turn our will and our lives over to the care of God, as we understand Him."[14]

---

[14] This is similar to Al-Anon's Step Three: "Made a decision to turn our will and our lives over to the care of God, *as we understood Him.*"

In turning my will over to God, I also had to turn my life plan for my son over to Him, too. In the past, I had often told my son, "You need to do this" when I wanted him to follow my plan. Now my son is also working the steps and looks for guidance from his Higher Power, too. When he tells me about his goals, I do not argue. If I am not sure that he's thought thoroughly about his goals, I simply ask, "How do you plan to do that?" I am curious and may ask other questions such as, "Do you have any ideas about…?" and "How did that work for you last time?"

Because this is a huge change from my past way of interacting with my son, I exert much self-discipline to do this. Yet, the conversations with my son are considerably more rewarding. I let go and let God help him and me live our lives with more peace and confidence.

Today's Reminder
I let my teen plan his life. As a parent my job is to instill values, set limits, and encourage my child to give careful thought to his life.

Why I Go to Parent Meetings   July 8

Parent meetings are a place where I can go and discuss my feelings about my son and his addiction. I do not worry about people judging or pitying me; at a parent meeting I feel supported. I can be totally open. People understand because of their own experiences. It is wonderful that no one argues there. After I share at a meeting, I find that people come up to me and either encourage me or thank me for sharing something which helped them.

Recently our son chose to leave the program; he decided to use other resources to help him. I continue to go to parent meetings because they help me.

I am grateful that our son found an Enthusiastic Sobriety program, which I believe was a stepping stone for getting him back to our Christian faith and, at the same time, brought more fun into his life. Furthermore, my attendance at Twelve Step meetings, working the steps, and reading the book, *Alcoholic's Anonymous*, has helped strengthen my own faith.

Today's Reminder
Meetings provide a support group where I can get things off my chest and also help others. If I cannot get to a meeting, I will call my sponsor or another parent, just to say, "Hi. How are you?" Knowing that we have each other helps us all.

Music as a Tool for Healing July 9

After going to Enthusiastic Sobriety parent and Al-Anon meetings for a while, I wanted to apply the principles I learned to my daily life. It was obvious that the prior months of suspicion, mistrust, worry, and fear—as a result of my teen's drug use—had given me a bleak view of life. Yet once my son started participating in outpatient treatment and spending most of his free time with sober teens, I felt some relief and wanted to be able to see and enjoy the good in life again. To prevent myself from falling into the bad habit of fear, worry, and expecting the worst, I decided to listen to upbeat melodies with a positive message. I found these from a variety of music genres. With the help of my now sober teen, I burnt a CD I could listen to while doing housework or while in the car. Some of the songs include:

Bobby McFerrin's, *Don't Worry, Be Happy*, the Beatle's *Good Day Sunshine*, Johnny Mathis' *Life is a Song Worth Singing*, the Sound Of Music's *My Favorite Things*, Natalie Cole's *Be Thankful*, Cat Steven's *Morning Has Broken*, Mahalia Jackson's *He's Got the Whole World in His Hands*, Johnny Nash's *I Can See Clearly Now*, and Nas' *I Can*.

Although there is always a benefit to reading Twelve Step literature, listening to music immediately catapults me into a deeply positive feeling in a way that reading cannot.

Today's Reminder
Whenever I fall into thoughts of worry, fear, or negative expectations, I will use music to turn my thoughts to the positive and bring joy into my life.

A Modified Serenity Prayer   July 10

A parent in the group once suggested a modification to the Serenity Prayer that I have found speaks to me on a deep level. Here's the modified version:

> God, grant me the serenity to accept the things I cannot change,
> The courage to change the things I can,
> And the wisdom to know *it's me*.

This simple change in the last line, always reminds me that I am the root of all the trouble *and* change in my life. I have the power to choose and to change—myself, my attitude, my perception of things, my own thoughts and my behavior.

Today's Reminder
I cannot change others, but today I can change my *own* words and deeds.

I am *Not* Responsible July 11

I used to feel responsible for my son's addiction. I felt guilty that I had very high expectations of him and that this caused his substance abuse problem. Yet I learned from other parents that I am not responsible. Addiction is an illness, and I did not cause this illness.

As a parent, I naturally had good intentions for my son. My husband and I provided for all his needs. Yet, other parents told us that, like them, we may have been overly responsible toward our son. For example, in the past when I knew he was going to a job interview, I asked him many questions and gave him unsolicited advice. Nowadays, if he has a job interview, I don't ask questions or offer advice. I simply say, "That's nice. Good luck!" He does much better in life when I let go and let him learn from his own experiences.

I also do not let myself feel guilty for being "overly responsible" in the past. The past is done. I can't go back. If I made a mistake, I can learn from it and handle situations better now.

Today's Reminder
I am not responsible for someone else's illness. I didn't cause it, can't control it, and can't cure it. Today I *can* let my child learn from his own experiences, and I choose to learn from mine.

Silence Can Be Golden   July 12

"Stating something once is a reminder, more than once is nagging," says my sponsor. It is acceptable behavior to remind a loved one of an important date, deadline, or task, but after that, let it go. What about those daily tasks such as getting up in time for school, treatment, or work; doing homework; or doing household chores? Even a daily reminder of these tasks can feel like nagging to our teens and invite a rebellious response.

Although it is very hard for me to break the habit of reminding my teens of their obligations when it appears that they have forgotten, I do find that *my* life goes better if I wait, keep my mouth shut, and do *not* remind them. Once my daughter forgot to return several library books and DVDs and owed a large fine, which she knew she would have to pay. She started to yell at me and blame me for failing to remind her. Instead of reacting by defending myself and blaming her, I kept my mouth shut and calmly walked away. She paid the fine and ever since has faithfully returned library materials by the due date. Keeping my mouth shut and staying out of my kid's business has been tough but rewarding.

Today's Reminder
I remind but do not nag. Once is a reminder, twice is nagging.

Feelings are Not Facts   July 13

One evening my daughter, who has a habit of leaving all her belongings strewn throughout the house, could not find something. She yelled at me for having moved her things into a pile in the corner of the room and continued to criticize me severely. Feeling defensive and upset, I called my sponsor. She didn't answer the phone, so I left a message.

The next day she returned my call, and I couldn't remember at first why I had called her! It was at this moment that I understood the meaning of the phrase I had heard at Al-Anon meetings, "Feelings are not facts." The evening before, I had been reeling in a painful "alternative reality" I had mentally created. Yet now, in the light of a new day, I was so removed from it that I couldn't even remember it.

After a few minutes, I recalled the night before. While I was being subjected to my daughter's yelling and criticism, I felt guilty. I reacted by thinking that I was a "bad mother" for disturbing her things.

Feelings and the negative thoughts, which often accompany them, are not facts; they pass. I don't want to react to feelings, make snap judgments, and do something which I may regret later. I need time to let the feelings pass and see what is real.

The next day when I thought through the incident clearly, I set clear boundaries with her. "Keep your belongings in your room. If I find anything in the common areas of the house and you are not able or willing to remove it, I will put it in the corner of the room where you can find it."

Today's Reminder
Today I will not immediately react to my feelings. I will take time to let the feelings pass and then, with careful reflection, decide if or how I will respond.

Parent Meetings   July 14

Most parents of alcoholics and/or drug addicts would like to write out a check for their teen's treatment program, drop the teen off, and then pick him or her up in six to eight weeks. However, we are told in the Enthusiastic Sobriety programs that we have to attend some parent meetings and it is suggested that we work the steps, too, if we want to have the best chance that our family will improve and receive the full benefits of the Twelve Step program. So what are meetings? Sometimes in meetings parents tell the stories of what their kid did to land in an Enthusiastic Sobriety program and how well their kid is doing now. While we need to hear that there are other families that have gone through similar experiences and that their kids are recovering, it is also very important to focus on *ourselves* and how we have used the steps to improve our own lives. Often, we find that if each parent and teen in the household is working the steps to the best of his or her ability, there is much more peace in the home.

One step I find very gratifying to do is the "tenth step" each evening before retiring. (Enthusiastic Sobriety Step Ten: "We have continued to look at ourselves and when wrong, promptly admitted it.") I review the day and see what I did that worked well and what didn't work so well. For those things that work well, especially for trying *new* behaviors, I congratulate myself for making progress. For those things that didn't work well, I consider my part in it. Where was I selfish, dishonest, fearful, or getting into someone else's business or responsibilities? How can I handle a similar situation in the future differently? Are there any apologies I need to make to anyone? (I've also learned that an apology is only worth it if I am sincerely willing to *change my behavior* in the future.) When we parents do our best to follow the steps and share our experiences at meetings, meetings are very illuminating.

Today's Reminder
At my next parent meeting, I will share from my experience, thereby providing strength and hope to other parents.

"For it is in giving that we receive." ~St. Francis of Assisi

Being Gentle with Myself — July 15

I am not very good at knowing how to balance my needs with those of my children and husband. I have frequently supported my husband's and children's dreams and goals over my own because it gives me pleasure to see them happy. I respect myself for trying to be a good person and follow the biblical quote, "Love is gentle. Love is kind; love does not insist on its own way...." However, I did not understand that *my* needs were important, too. Recognizing them is different than insisting on them. Putting myself last comes naturally to me. I grew up in an alcoholic family where my needs were not considered and I felt responsible for meeting the needs of everyone else.

I am working on taking responsibility for recognizing my individual needs, expressing them, and finding a way to get them met. I am often first aware that I need something when I feel angry. Rather than blaming others for not meeting my unexpressed needs, I can use my anger to flag the fact that I need something. After I recognize my needs, I can request that they be considered by my family. Ironically, then there is less pressure on them to meet my needs for me.

My progress seems painfully slow, and I struggle to not criticize myself for passing on behaviors that may have hurt my children despite the fact that I have tried so hard to change. My Al-Anon friends remind me to be patient and kind to myself in changing long standing behaviors.

Today's Reminder
I will be gentle with myself today. This will help me to know that my needs are important and meeting them is part of my life's work.

Household Rules and Divorced Parents   July 16

When parents are divorced, it is often likely that they will have different rules in each home for their kids. Some parents are not able to present a "united front" with regard to a stand on drugs and alcohol. This has been the situation between one set of parents I know. Their son lives with his mom; she knows that he drinks and realizes that his behavior while drunk is very poor. Nevertheless, she will not insist that he become sober or go into a treatment program in order to live in her house, and she asks him to go live with his dad. The dad, a recovering alcoholic himself, told his son that he is welcome to live with him so long as he agrees to go into treatment and become sober. The dad is firm about the sobriety rule for his home, and the son knows it. So he refuses to go live with his dad.

The father is frustrated, but he knows he has no control over other people. The mother is frustrated, because living with an alcoholic teen is too much for her. Yet she is unable to get help for herself and create a sobriety rule for her home. Someday she may. Someday the son may decide to get sober. Meanwhile, the father works his own program and trusts that a Higher Power is guiding each member of the family.

Today's Reminder
Although a united front between parents encourages a child's recovery, I know that I have no control over other people. I will do my best as a parent to control myself and take advantage of the tools of the Twelve Step program.

Sanctuary   **July 17**

When I learned that my son had relapsed, I felt shock at first. He had been sober long enough that I had "forgotten" what it was like before sobriety. Then I felt a great sadness for my child, who deeply regretted his slip and was berating himself. He had called his sponsor and then the counselor immediately after drinking some alcohol. I remembered that alcoholism is a disease; there is no cure, only remission by working the steps *on a daily basis*. Knowing my son had a disease, I felt compassion. It was as if he had diabetes, controlled by diet for a while, and then knowingly indulged in a holiday meal causing a dangerously high blood sugar count. Before working a Twelve Step program, I would have been angry. After our time in an Enthusiastic Sobriety program, I knew I needed to stand by him, love him, and give him the opportunity to recover again, which he sincerely wanted.

The outside world can be challenging on some days. We all need a place to re-group, feel loved and be reassured that whatever challenge we face, "this too shall pass." I want my home to be such a place.

Today's Reminder
My home is a sanctuary where everyone in my family feels loved and supported in facing life challenges.

"Lord, make me an instrument of your peace.
Where there is hatred, let me sow love;
Where there is injury, pardon;
Where there is doubt, faith;
Where there is despair, hope…"
~from the Prayer of St. Francis of Assisi

Supporting Versus Enabling Our Children July 18

One of the most difficult parts of the Twelve Step program for parents of addicted children to understand is the difference between providing appropriate parental support and "enabling" them to continue using drugs and drinking alcohol. What has worked best for my husband and me is *not to do for him what he can do for himself.* That barometer works well, because it changes with age. Parents do more for their kids at age fifteen than at age eighteen or older.

For us, a large part of what our high-school aged son could do was related to school, the "job" of teenagers. When we realized our son was not doing his "job"—that is, he was cutting classes and not doing homework because of his drug and alcohol use—we stopped giving him spending money. When we had evidence of his drug use to confront him with, we insisted he participate in a drug and alcohol treatment program, or else no cell phone, no permission to go outside of the home other than for school, no rides anywhere except school, and no extra goodies—such as new clothes, video games, etc. We paid for the treatment program period. Once he started participating in the program and got sober, he got to keep his cell phone, we gave him some spending money to go out for coffee after meetings with the other (sober) Enthusiastic Sobriety kids, and occasionally bought him some extras. By withdrawing financial support when he was using and later providing more financial support to encourage his sobriety, we slept better at nights knowing we had not supported his drug habit.

Today's Reminder

As the parent of a minor child I have a duty of support for my child, but I have no duty to provide him with extras, especially extras which might be used to purchase or to barter with for drugs or alcohol.

We Do Not Clap for Our Kid's Sobriety   July 19

In parent meetings we do not clap for a parent who says his or her child has been sober for a length of time. Why? Because we, as parents, did not cause our kid to become sober. Certainly, we may have influenced our child by bringing him or her to a drug treatment program, but it was our child's choice to actually stay and work the program, just as it is *our* choice whether to go to meetings and work the Twelve Steps ourselves. Just as we are not responsible for our child's alcoholism or drug addiction and cannot blame ourselves for their condition, we are not responsible for their recovery and cannot take credit for it. We *are* responsible for our own health, and we can take credit for the work *we* have done by using the tools of the program: going to meetings, telephoning and sharing with other parents, applying the slogans and principles of the program to our daily lives, working the steps with a sponsor, sponsoring others, and using prayer and meditation to improve our conscious contact with our Higher Power.

Today's Reminder
I will not "own" my kid's sobriety: I didn't cause it nor can I control it. However, I will own my own emotional sobriety. My ability to find peace, whether my child is sober or not, depends directly on my working my own program.

Looking at Motives   July 20

Often my husband and I discuss how to handle a situation involving our teenagers. We have found that the best way to look at any situation is to consider our motives. For example, once our son finished high school and got a job, we thought about asking him to move out. Yet we wanted him to live with us for a while. What was our motive? We decided that we wanted to give him some time to adjust to his newly sober life. His staying with us did not inconvenience us, because his younger sibling is still in high school and living at home. However, we were fearful of the "Failure to Launch" phenomenon we had seen in families (even where drug addiction and/or alcoholism were not an issue). We considered the fact that many middle-class young adults go through a transition time between ages eighteen and twenty-one in which parents partially support them. We decided we were motivated by the parental desire to help our son learn to budget and transition into financial independence in a safe environment. We would let him continue to live in our home for the time period his younger sibling is still here; meanwhile, we asked him to pay rent and contribute toward the family grocery bill. We were able to clarify our thoughts by talking with other parents in the program and especially by talking with our sponsors who asked us probing questions. They helped us see our own motives clearly and plan accordingly.

Today's Reminder
If I am unclear how to handle a situation involving my teen, I will use my sponsor as a sounding board to achieve clarity about my motives and goals.

Avoiding Resentments   July 21

When doing an inventory, you list your resentments. I learned that a way to avoid building resentments was to become more aware of them. For instance, I would jump to do something for my teenager, which inconvenienced me and which he could handle himself, if given the opportunity. The first time I became aware was when he asked me to drive him to a town about 45 minutes away to spend time with another (non-driving) teen in his Twelve Step group. I was exhausted and didn't feel like getting into my car and driving for an hour-and-a-half round trip. My old pattern would have been to jump up, agree to drive him, be very quiet on the way there, and drive with a feeling of self-pity. Then I would be angry with him for "making" me do this when I was tired. It became clear to me that each time I did something for my son that I really didn't want to, I would begin to build resentment toward him. So, I said, "I'm too tired to drive. If you really want to see your friend, you may go but you'll have to arrange other transportation." And he did! He felt good about it and so did I.

Today's Reminder

Before doing something for my teen today, I will ask myself, "Is this something he can do for himself?" If so, I will help him develop self-reliance, independence, and confidence by letting him do it for himself.

Mouth Closed and Mind Open   July 22

In parent Enthusiastic Sobriety program meetings, Al-Anon and Alcoholics Anonymous meetings the chair announces a topic and each person may share on that topic. Each share is uninterrupted and there is no "cross-talk." Each person speaks from his experience and does not comment on anything that another has shared. This format allows everyone to state what is on his mind without fear of being judged or criticized.

At open AA meetings, because I am not an alcoholic, I cannot share. Going to open AA meetings was a great experience for me. Instead of spending all or part of the meeting thinking about what I might share, I focused on listening to what other people had to say and learning from them. With my mouth closed and mind open, I was truly able to listen and learn. After this, I decided at parent meetings and Al-Anon meetings that I would not think about what I would share until it was my turn. I focused my attention on each speaker. I listened and refrained from mentally judging, criticizing, and believing that I knew best. I tried to feel what it must be like for them. I gained much more out of meetings. Furthermore, I got into the habit of listening without jumping to judge, criticize, offer advice, think I know best what the person's next step should be, etc.

With my kids, I listen more and let them finish what they have to say. When I keep my mouth closed and mind open, I hear so much more. I also have stopped offering advice. I let them solve their own problems—unless they ask for advice. I let them know that I believe they are intelligent and that they can handle things. It is amazing how much more my children tell me and how our relationship has improved. I am truly grateful.

Today's Reminder
I keep my mouth closed and mind open. I listen and show my children I have confidence in their ability to solve their own problems.

Responding to Manipulation July 23

"The program is a cult. It damaged me and other kids into thinking we are addicts or alcoholics." Some kids say this after leaving an Enthusiastic Sobriety program. I believe this statement is often a rationalization to drink and/or use drugs again.

It is also an attempt to manipulate a parent to feel guilty. I certainly would not feel guilty if I were to take my diabetic child to a doctor and have him follow an insulin treatment. If that child, as a young adult, were to choose not to take insulin anymore, I would have no control over him. He would have to learn from his own experience what his body needs. Likewise, I feel no guilt for having found help for my child who suddenly lost all interest in school and sports and cared only about drugs and alcohol. The Twelve Steps of Alcoholics Anonymous, upon which the Enthusiastic Sobriety programs are based, is a proven way for an alcoholic and/or addict to get sober.

Many alcoholics and drug addicts need to do some more research, i.e. return to alcohol and/or drugs to decide if they really have a problem. As the Big Book of *Alcoholics Anonymous* says:

To be gravely affected, one does not necessarily have to drink a long time nor take the quantities some of us have...We, who are familiar with the symptoms, see large numbers of potential alcoholics among young people everywhere. But try and get them to see it!

As we look back, we feel we had gone on drinking many years beyond the point where we could quit on our will power.[15]

Today's Reminder
I no longer allow my child to use guilt to manipulate me into enabling him to continue drinking or drugging.

Avoiding the Escalation Trap   July 24

How many times has my teenager yelled at me and I reacted with an equally loud retort? What did my yelling back accomplish?

1) escalation of an already bad situation
2) more harsh words reaching a crescendo
3) my teen's dramatic exit with a slammed door

In the short term, I felt justified in expressing my anger. In the long term, returning yells with yells made me feel worse because it accomplished nothing.

---

[15] *Alcoholics Anonymous, pp. 33-34*

In a situation where my teen treats me disrespectfully, I need to mentally acknowledge that it is appropriate for me to *feel* anger but that I have a *choice* as to what I do with my feelings. Modeling the very behavior I find objectionable only adds fuel to the fire. I have to be the adult in the situation and exercise logic and self-restraint, no matter how provoking my teen can be. (Boy, does she know how to push my buttons!) The best I am usually able to do "in the heat of battle" is to keep my mouth shut and quietly walk away. Sometimes I am able to say fairly quietly, "I'll talk with you about this later." Then I leave and call my sponsor or another parent in the group to vent my anger and decide on the best way to handle the specific issue.

Today's Reminder
If my teen treats me disrespectfully today, I will exercise self-restraint. As the adult in the situation, I will model mature behavior.

Poor Choices Have Consequences   July 25

I used to believe parents had no rights, just responsibilities. Our children come into this world because of us. We love them and have a responsibility to care for them, teach them right from wrong, and reinforce that teaching by setting appropriate consequences for their actions. I recall agreeing to drive my son and his friends to the local gym one day. My son started acting inappropriately in the car, and I warned him to correct his behavior. He did not. When we arrived at the gym, I told all the other kids to get out and have a good time but insisted my son stay in the car. I took him home; he kicked and screamed the whole way.

Years later I told my son that although I would like to protect him from consequences of poor choices he might make, this would not help him. At some point there would be a situation in which the consequences were taken out of my hands, and he would have to face the outside world. He learned his choices were up to him.

When he became addicted to drugs, he ended up in court and was required to seek drug treatment. He chose an Enthusiastic Sobriety treatment program. This delayed his schooling, and he was unable to graduate with classmates he had known since pre-school. He experienced the consequences of his choices and there was nothing I could do about those consequences. Yet, I *was* able to love and support him as he began to make better choices.

Today's Reminder
I cannot protect my teen from his poor choices in life, so I will not enable him to make poor choices at home without consequences.

Type A Personality Relief July 26

I attend parent meetings with my husband because of my son's drug abuse. I started incorporating the slogans into my life as coping skills for whatever life situations arose. As a Type A personality, I especially liked the concept of living in the moment. Planning is helpful, of course, but I learned not to get too far ahead of myself. No matter what is happening in my life I can let go of my troubles and maintain an "attitude of gratitude" in the present moment by enjoying the natural beauty around me as well as appreciating the people in my life. Watching my son and the other teens get and stay sober while living life, I now see so many positive attributes in these kids. I have learned much about acceptance, especially accepting people where they are and just loving them. I am enjoying life more these days and still manage to get things done.

Today's Reminder
Today I remember to live in the moment and enjoy what I can.

Journaling   July 27

Shortly after our son finished outpatient treatment, my husband and I separated and later divorced. This was an especially difficult time, since I was concerned about my son's maintaining his sobriety once he completed outpatient treatment. What did I do to cope with these two stresses? I saw my sponsor once a week and spoke with her on the phone frequently. I worked the steps. I attended more meetings, and read literature about co-dependency and alcoholism/drug addiction. Especially valuable was journaling. When upset, I wrote in my journal. Later, I read it and saw that earlier entries were filled with negative thinking and feelings of resentment, frustration, and self-pity. More recent entries revealed a more positive and healthier outlook. I was moving on with my life. I also found that a number of the prayers I had written in my journal had been answered over time. It was very helpful to let my feelings out in a safe way and maintain a record of my progress. Today I am much happier and so are my kids.

Today's Reminder
When times are stressful, I will use the tools of the program to help: sponsorship, meetings, literature, phone calls, and journaling. I will remember that this is a program of progress, not perfection. I will find what's good in each day.

The Twelve Steps Changed Us   July 28

When my kids were using drugs and alcohol, life was miserable. My son's grades nose-dived. He used so much, so often that he could not get up and function the next day. On the contrary, my daughter maintained good grades and kept up with her extracurricular activities. Yet, I later learned that she was not only using marijuana, but drank regularly at a girl friend's house. Apparently, the friend's parents were of the opinion that "it's better if they do it under our roof than elsewhere and drive home drunk." In due course, though, her grades began to suffer and she could not keep up with her schedule.

After putting my son and daughter—with their permission—into an Enthusiastic Sobriety program, I started working the Twelve Steps myself and attending parent meetings. The results have been the answer to my prayers. My son had tremendous resentment toward his father whom I divorced. Yet, my son worked the steps and consciously worked through his feelings and has established a relationship with his father today that works for them. He also took ownership of his drug-related legal problems. He got a job, worked, and paid his legal expenses. He eventually moved out and now lives as a responsible young adult who supports himself and is a contributing member of society.

My daughter started earnestly working the steps and was doing quite well in her program. She even was sponsoring a few kids. Yet, she began to have boy trouble; she liked two boys and they both liked her. The stress of having to choose between them caused her to be irritable. While I relapsed into worry and fear, my daughter sought the help of her drug treatment counselor. She decided to let go of both boys and renewed her commitment to sobriety. It was a great reminder to me that my daughter has her own Higher Power, too, and I can simply "Let go and let God."

Today's Reminder
I take charge of my own life and let my kids take charge of theirs. I apply the steps to my life and have faith in a Higher Power.

Trust in a Higher Power July 29

Once my daughter entered an Enthusiastic Sobriety program, I worried that she would secretly be using and not letting anyone know about it. I worried that the other kids wouldn't be able to tell that she was using, if that were the case.

One day she came home with one of the kids from the program. She handed him a bottle of pain pills. Right in front of me, he threw them in the trash. She then expressed her relief and, with smiles, they both departed. I took care to dispose of the contents of the trashcan immediately!

This incident helped me to trust the program. The counselors and her peers were obviously influencing her to a great extent. She was able to be honest and open about her actions, probably for the first time in many years.

After working with my sponsor, I learned that I could have saved myself a lot of anxiety by putting my daughter's recovery in her hands and the hands of God. My sponsor explained that this was Step Four. (The Enthusiastic Sobriety Programs' Step Four is: "We made a decision to turn our will and our lives over to the care of God as we understand Him.") I continue to work the steps, and they are all important, but Step Four was a big milestone for me and gives me a measure of serenity to this day.

Today's Reminder
I let go of worry and trust in God and the Twelve Step program.

Two Ways to Look at It July 30

I saw a poster one of the kids had made to decorate the room of our parents' meeting which read, "Expectations breed disaster." On the poster was also the ambiguous picture of the vase/faces perceptual illusion. Initially, I reacted to the poster by thinking that I shouldn't expect anything from my son. I shouldn't expect that he would go to school, work hard, and get good grades; that he would come home by curfew; that he would have positive goals for his life and associate with like-minded teens. I certainly should drop the expectation that he would be sober. Sinking into self-pity, I compared my child to other teens who were meeting these expectations.

I suddenly realized that I could look at my expectations in two ways. One way I could see my son as ruining his life (and mine) by failing to meet my expectations. The second way I could see myself as being master of my own fate. I, not my son, was choosing to ruin my life by obsessively comparing his life with other teens and constantly feeling depressed. By accepting reality, refusing to think obsessively about his life, and letting go of my expectations, I could spare myself from at least some pain and anguish. I could focus on my own life and what I have control over—my thoughts and actions—and start thinking about what I could do to bring myself some happiness.

Today's Reminder
There is more than one way to look at every circumstance. Today I choose acceptance and looking for the good that I can do for myself.

Responding Instead of Reacting   July 31

My family has been in an Enthusiastic Sobriety program for over four years. Now both my son and daughter are sober. My son began working and going to community college part-time. A short time ago, I was planning a business trip. Before I left I asked my son how he had done on a math test that day. He told me that he thought he had done ok. Then I left on the trip. When I arrived home, my son greeted me anxiously. He confessed that he had lied to me about the test; in fact, he had gotten behind and not taken the test. Before program, I would have been very angry and reacted with critical remarks. But these days I know to think before I say anything.

I reminded myself that on the scale of life events, his algebra test was not so important. His recovery was. It took courage for him to tell me the truth about something I would have never discovered had he not told me. I was grateful that he was being honest with me, so I told him that I appreciate his honesty and that I know that he is trying to balance school, work, and his meetings, a new experience for him.

We all have progressed through working the steps. I know that by responding instead of reacting I can encourage and support my kids in their sobriety so that they can have better lives.

Today's Reminder
When my kids tell me something I do not like hearing, I will pause and breathe. I will do my best to let go of angry remarks and look for the good and acknowledge it.

AUGUST

Peace of Mind — August 1

At the time we looked at our local Enthusiastic Sobriety treatment program, we desperately desired our child's sobriety and our own peace of mind. After he spent some time with the counselors and went to a function and meeting, he agreed to enter the intensive outpatient program. We decided to leave him in the care of the "experts" and "take a break" from trying to get him to do everything we wanted. A parent working the Twelve Steps suggested I do what she did when she first began working her program: write every hour a "gratitude list" (a list of people, things, events, or circumstances in my life for which/whom I was grateful.) Although I didn't always write the lists, I did make hourly mental lists and was amazed how this helped. These lists seemed to shift my mind from a strained, racing motor to a steady, easy-going motor in its proper gear. Simple, yet very effective, this technique worked whenever I chose to use it!

Today's Reminder
Today I will let go of stress, worry, and concern by creating gratitude lists.

Removing the Insanity — August 2

I thought I could solve any of my or my family members' problems given a few months. Yet my daughter was driving me crazy. She lied to me about where she was and with whom.

Several nights I stayed up all night, drove around looking for her, called and texted her and all her friends. She was having trouble in school and hanging out with the wrong crowd. She ran away and was gone for several days. When she overdosed for the second time on methamphetamines, she was put on a 72-hour mental health hold. When she was released, we drove directly to our local Enthusiastic Sobriety drug rehabilitation program.

Despite the fact that she was struggling with the program, I kept attending parent meetings and gained strength and insight. More importantly, I learned to set rules and enforce them. While I have no control of her choices, I do control my own. I know that by making choices which encourage my daughter to choose sobriety and other healthy actions, I can feel good about myself. I stopped choosing to worry obsessively and let her experience the consequences of her choices. My insanity—i.e. useless worrying, driving all over town, and calling everyone—has been removed and I have gained peace of mind.

Today's Reminder
I make rules for my child to encourage her to choose a healthy lifestyle. I have no control over her choices, but I can enforce my rules with consequences I have control over—what I am able to do.

Staying on Our Kid's Side August 3

Our daughter wanted to go on a camping trip with her classmates. She asked us for permission. The teens planned to stay up most of the night talking, playing cards and games, eating snacks, and "partying" (which undoubtedly meant underage drinking).

Because her older sibling was in the local Enthusiastic Sobriety drug treatment program, she knew well our household rules: absolutely no alcohol or drugs "in you or on you." The Enthusiastic Sobriety programs suggest that we parents stay on our teenager's side and let her make her own decisions. If she makes her own decisions and faces the consequences, she will learn more from the experience than from our trying to control her.

After talking with a few other parents, we decided to tell her all of the possible consequences of the trip that we could foresee and let her decide. We mentioned the temptation of joining others drinking alcohol, facing arrest, and even being assaulted by an angry drunk. We admitted that possibly none of these might happen, but said we wanted her to think about this. We added that the decision was hers. She chose to go.

After the trip, she told us something unpleasant had happened. A drunken classmate vomited all over her, and she helped clean him up. She told us how "disgusting" his getting drunk was. Once again, life was a better teacher than mom or dad!

Today's Reminder
I stay on my kid's side and let her make an informed decision so she can learn from her own experience.

"When parents are strong enough to act with such confidence, their children ...clearly understand that their parents accept them unconditionally, but refuse to accept wrong behavior." ~*Beyond the Yellow Brick Road*

Influence Instead of Control August 4

It is clear that no one person can control another; in particular, "controlling" a teen-ager is like fitting an elephant into a Ferrari. As parents, my husband and I were powerless to make our teen do *anything*, especially when he was under the influence of drugs and alcohol. However, we soon realized that to meet our parental responsibilities, we did need to influence our teen. The first major influence we exerted was a requirement that he *had* to enter some kind of treatment program and participate in it. We let him choose the program. He chose an Enthusiastic Sobriety Program for teens and young adults. This program is based on the Twelve Steps adapted from Alcoholic's Anonymous, which appealed to us.

We have also influenced our children by our examples. My husband and I are both sober. We went to meetings, met with our sponsors, and worked the steps. My husband went to work each day, worked hard, and took pride in a job well done. He came home and tutored our teens in math each evening. I worked during the day and went back to school at nights to get another degree. I came home from work, made the family dinner, went to class and returned home to do homework until midnight. I got the degree. We did not say that we value sobriety, working the steps, hard work, persistence, education, or setting and reaching goals. Yet, our teens got the message. Nagging is unnecessary when our example says it all. While a teen may not always choose to follow parental example, our experience is that both our teens continued to make better choices as they watched us and matured.

Today's Reminder
Today I will do my best to live my life as well as I can so I can be a good example for my children.

Balance and Fear August 5

There are two kinds of fear. The kind of fear that's in response to an immediate threat and requires immediate action is healthy fear. I experienced this when I was mountain climbing and reached for a hold that wasn't stable. I had to do something right away to save myself. As I began to fall, I found something else to grab onto which was stable and steady. So I've lived to tell the tale.

However, the F.E.A.R.—"False Events Appearing Real"—that the program warns us against is the unhealthy kind. It wastes mental energy with worry about the future. When my son was newly sober and not home, I worried about what he was doing and feared he might use again. That fear was unhealthy because it was about a false event that appeared real to me as I played the scene out in my fearful mind. Perhaps more important, it was a fear about a situation over which I had no control.

Today, I plan to strike a healthy balance with fear. I will listen to real fears which may help me save myself, and avoid unhealthy ones.

Today's Reminder
I will not spend time being fearful of events that have not happened and may not happen. I will turn my mind to my own present situation and what I can do, right now, to improve it.

"It's the Disease, Not the Person" August 6

To be able to detach from obsessive thoughts about my addict-child, I had to remember, "It's the disease, not the person" when he acted particularly badly. I recall one time that he was stoned and being verbally abusive. I went into my bedroom, shut and locked the door. He was pounding on the door with such force that I was afraid it would break. I called his father to leave work and come home. Although it was easy to see that it was the disease which was driving my son's behavior, this did not excuse the behavior, and I did need to detach physically and find a safe place.

Nowadays, he is physically sober. Yet all our family members have emotionally non-sober moments at times. We may get irritated and snap at each other or make other poor choices. I have learned to remember that we are all human beings and we all make mistakes. Instead of being critical, judgmental and self-righteous when another makes a mistake, today I choose to see that we are in this together. While not excusing poor behavior or choices, I can choose to walk away and get some space from someone doing something I don't like. Or I can communicate my discontent matter-of-factly, without anger. Now, when I make a mistake or poor choice, it is easier for me to be kind with myself. I need not obsess about what I did or stay angry with myself. I can let go of the anger, accept I've made a mistake, and just go about doing something to correct any harm I may have caused.

Today's Reminder
When anyone snaps today, I will not take it personally. I will either remove myself from the person or let him know that I did

not like his remark. I will treat the person who snaps the way I would like to be treated if I snapped at someone.

Turning Our Will Over to a Higher Power — August 7

I was familiar with Al-Anon's Step Two, "Came to believe that a power greater than ourselves could restore us to sanity," which is essentially the same as the Enthusiastic Sobriety programs' Step Three, "We realize that a Higher Power, expressed through our love for each other, can help restore us to sanity." One of the advantages to the Enthusiastic Sobriety's Step Three is the express mention of a Higher Power "*expressed through our love for each other.*" This phrase reminds me that whatever our concept of a Higher Power, we often receive encouragement and good ideas from others in the program.

After completing his outpatient treatment program, our newly-sober son sat home and played video games when he wasn't with the group. He did not seem to have any interest in going to school or getting a job. We were frustrated and eager to see him "get on with his life." My husband and I talked with other parents about what they did once their child had completed the out-patient program. Some simply loved and encouraged their children to stay sober, while others told their kids to do something constructive —school, work, or volunteer work —and gave them a deadline.

We decided to tell our son to do something constructive within thirty days. We were ready to talk with our son and present a "united front." Ironically, he came to us first and told us that he wanted to get a job and return to school the following semester. We were pleased and relieved. Looking back on our experience, I believe that just as the parent group was guiding us to healthy decision-making and parenting, so the teens' group was guiding our son in deciding what next to do with his life.

Today's Reminder
The support of other parents in a Twelve Step program is one expression of a Higher Power which can guide me in making decisions about my child.

Why I Still Go to Meetings   August 8

Attendance at parent meetings has taught me many life lessons. At first, my husband and I received good ideas from other parents about how to handle situations with our son. There were many creative solutions to common problems we faced as parents of drug addicts. For example, we learned we did not have to accept unacceptable behavior like verbal abuse. My husband and I also received support from other parents for not allowing our son to live in our home when he chose to use drugs. In the end, this was beneficial for all of us. He later decided to follow the Twelve Steps, learned how to live on his own, completed his treatment program, and returned to college.

I started using other parts of the program as good life lessons. I use the Serenity Prayer for other aspects of my life. (It's great when stuck in traffic!) I remember to be grateful for all the blessings in my life. And I really like the step about making amends. I can't undo the past. Perhaps I was not conscious of what I was doing then and how I may have hurt others. Today I can examine my part in any life circumstance and see how I can do better. Because the parent meetings help me learn life lessons, I enjoy going even though my son has completed his treatment program and is an adult on his own.

Today's Reminder
The Twelve Steps can be applied to many aspects of life. I attend meetings, listen and learn.

Learn to Park, Idiot August 9

I was having a bad day and rushing to pick up my youngest from day care. I drove into the small parking lot and grabbed a space—actually I took up more than one space and did not bother to fix it before rushing to get my child. I spent some time talking with one of the teachers and when I got out, I found a note on my car windshield, "Learn to park, Idiot," written by someone who could not find a space. I really took the note to heart and felt awful. Having been very critical of myself all day, I went to bed that night feeling much worse about myself.

The next morning I woke up, the sun was shining, and I got some good news. I began to wonder why the note had bothered me so much the night before. Insight came. My perspective had been distorted by my negative thinking all day, so I readily accepted more criticism. In the morning I realized that I had blown a small mistake out of proportion.

Today when I, or one of my family members, is having a bad day, I stop to think. I do not want to add to the existing heap of criticism we may already have piled on ourselves. I check my thoughts and hold my tongue, remembering that if I don't have anything nice to say, I will say nothing at all.

Today's Reminder
People can be more sensitive to criticism on some days, so I think before I speak.

Under Foreign Management — August 10

When I discovered that my teen had been involved in shoplifting and petty theft to support his drug habit, I was devastated. At first I wondered, "How could he do such things? Hadn't his father and I taught him right from wrong?" I actually asked him these questions, and in an honest moment he answered, "Yes but I didn't care."

Later, I began to read Al-Anon literature and Bob Meehan's *Beyond the Yellow Brick Road*. I read that while under the influence of drugs, a teenager's mind is "under foreign management." His voices of conscience as well as self-doubt are silenced in favor of the high or relief drugs bring; his thinking becomes distorted. From Al-Anon, I learned about detachment. I realized I had to separate the person from the disease. I still loved my son, but not his disease or the awful behavior resulting from his disease. I was grateful for the glimmer of hope I received from his answer to my question that day. Underneath the disease there was still some remnant of the frank, honest young man I had raised. I began to believe that once he started working the steps, I'd get back the son I had known and loved.

Today's Reminder

I cannot believe anything my child says while "under foreign management." Yet, I will continue to love my child even though I hate the disease.

This Kind of Thing Happens to Other People — August 11

Until I found out my son was a heroin addict, I always thought this type of thing happened to "other families". Certainly this could not happen to me. My wife and I are both college-educated professionals. We were both raised in solid, middle-class families. I was a Boy Scout leader, coached my son's soccer teams, and went to almost all the parent teacher conference…everything you are supposed to do. Our son excelled in sports. He consistently made the honor roll, had lots of friends, and always had a girlfriend. Drug addicts were from families completely unlike ours! This could not be happening to us!

One of the first things I heard at an Enthusiastic Sobriety parent meeting was the three Cs. We, the parents, didn't Cause it, can't Cure it and can't Control it. I had trouble believing I did not cause it in some way. Hindsight is 20/20. Looking back, I could think of several things that I could have done differently that may have changed the way things turned out. I remember the day I was talking about this with a parent who had a lot more experience. He asked me, "Did you ever do anything intentionally that in your wildest dreams would cause your son to become addicted?" Of course not. He then said, "You can waste your time looking back on things you can't change, or you can spend your energy helping your son and yourself."

Today's Reminder
I will not waste my time looking back; I will use my energy productively today by working the steps. This will help me, and indirectly, my child.

"He who spends time regretting the past loses the present and risks the future." ~Francisco de Quevedo

When in Doubt, Shut Your Mouth   August 12

In our Enthusiastic Sobriety group other parents have reminded me frequently that I need to listen and avoid talking when my kids tell me something. I often want to jump in and tell them how to "fix" their problem. Sometimes I feel anxious as my kid shares something with me that I'd rather not hear. At times like these when my mouth gapes open, I can quickly bite my tongue and say nothing. My personal mantra has become: "When in doubt, shut your mouth." One of the counselors suggested that parents keep comments short when responding to a kid. He told us that our responses can easily be limited to three words stated at appropriate times: "cool," "bummer," and "wow." (Being an old fogey I sometimes substitute, "nice" for "cool" and "too bad" for "bummer.") That's it. And it works!

Today's Reminder
Silence is golden.

Forgiveness   August 13

I didn't realize that I had grown up in a family affected by alcoholism until I heard someone say that he was the adult grandchild of alcoholics. His parents had done their best to keep alcohol out of their home, but growing up with alcoholic parents who had constantly found fault had scarred them both. They had developed a very critical viewpoint of themselves. He had unconsciously adopted their perfectionism. He said that now he was striving to become more forgiving and tolerant of his own imperfections.

With similar circumstances I, too, had adopted this perfectionism, and I could see that it had already impacted my children. Often when chaperoning my children and their friends I had been critical of my own children's misbehavior but more relaxed and forgiving with the others. I realized that, I, too, wanted to become less perfectionist and more forgiving of others as well as myself.

All children need to develop and test limits; they also need parents who set boundaries, let them know the consequences, and kindly but firmly enforce the consequences when necessary.

Today's Reminder
I will be firm but kind in enforcing boundaries. I will make an effort to stop before I say anything critical and use the acronym, **think**: Is it **t**houghtful, **h**onest, **i**ntelligent, **n**ecessary and **k**ind?

Getting Rid of Negative Thoughts August 14

In working the steps, I did a personal inventory and learned that I have a tendency to be overly critical and to see the glass "half empty" instead of "half full." In fact, I remember that long before my teen got involved with drugs, I was very critical. When he was only five years old, I was leaving a shopping mall with him and his younger sister, who was in a stroller. Struggling with the stroller, I pushed hard and walked the stroller ahead of my son. After I got out the door and had walked several yards, I realized that he was not directly behind me but at the mall door. I immediately thought, "Why is he dawdling?" Then I became aware of the fact that he was holding the door open for another mother who also had a stroller. Contrary to my initial thought, he was being quite the little gentleman. I was proud of him and his desire to help. This was the first time I became aware of my propensity to jump to negative conclusions and be critical of my child.

Today, rather than berate myself repeatedly for past behavior, I am grateful that I am more conscious of these thought patterns. Awareness of a critical and unfounded negative thought allows me to choose. I can stop and think: what is a more positive way to look at the situation? Changing behavior is a slow process, but if I work at it steadily, I feel good about the progress I make.

Today's Reminder
When I become aware of jumping to a negative conclusion, I will back off and ask, "What other way can I look at this?"

Is Anyone Out There?   August 15

For a long time, we felt alone. Our extended family knew something was wrong but did not want to interfere. Yet as our daughter's addiction and its consequences worsened, I could no longer hide my distress at work. A coworker handed me a printout from our local Enthusiastic Sobriety program's website and said, "I want to give this to you. They saved our life."

We entered the program as a family. I vividly remember our first parent meeting. I cried the entire time. I don't know if I cried because we were there, because it took us so long to get there, or just from the relief of being in a safe place. We spent every Thursday for months attending parent meetings. There were days that I tried to find an excuse not to go. However, I always made myself attend. Without fail, I came away from every meeting feeling validated and supported. We listened to the counselors discuss addiction and the recovery process, or we discussed topics with other parents. When our daughter relapsed, there were ten other parents that had experienced the same thing and were there to support us and discuss solutions.

We do not know what the future will bring. What we do know is that we need to continue to work our program. With the help of our higher power we will meet the challenge of sobriety.

Today's Reminder
Meetings are an important part of recovery for parents, too. I will go to meetings, listen, and share. I will learn from others' experiences and they will learn from mine.

"People become better parents when they get together and share their mistakes and successes—when they educate one another. This is particularly true when parents confront a drug-abusing teenager. They have no precedent to act upon; the problem is unlike any other they have ever faced, and their best resource is someone who has faced it." ~*Beyond the Yellow Brick Road*

Variations on Gratitude Lists   August 16

When I first started program, I wrote gratitude lists hourly to stop obsessively thinking about my son's addiction. This calmed me and prevented my spiraling into "doom and gloom" thinking.

Later, I found that I could use a variation of this technique whenever I worried about anything. I would list all the good I saw in the people and the situation. When my son first learned to drive, I would worry every time he borrowed the family car. So I decided to list all my son's strengths as a driver. He is alert, has excellent eyesight, fine eye-hand coordination, good reflexes, great sense of spatial relationships, etc. Reminding myself of his strengths put my mind at ease. In like manner, when I was job-hunting and worried about finding a job, I listed my skills and talents. This increased my confidence and provided practice in selling myself on job interviews!

Today's Reminder
Today if I start to worry about something, I will stop and list all the good I see in the situation and people involved.

This Too Shall Pass   **August 17**

One day as I was walking home I saw my son in his car. He rolled down the window and I smelled the aroma of marijuana. My son secluded himself for months in the basement claiming he had stomach problems and refused to go to school. After the family physician and a specialist could find nothing wrong with his stomach, I persuaded my husband that we get drug treatment for our son. We took him to our local Enthusiastic Sobriety program.

I faithfully went to parent meetings. My husband went less often. He made comments to me after the meetings that he thought addiction was simply a choice, not a disease. He criticized the program, especially the fact that the kids stay up late and many smoke cigarettes. I realized that he was unhappy with the program, but he had also been unhappy when our son was using drugs. I decided to detach from my son *and* my husband. I have no control over my son; whether he is sober or not is up to him. Likewise, I have no control over my husband or his opinions.

Despite my husband's unwillingness to believe that addiction is a disease, he did agree to allow our son to continue in the program until he graduates. He also graciously allowed other Enthusiastic Sobriety teens to stay temporarily in our home. Today I let go of our disagreement on the reason for addiction, since it does not affect how we are treating our son. I remind myself that "this too shall pass." Our son will become an adult and learn to live on his own. For my husband and me as a couple, I keep in mind that there is life after children.

Today's Reminder
Presenting a united front regarding treatment of addiction does not require agreement about the reason for addiction.

Breaking Out of Ruts   August 18

I think I love my ruts. I am used to doing things one way and get very uncomfortable when I must try something new. I settled into certain disciplinary routines with my kids. Some techniques would only work for a short time. I searched for more effective techniques, but was fearful and hesitant to try them, lest they make matters worse. I continued with the ineffective techniques, despite the fact that they no longer worked. This was "insane." ("Insanity is doing the same thing over and over again and expecting a different result.")

Opening my mind to suggestions of other parents in the parent meetings helped. It took a leap of faith to actually try the new ideas suggested. Especially hard was breaking my habit of rescuing my son from the negative consequences of his poor choices. The more I was willing to suspend disbelief and trust that a new idea could work, the better I was able to implement it.

When I let my son fall flat on his face—metaphorically—he was able to learn more quickly the lessons I wanted him to learn.

Today's Reminder
I will break my habit of using ineffective parenting techniques. Today I will be open to new ideas from other parents in the program.

Recognize It — August 19

Our daughter was traveling a path of destruction, and we did not recognize it. She began using drugs. We thought it was rebellion, a natural progression to maturity. We did not want to see the truth. In our effort to support her every endeavor, we pampered and spoiled her. She adopted an entitled mentality. Finally, when she was in trouble with the law again, she admitted she needed help. To keep a roof over her head she agreed to attend our local Enthusiastic Sobriety program.

We entered the program as a family. What a huge relief! We found a group of people that not only understood but could also offer friendship and guidance. Our daughter found it very difficult to accept shots and walls. We, on the other hand, found shots and walls comforting. As our daughter relapsed over and over again, we were able to turn to our sponsors and our own program to find peace. We do not know what the future will bring. We do know that with the help of our higher power, we will meet the challenges.

Today's Reminder
I will be alert and not deny signs that my child may be abusing alcohol or drugs. If in doubt, I will find a Twelve Step group to get support.

Needs vs. Wants August 20

How should we support our children while they are in a recovery program? The guideline that my wife and I decided upon is the distinction between needs and wants. We provide for our son's needs. It is up to him to take care of his wants. Food, shelter, and clothing are basic necessities. We believe that there's no point in asking him to take on a challenge – and certainly overcoming an addiction is a challenge – unless his basic needs are satisfied. Otherwise, he will be so distracted or overwhelmed with trying to meet basic needs that he will not have enough energy to focus on getting and staying sober.

In the case of our local Enthusiastic Sobriety program, there are a few other needs to consider. I believe my son needs, first, to focus on learning to live sober and clean. A major part of the Enthusiastic Sobriety concept is learning to have fun without substances. That means hanging around together at the Enthusiastic Sobriety social functions as well as going out to have coffee together. We have considered these needs of our son during his early sobriety.

Parents may wonder, "How long should parental support continue?" That depends on many factors such as the parent's ability as well as the young person's age, education, maturity, employment and length of sobriety. As a young person's matures, he or she naturally wants to do and have more. At this point, most Enthusiastic Sobriety parents either end support or slowly wean our youngsters from financial dependence. As they begin to provide for themselves and explore what they want to do in their lives, their self-esteem and confidence are boosted.

Today's Reminder
I will consider how best to encourage and support my child in his recovery program and discuss this with my spouse so that we can present a united front.

"Get Off Your Asphalt" — August 21

In Bob Meehan's book, *Beyond the Yellow Brick Road*, he describes a parenting pattern he has seen often with parents of kids with addiction issues. The parent "rescues" the child, fails to allow the child to experience the natural consequences of his actions, and then blames the child for the harm caused to the parent by the rescue. Meehan illustrates this with a scenario in which a parent, trying to teach his child how to ride a bicycle, sees the child losing his balance and hurls himself to the ground so that the child falls on top of the parent. Then the parent blames the child for falling on him!

Since reading this I have tried to avoid this destructive pattern of not letting my kid feel the feelings and experience the consequences of his actions. For example, one day I was watching one of my younger kids play in a ball game. He struck out—the third out—when the bases were loaded. He felt really bad. Instead of trying to gloss over this, I let him experience the disappointment. I acknowledged that it was ok to feel bad, that he needed to feel it. Perhaps after feeling this, he could more easily let the feeling go and be ready for the rest of the game.

Today's Reminder
I will no longer "save" my kid from his disappointments and frustrations, nor will I prevent his experiencing the consequences of his actions.

Helping Our Kids Become Independent   August 22

The goal for our children is that they become capable young adults who can handle their lives independently, without constant assistance and parental intervention. As I listened at the parent meetings and also remembered the Enthusiastic Sobriety counselor's advice to "back off" and let my child solve his own problems, I realized that the way we learn is by making mistakes and correcting them. If we parents are always intervening and "helping" our children, any success or failure they experience is diminished. If I can let go and not "help" my child do something he can do for himself, his efforts are rewarded by the lesson he learns. His failures are stepping stones for later success. And his later success becomes a source of satisfaction.

Today's Reminder
I do not want to deprive my child of stepping-stones for success. Today I will resist the temptation to "help" him. My self-restraint will benefit us both.

Keep a United Front   August 23

One of the points stressed in the Enthusiastic Sobriety Programs' parent meetings is to "keep a united front" to avoid conflict and provide consistent rules for the teens. Before the program many parents found themselves in conflict because of inconsistent rules. In a typical situation a kid asks permission from the parent most likely to say yes to a request. The parent says yes without consulting the other parent. When the other parent discovers that the kid has done something for which parental permission was given without consultation, he or she gets frustrated and angry. Then the parents argue over the wisdom of granting the request, but the kid has already done it.

This scene occurred often in our family for years before our son turned to alcohol and drugs as a teen. It's amazing to me that my husband and I didn't recognize our pattern before it was pointed out to us at the parent meetings. Now when a request is made, my answer is "I'll talk with your father and we'll get back to you about that." We then discuss our kids' requests with each other. Today our kids know that we will not be bamboozled by their attempts to make a quick sales pitch. If they ask for permission for something immediately before a decision must be made, they won't get it. My husband and I feel closer now because we have spent more time talking about our values and less time being frustrated because we were not consulted about a decision.

Today's Reminder

Whenever our teen asks for permission to do something, my spouse and I will consult each other before we answer. We will keep a united front and not allow our teen to "divide and conquer" us.

"Your game plan for the second half must consist of concrete guidelines upon which you both agree. These guidelines, which will reflect your own philosophical, ethical, and moral attitudes, are the "walls"...Whatever you decide, stick with your principles and remain both logical and loving—and always remain united and consistent." ~*Beyond the Yellow Brick Road*

It Is Not *My* Job   August 24

Enthusiastic Sobriety Program counselors often tell parents to let their children own their own behavior. It is not *my* job to solve my kid's problems. It is not *my* job to see that my kid gets to his therapy. It is not *my* job to pay for my kid's traffic tickets. It is not *my* job to arrange a ride for my kid to a meeting. I have also heard counselors say that if a kid gave half as much thought and energy to solving a problem as he did to getting his next drink/drug, the problem would be solved. So I can have faith that my kid has demonstrated that he has the ability and persistence to solve his own problems.

Of course, as a parent of an underage person, it *is* my job to nurture, encourage, and support healthy choices of my maturing child. It *is* my job to go to court with my juvenile-aged son; it *is* my job to financially support my child within my means. I can support my child in his recovery by providing some resources, such as: letting him use my telephone to call for a ride to a meeting, giving him some money for bus fare or car pooling to a meeting, or giving him use of a car to drive to meetings. Also, it *is* my job to let my child know what I consider unacceptable behavior in my home and to set firm consequences.

For a person who has always felt responsible for everything that goes on in my family, it is challenging to "let go and let God." With the help of my Higher Power, and the love and support of other parents in a Twelve Step group, I can meet the challenge one day at a time.

Today's Reminder
As my child grows, my specific parental tasks change. What was appropriate for me to do for my child when he was younger is no longer appropriate. Today I will not do for my child what he can do for himself.

"What we have to learn to do, we learn by doing." ~Aristotle

Overcoming Denial August 25

Our child is bright and talented. In high school she was very active in extracurricular activities. Because of her scholastic and extracurricular success, I did not notice any problems. At the beginning of her high school experience, her friends were very intellectual, discussed philosophy and played chess. At some point she spent much less time with these friends and much more time with friends whose main activity was to "party." Shortly before she left for college, I found a bottle of liquor in her closet. I assumed it was a graduation present from a friend and did not question her. I also saw cigarettes and asked her about them. She told me she was holding them for a friend whose parents would not approve. I believed her.

After she had been at college for a few months, she begged to return home, saying she couldn't tolerate the "small town" atmosphere; there was nothing to do there but drink. She said that she thought she was becoming an alcoholic. When I mentioned this to my friend, she advised me to go to Al-Anon.

My daughter came home and got a job. Yet, I became upset when she fell asleep daily on the sofa after work. I got a call from a counselor at our local Enthusiastic Sobriety treatment program; my daughter had gone to see him and was interested in the drug and alcohol treatment there. When my husband and I met with the counselor, I was shocked to find out that her sleeping on the sofa was really sleeping off cocaine. Yet, she was aware of her problem and wanted help. She was no longer in denial, and I, too, began my own journey into recovery.

Today's Reminder
I tend to see my child in the best light, but I need to keep my eyes and mind open.

Worry and Fear **August 26**

When I first learned that my son had an addiction problem, I was consumed with guilt, worry and fear. What had I done wrong? Should I not have let him go to the school where he was introduced to drugs? Should we have had every dinner together as a family? What would happen to him now? Would he ever be willing to get sober? What if he ran away? What if he drove a car while under the influence? These kinds of thoughts swirled around in my mind.

At a parent meeting someone suggested that, while our kids are addicted to drugs and alcohol, we might be addicted to worry and fear. While some fear might be healthy to help us make better choices, the obsessive fear and worry that I was experiencing at the time was driving me crazy. I couldn't function well at all. I had to admit my life was unmanageable!

To prevent myself from being consumed by obsessive worry and fear—which focuses on the past, which can't be changed, and the future, which is still unknown—I began focusing on the present by creating gratitude lists. I would write—or mentally note—whatever I had to be grateful for at that moment. This focused my thoughts on the present and calmed me down. I became more aware of my physical condition; my heart stopped racing and I was able to breathe slower and more deeply. I could place my problems in perspective and be more rational in solving them.

Today's Reminder
Now whenever I have trouble letting go of obsessive thoughts, I will focus on the present, count my blessings, and take deep breaths.

Extending the United Front to School   August 27

In addition to our household rules and consequences, my husband and I coordinated with our teen's school to be sure that consistent rules and consequences would flow from his failing to meet his responsibilities there. We met and worked with a very understanding school administrator. We let the school know that we valued education, wanted to be on the same page with the school, and encouraged the school to use consequences which we would support at home. Our son had skipped enough classes that he was on the verge of losing credit. The administrator calmly explained the consequences to our son and consistently meted them out in a matter of fact manner. By not backing down on consequences at home, we felt good about ourselves as parents.

The united front between home and school—having consequences for *all* his behavior—finally got to our son. He knew that he had to choose between home and school or drugs. Fortunately, he chose to go to the Enthusiastic Sobriety sober living facility, called Step 2. Evidently he had reached his bottom. I am grateful for learning the Enthusiastic Sobriety parental tools of "shots and walls" and a "united front." By extending the united front to our son's school, my husband and I were able to get through a very challenging time.

Today's Reminder
Keeping a united front with my spouse and my child's school helps us to be consistent in enforcing consequences for unacceptable behavior. Today I will make sure we are all on the same page.

Handling a Relapse   August 28

I was told that relapse is often part of the recovery process. After several months of being in an Enthusiastic Sobriety program and being sober, my son began expressing his anger verbally with everyone in the program. He found reasons to distance himself from the group of sober teens. I met with the counselors and spoke with my sponsor. I kept working the steps myself. Eventually, my son relapsed and left the program.

However, my husband and I did not give up. We wanted to send our son the message that sobriety is important to us, and that just because he had quit, we were not going to. We kept attending the weekly parent meetings and spoke with many of the parents who had weathered relapses of their kids. We held fast to our household rules and consequences. We stopped giving him money and created a very early curfew; when he violated that curfew, we grounded him. He accepted our consequences and eventually responded and returned to the program. By continuing to do what was right for me—using the support of the group, attending parent meetings, working the steps and talking regularly with my sponsor—I was able to handle this rocky period. We were indeed fortunate. Our son had tasted enough benefits of sobriety that it only took a few months for him to decide to return to his Enthusiastic Sobriety treatment program.

Today's Reminder
By using the tools of the program: meetings, making phone calls to other parents, working the steps with a sponsor, and applying the slogans, I can live with the good times and the bad.

Trust Your Instinct   August 29

No parent wants to believe his or her child is a drug addict or alcoholic. This creates a strong tendency to downplay or deny certain clues that our intuition recognizes clearly. Looking back over my experience with my daughter's journey into addiction, I can see that I should have trusted my instinct.

When I first suspected she was trying drugs, I told myself that it was just a reaction to a very disappointing event in high school. I tried to reason with her that drugs only masked the problem. Under a doctor's advice, I grounded her all summer to keep her close to home and to rebuild her self-worth, but in the fall at school, she skipped classes with a friend to get high. I took away her allowance, cell phone, iPod, and all driving privileges. She continued getting high with her friend during school. The doctor then diagnosed my daughter with bipolar disorder and prescribed some pills. She was told that she could not get high while on the medication. She agreed, but within one day, started getting high. She also seemed angrier. When the doctor learned how much marijuana she was using, the diagnosis was rescinded. I wish that I had trusted my instinct about the friend and the seriousness of the addiction instead of letting the doctor's opinions sway my confused mind and worried heart. Nevertheless, I am grateful that my daughter is in a drug and alcohol rehabilitation program now, and that as a family, we are all recovering from the effects of mind-changing chemicals which were making our lives unmanageable.

Today's Reminder
Let me use my parental instinct to see my child as she truly is and find appropriate treatment.

Chores and the Clean Room Battle   August 30

I have learned that I have to let my daughter "own" the consequences of her behavior. For example, it is reasonable for every member of the household to have certain chores to help maintain the home we live in, and I know that *asking* her to do her part is appropriate. If she chooses not to do these chores, I have the right to decide how I will respond. Today I have learned to select only *enforceable* consequences, ones that are solely within my control, such as not giving her an allowance and/or not letting her use the family car until the chores are done. As for her maintaining a clean room, I decided that that battle was not important enough to fight. I have stopped cleaning her room and fighting with her to clean her room. She has begun to experience the consequences of a completely disorganized room. There have been several times when she was unable to locate something of importance to her. Her room is still a mess. Someday, I hope, she will choose to be more orderly. For now I can live with the knowledge that I haven't interfered with her learning from the consequences of her actions/inactions.

Today's Reminder

I have a right to set rules in my house for my child. If my child chooses to break a rule, it is my parental responsibility to see that she experiences consequences. They may be natural and flow from the outside world, or they may be logical and enforceable by me. Either way, my child learns a lesson.

Staying Sober–The First Priority　　　　　August 31

Dropping out of high school was unthinkable. Could I really let this go? It came down to what was the most important thing in my life. The answer was life. The life of my son. Did I want the high school diploma or did I want my son? Prioritizing was key. I had to stop comparing and judging and take a good look at the situation. I couldn't control his actions, but I could control my own. I had to get my life together before I could assume I had any effect on his. He had to get his life together before he could add another responsibility. Staying sober was the first priority. Everything else really didn't matter until sobriety was real. This was a hard fact to accept. And so was the fact that he had to do this without me. It took a complete shift in my thinking. I had to work on me. He had to work on him. I began to read Al-Anon literature, attend meetings, and talk with my Enthusiastic Sobriety sponsor. For the first time in years, my son and I slowly started talking the same language, the language of the Twelve Steps. It gave us common ground to walk on, and something to share.

Today's Reminder
First things first.

SEPTEMBER

Keep an Open Mind   September 1

Whenever my kids would misbehave in a way I had not anticipated, I used to state a "new rule" which inevitably began, "From now on..." My tone would suggest the rule would last until the end of time, or at least until the rule didn't work anymore! I have a very hard time living without structure and rules, so I used to require numerous rules for my kids. This didn't work so well, because invariably my kids would find some way around the rule or life itself would "defeat" my control.

After attending some Enthusiastic Sobriety parent meetings, I realized that having many rules for my teens was ineffective and exhausted me. I became willing to open my mind to other ways of parenting. It was suggested that parents have between three to six "shots", non-negotiable rules, in their home. The program itself has three "shots," the "3 f"s": no "fixing" (drug or alcohol use), no fighting, and no fornicating. A young person who violates one of these is asked to leave the program.

After discussing our values, our own experience as teenagers, and our hopes for our children, my husband and I developed a united front of our "shots" at home: no drugs or alcohol in you or on you, no sex, and no breaking the criminal law. (Breaking a minor traffic law would result in a consequence created by the traffic court, but we would not consider it a "shot" requiring our teen to leave our home.)

Having very few rules and being flexible really helped eliminate tension in our home. Our teens have responded by behaving more responsibly. They admit when they've done something wrong. Then we can suggest ways to make it right; it's a win-win situation.

Today's Reminder
My own parenting style has not worked so well. I keep an open mind and consider suggestions from other parents working the program.

Courage to Change   September 2

My son's school counselor told me that the school had evidence that my son was selling drugs to other students and that the school was likely to take action the next day. This motivated me to confront him that evening and get him to agree to enroll in a local substance abuse program. Also I started going to weekly Al-Anon meetings.

One evening I drove my son and one of the other teens to their meeting at the treatment center. I was to pick them up at 9 p.m. I arrived on time, but they were not there. They had left the meeting earlier, which would result in their being expelled from the treatment center. I went home. Later I received a call. My son had returned to the treatment center and the center personnel had let him in, but were not letting him out until I came to get him. Before Al-Anon, I would have rushed to get my child. But now, I thought before I acted. I would be inconvenienced by making another trip to get him. I decided to let him sit there for a while. After I picked him up, I let him know that I was not pleased that he had chosen to leave the treatment center. I made him sign a contract with me. If he would stay sober (as reflected by weekly negative urine analyses) and enter another treatment program, he could keep his driver's license and use his car. If he lost his sobriety and/or left the new treatment program, I would take away his license and the car. Influenced by Al-Anon meetings, literature, and discussion with Al-Anon members, I had developed the courage to set limits with my son and be able to enforce them. In a few days after researching programs, we found an Enthusiastic Sobriety program which is working well for both of us.

Today's Reminder
I will take care of myself. I will not rescue my child from the negative consequences of his poor choices today.

Why Does This Keep Happening to Me? September 3

When situations bothered me and seemed to repeat over and over again, I found myself thinking, "Why does this keep happening to me?" I felt like a victim of circumstances. Later, when I started doing my inventory, I saw my unhealthy patterns of behavior which attracted the same results. Only when I saw my part in the situations was there hope of a change. For example, I used to get angry when my husband worked late, did not call, and left the kids and me wondering when he would get home. I would call him at work to ask when he would be home and receive a vague response. The kids and I would become irritable and hungry while we waited for him to arrive. I would take out my frustration on the kids, finding things to criticize them for, such as not picking up their things or not finishing homework before watching television. Plus, I would feel sorry for myself. After doing my inventory I realized that I married someone who was devoted to his work and lost track of time; I was not a victim, but a volunteer.[16] I started to change my behavior. Not only did we eat dinner without him, but, more importantly, I stopped being angry and taking it out on my kids. Doing an inventory helped me to accept that I can't change others' behavior, but I can change myself and improve situations.

Today's Reminder

If I wonder, "Why does this keep happening to me?" I will recognize that I have a part in this situation. I am not a victim, but a volunteer. I can choose to change my behavior.

Mothering and Responsibility — September 4

I used to feel responsible for everything and everybody. I was consumed with mothering and managing my children and the household. When my children were very young, I was responsible for their care, which included scheduling all their activities and providing transportation. Mothering and managing were justified at that time. Yet, once my children became teenagers, I spent too much time running around and orchestrating their lives. They did not appreciate my efforts and were angry with me. Meanwhile, I felt frustrated.

Now I realize that my teenagers are engaged in the developmental task of becoming independent. I must let go and allow them the opportunity to schedule their own activities and to meet their own academic, business, and social commitments. Those things are not *my* responsibility.

---

[16] "Volunteer" is being used in the sense of choosing one's response to a situation. In *Bumper Stickers*, Meehan explains: "Own your own behavior, and stop blaming those around you for what's happening to you. You must get out of a complete victim way of thinking."

Today I know that I am only responsible for myself: my thoughts, words, and actions. I want to keep my thoughts on *my* commitments for the day and not worry about my family members meeting theirs. I can take the steps necessary to accomplish *my* daily goals and refrain from doing for others what they can and should do for themselves. By keeping the focus on me, I experience relief and improve my own life.

Today's Reminder
I will give up managing my teenager's life and start truly living my own.

Be Here Now   September 5

At a recent parent meeting, some of us were sharing about our concerns regarding our kids' return to school. We were worried that they would not be able to handle the stress and might relapse. I remembered when my kid started using drugs and stopped putting any effort into school. I *could* think that he might do the same again. I *could* fill my mind with worry and fear. I *could* wonder, "What will our extended family and neighbors think if our kid relapses?" All these thoughts are examples of F.E.A.R.—"Forgetting Everything's All Right."

I don't have to indulge in negative thoughts about a possible future. Today I can choose to avoid "doomsday" thoughts. Whenever my child or my family faces a new life situation, I can remember that the past does not necessarily predict the future. Also, keeping my thoughts *in the present* is much more productive. I can plan for tomorrow and live in today. If I look at my life right now, I can see that everything is okay. I can take time to enjoy the present moment.

Today's Reminder
I will not "futurize," that is dwell on all the possible bad things that could happen in the future. It is also possible that good things may happen in the future, so I will simply focus my thoughts on the present and what I can do now to enjoy and improve my life

It's Hormones! September 6

Interactions with my daughter often caused me much angst. She was always overdramatizing. It really bothered me. I would spend an entire day reacting to her moods and worrying about the particular issue she raised in the morning.

Then I remembered a comparison between the emotional onslaught caused by hormones in teenaged girls and that of an adult woman taking 50 birth control pills a day! This helped me see that I need not get caught up in my daughter's emotional tempest. Her daily changes did not have to send me reeling, too, into daily obsessing about her future well-being. I had been "addicted" to worry about her. I chose to let go of this addiction and work the steps: believe that a Higher Power could restore me to sanity and that I could turn my life—*and hers*—over to the care of the benevolent and loving God (my concept of a Higher Power). When I chose to let go and let God take care of her day while I did my part to live my own life that day, my days improved dramatically!

Today's Reminder
Today I will not let my teenager's moods upset me. I will find a quiet spot to breathe, get a calm perspective on our lives, be glad

that God is watching over us, and then go about my activities for the day.

Being a Winner for Our Kids — September 7

The Enthusiastic Sobriety Programs' Step Two states: "We have found it necessary to stick with winners in order to grow." How can we parents be "winners" for our kids so that they actually want to spend some time with us?

We need to work the steps ourselves. A number of parents have found that in working with a sponsor and writing an inventory,[17] we have been able to identify some behavior patterns which cause difficulties with our kids. Some examples of behaviors we became aware of while doing inventory are: insisting that our kids communicate with us at times and places convenient to us, not them; criticizing our kids more often than complimenting them; getting angry with our kids because of our belief that they are just "using us" for money; and invoking guilt with phrases like "after all I've done for you" to try to control their behavior. Becoming aware of these negative patterns is the first step to changing our behavior and developing healthier relationships with our kids. Personal reflection and discussion with our sponsor and other parents can help us develop a plan for better ways to interact with our kids.

---

[17] For methods of writing an inventory see pages 62-71 of the Big Book, *Alcoholics Anonymous*, or the Al-Anon publication, *Blueprint for Progress: Al-Anon's Fourth Step Inventory*.

Today's Reminder
I will be a winner for my kid by focusing on how I can improve my own behavior and set an example of working the steps.

Sponsors   September 8

A sponsor is a trusted friend who has been working a Twelve Step program longer than the sponsee. A sponsor listens, in confidence, to the specific details of the sponsee's story and offers experience, strength and hope. A sponsor does not give advice, although he or she may share how the Twelve Steps, the slogans, and the Serenity Prayer helped in handling a specific life situation. Because each family situation is unique, one person's story is only an example of how the steps and slogans worked for that person, not directions for how to use them.

When I speak with my sponsor about a specific problem I'm having with my teen, I sometimes get bogged down in self-pity. After giving me a chance to vent my frustration and agreeing that the situation is frustrating, my sponsor gently helps me see that my descent into self-pity does not help. She can steer me to thinking about the steps or slogans, the mainstays for recovery. Often, after just being listened to, I feel better and can begin to think more clearly about how I might solve my own problem.

Similarly, when a sponsee calls me, I am able to listen objectively to her situation. Because it is not my problem at that specific time, I can easily remind her of specific steps or slogans which might be beneficial. Frequently I am often reminding her of steps or slogans which I need to hear and which I can use in my own, albeit different, problem of the moment.

Today's Reminder
Today I will call my sponsor and let him or her know what progress I am making in applying the steps, slogans, and Serenity Prayer to my daily life.

Ownership September 9

As parents we felt it was our responsibility to ensure the success of our children. We gave them books and a quiet place to study. However, when our son didn't want to do his homework, we took ownership of it and made him complete it. My husband and I spent four hours a night getting our son through his homework. This process was ruining our lives. Then my husband and I became aware of our son's abuse of drugs and alcohol.

Something had to change. We took him out of school and enrolled him in an Enthusiastic Sobriety outpatient treatment program. We were concerned about the effect of his missing a semester of school, but we knew that our son had to focus on recovery from his addiction before he could concentrate on education.

When he was ready to return to school, the three of us agreed that it would be best for him to enroll at a school for at-risk teens. We were tempted on many occasions to take back ownership of his homework but resisted. The Enthusiastic Sobriety counselors advised us to let the natural consequences of his schoolwork flow. Our son struggled. We were concerned, but we did not help him with his homework. We told our son that although we continued to believe that education was important, we were no longer going to make him do his homework. Although there were some bumps in the road, *he* now owned his actions and decisions. Some of his grades were good, others were not so good, but he did not fail any classes. Two and a half years later *he* earned his high school diploma.

Today's Reminder
Today I will let my kids make their own age-appropriate decisions and learn from them.

This Learning Journey   September 10

For parents of drug addicts and alcoholics, patience is more than a virtue. It's a necessity! I found that reading as much as I could about the addiction process really helped me. The process itself is predictable, so reading helped me see where we were in the cycle. This reassurance helped me to accept our situation. With acceptance came patience. The recovery process takes so much longer than I ever thought.

I stopped trying to solve my son's problems and stopped worrying about him. Instead, I focused on my own life and attended parent meetings. There I found people from all walks of life. Some mothers worked full-time, some part-time, and some were full-time homemakers. We were all there with the same problem. As a newcomer, I found hope. There were people in all stages of recovery. I noticed the "old-timer" parents had a peace of mind that I really wanted. They were able to let go of whether their kids were doing well or poorly. I learned that I didn't cause my son's addiction, I can't control it, and I can't cure it.

Hearing others' experience has helped me on this "learning journey." After three years, I no longer identify myself as a parent of an addict. I have learned that this is just a part of who I am.

Today's Reminder
I accept the fact of my child's addiction and know that recovery takes time. Today I will be patient and take actions for my *own* healing.

"Patience and perseverance have a magical effect before which difficulties disappear and obstacles vanish." ~John Quincy Adams

Praying Daily   **September 11**

The most valuable practice I have gained from the Twelve Step program has been that of praying daily. In the past I had prayed for things for myself, known as prayers of petition. My sponsor suggested to me that to get over resentments, I could pray for the persons resented, especially praying that others receive what I want for myself. Thus, if I want family harmony and recognition for my efforts at work, I would pray for these for the people on my resentment list. For a while I prayed for others to get things. When I got to the Eleventh Step, "Sought through prayer and meditation to improve our conscious contact with God, *praying only for knowledge of His will for us and the power to carry that out,*" I realized it is best to pray for others as well as for myself that we all gain knowledge of God's plan for us and have the courage to carry it out. Today, I pray this way daily. If during the day, I do not feel that things are going well, I stop and restart my day with another prayer which reminds me that it is "Thy will, not mine, be done."

Today's Reminder
Let me remember to pray only for knowledge of the higher power's will and the courage to carry this out.

"In His will, our peace." ~Dante

"Second Class Citizens Get High" [18]   September 12

At first, this principle, from Bob Meehan's *Bumper Stickers,* was the hardest for me to apply and understand. After all, didn't the fact that I did my kids' laundry and cleaned their rooms mean that I treated them like "first class" citizens? I myself would *love* to have a maid! Now, that's first class!

Today I finally get it. First class really has nothing to do with what I did or did not do for my kids. It has to do with the point of view (and self-esteem) of the actor and recipient. My self-esteem was suffering, because I *expected* my kids to show appreciation for what I was doing and I needed it to feel okay about myself. On the other hand, my teen-agers *expected* me to do their laundry and got angry whenever I missed a piece of clothing. Between the counselors telling me I was treating my teens like "second class citizens" and the protests of my teens, I felt like I was in a no-win situation.

Developing more self-esteem takes time; it does not happen overnight. We were in the program for four and a half years before my son "graduated" to Alcoholics Anonymous. Now I know that the reason my teens got angry about my missing a piece of their clothing is that they themselves knew that they

---

[18] *Bumper Stickers.*

were old enough to take care of it; they were really angry with themselves for choosing to be dependent when they wanted to feel independent! Also, I do not need to please others to feel good about myself today. I am no longer a victim; I choose what to do with my life. Today, if one of my kids wants help, he or she may ask me. Sometimes I choose to help. Our attitudes are different. I do not feel obligated to take care of their responsibilities and they are grateful when I do lend a hand.

Today's Reminder
When each family member knows what his own responsibility is and takes care of it, the self-esteem of each person is enhanced.

Letting Go of My Will — September 13

I received another lesson in letting go lately. I was fighting with my garden hoses to try to get them to stay in a spiral around my garden. They just kept flopping and wanted to go another way. I finally let them go into a figure eight, the shape they seemed to prefer. I stopped and wondered why it was so important to me that the hoses be spiraled. I became conscious of my desire to have my yard look good to my neighbor from the side! I realized I need to stop worrying about what the neighbors will think. I also want to remember to let go of my will and "go with the flow."

Today's Reminder
Today I will not wrestle with situations or things to try to make them as I wish; I will accept things I cannot change and live with them.

"Seek not that the things which happen should happen as you wish; but wish the things which happen to be as they are, and you will have a tranquil flow of life." ~Epictetus

Curiosity: Antidote to Resentment and Anger September 14

I first heard this idea from a parent in a weekly meeting. He said that his solution to feelings of anger and resentment is to replace them with curiosity. For example, suppose someone says something hurtful. Regardless of that person's intention, it is really my choice as to how to react. I can choose to feel anger and resentment, or I can choose to feel curious instead. My thoughts go like this: "I wonder why he/she said that?" or, "I wonder why he/she did that?" This has two positive effects, one immediate and one delayed. The immediate effect is that the negative feeling is replaced by curiosity.

The second, somewhat delayed effect, is understanding. By pursuing the answer to my question, I often discover things that help explain, mitigate, or even excuse the statement that offended me.

I tried this with during my son's recovery. I found things that would normally have launched me into orbit with anger were diffused. For example, one time he and his girl friend decided to sit on the top of his car – on the sunroof – to watch the sunrise. It cracked in dozens of places. Fortunately, it did not shatter, so no one fell through or was injured. When he told me what happened, rather than rail at their lack of judgment, I asked to see the car. I was genuinely curious about how it would appear. The pattern of cracks was almost artistic. Regardless, whatever anger I might have felt became curiosity, then fascination, then laughter.

Today's Reminder
The next time I start to feel angry, I will stop and switch to curiosity, thinking, "What was s/he thinking when s/he did [or said] that?" By changing the focus of my thoughts, I will use my energy to repair my relationship with the other person

Divorce and a United Front September 15

After our divorce, my ex-wife and I had a very strained relationship. We were not showing a united front to our daughter. When our daughter got arrested for drug possession, it motivated her to change and she enrolled in an Enthusiastic Sobriety program.

I attended parent meetings for a while and talked with a friend who is a sober alcoholic in AA. Then I decided to treat my commitment to the Enthusiastic Sobriety parent program like one to a sports team. When I played sports, I would attend every practice and every game. I made a 100% commitment to the Twelve Step program. I went to the men's retreat, got a sponsor and worked the steps. I looked at my resentments and asked myself, "What's my part in it?" As I looked deeper and began to apply the principles of the Twelve Step program to all facets of my life, I found that my relationship with my ex-wife improved, as did our cooperation in co-parenting.

An added benefit was that this brought me closer to my daughter. We had a common activity, working the steps.

Today's Reminder
Each day I am going to make a 100% commitment to practice the principles of the Twelve Steps.

Abandon Blame All Ye Who Enter Here September 16

Writing my inventory and sharing it with my sponsor was both enlightening and lightened my spirits. I saw that fear was a big pattern in my life, fear that came from my childhood. I was the youngest child in a large family and often feared my needs would not be met. I became a perfectionist and blamed myself for anything that went wrong. The Twelve Step program is one of *hope*; it stresses *progress not perfection*. After sharing my inventory with my sponsor, I felt some relief from the fear that I had caused my son's addiction. I realized I needed to be kind to myself and not blame myself for everything that went wrong.

Now instead of berating myself for my shortcomings, I pause and ask my higher power to help me see situations logically. Sometimes I also need another person in program to help me.

Today's Reminder
Today, by diverting my thoughts from blame and fear, I get a more realistic view of a situation and often feel more hopeful.

Overcoming Grief September 17

When I found out that my son was so addicted to drugs that he had abandoned all the goals we had had for him, I was crushed. He was only beginning high school when we took him out of school to participate in the intensive outpatient treatment program. I was doubtful, at first, that he would *ever* be able to relinquish the hold drugs had on him. "If he doesn't die or end up in jail, what kind of life will he have with only an 8th grade education?" I wondered. I was afraid, sad, and grief-stricken, because my dreams for his life had been shattered.

After attending parent meetings, talking with my sponsor, and working the steps for a while, I began to work through this grief. Today my life goes more smoothly when I accept my son as he is. I no longer dream for him. He creates his *own* goals for his life, and I encourage him and have faith that his Higher Power helps him just as my Higher Power helps me.

Today's Reminder
I let go of my dreams for my child and realize that he has his own life journey.

Rules, Walls, and Shots September 18

The parenting books call it "setting limits" or "boundaries with logical consequences." In the Enthusiastic Sobriety programs, we call it creating "walls", (rules which are negotiable) and "shots" (non-negotiable rules). We are advised not to have more than six shots. However, I found it very difficult to hold to my shots. The counselors told me that if my son was resourceful enough to obtain illegal drugs, he could turn it around and be resourceful in a positive way.

When our nineteen-year-old son was arrested and telephoned us to get him a lawyer, my husband and I didn't do it. Our son had gotten into trouble as a result of returning to drugs, and he was no longer welcome in our home. He would have to use his resourcefulness to cope with his problem. My sponsor reminded me that I had to have faith in my son's ability. When I spoke with my son, I told him, "You can handle this."

It was very painful to know he was in jail. He stayed there for three weeks. I knew I had to detach. At first, I could only detach with anger. Later I told myself that just for today, I would not worry or lose my healthy boundaries. (I saw how telling myself not to worry just for today was similar to an alcoholic's telling himself not to drink just for today.) I would live my life; my son would live his. I knew that I loved my son, yet disliked his behavior. As time went on and my son did deal with the situation, it became easier to detach. Today I can detach with love.

Today's Reminder
I fulfill my parental responsibility by setting limits and enforcing consequences, using "walls" and "shots." Although I love my child, I do not like and will not support his self-destructive behavior

"Say What You Mean,   September 19
Mean What You Say, and Don't Say It Mean"

This saying helps me to communicate directly with my family members. I used to say things that were meant to indirectly communicate my needs or desires to family members. For example, while we were traveling in a car, I might feel cold and want to have my son close his window. Instead of saying my feeling and what I would like (I'm cold. Would you mind closing your window?) I would ask, "Is there any reason you have your window open?" This might lead to a long discussion before I would decide to make my request or completely censor myself and refrain from requesting anything.

In our local Enthusiastic Sobriety group, I was told the basis of a Twelve Step program is honesty, open-mindedness, and willingness. I also heard the teens say we have to realize "C.R.A.P." (Communication Resolves All Problems.) When I keep things simple and state what I feel and what I would like, life gets simpler.

Today's Reminder
I will directly and honestly communicate my feelings and requests.

Taking Care of Myself — September 20

At the time I started going to Enthusiastic Sobriety parent meetings, I felt that my own life was "out of control." Not only had my stepchild been using drugs, but I had had trouble dealing with my own grown kids. After being burned on a loan I had co-signed for one of them, I learned through attending parent meetings, talking with my sponsor, and working the Twelve Steps that my kids had to "own" their own behavior. As adults, they needed to learn from their own financial choices and from the consequences of those choices. I didn't have to "rescue" them. I got rid of the guilt I had felt for setting financial boundaries with my adult children. I realized that there was no reason to feel guilty for taking care of myself.

Today, with the help of my sponsor, the Twelve Steps and meetings, I have acquired the tools to take care of my family and problems in life. I especially like the "attitude of gratitude" which I use regularly and which really improves my life.

Today's Reminder
I do not rescue my adult children from the consequences of their poor choices, financial or otherwise. I take care of myself and set appropriate boundaries with them.

Letting Go September 21

My son hasn't had a job in over a year. The "now hiring" signs flash in bright neon. He doesn't even notice. Every aspect of life seems difficult for my son: school, a job, finding a place to live. I used to help him fill out applications, point out "opportunities," question him about when assignments were due. I've changed. I let it go now. I let go so he can have the opportunity to grow. I can't control his actions. One definition of insanity is doing the same thing over and over and getting the same results. Trying to do for my son got the same results: none. When I could finally let him go, I realized that he could stand on his own two feet. Not on my time table, but on his.

Today's Reminder
Sobriety is important, so I am patient with my newly sober teen's progress in other areas of his life. I no longer "help" him do what I think he should; I let him learn in his own time.

Parenting an Addict and Becoming Free September 22

As parents we come to the realization that we cannot keep our children sober. We can neither make our kids use nor not use. This is not in our power. However we do have some control or power. We have control over our choices: how we respond to the situations in our daily lives.

Herein lies the challenge: how do we, as parents, continue to fulfill our roles as people of "authority," with the inherent responsibilities of parenthood, and at the same time become free from the unmanageability that has manifested in our lives? I have used a two-fold strategy. The first part of the strategy is to create a home environment that supports the recovery process. Suggestions can be found in the parent chapter of the book *Beyond the Yellow Brick Road*. The second part of the strategy is to completely evaluate my role in our family's situation by working my own Twelve Step program. Attending parent meetings, getting and working with my sponsor, and playing an active role in the parent step study are actions I have taken to carry this part out. This has given me confidence in fulfilling my parental responsibilities and in becoming free from the unmanageability of living with an addict.

Today's Reminder
Today I create a sober home and set limits with enforceable consequences for my child living in my home. I also work the Twelve Steps and go to parent meetings to help me live with an addicted child.

From Denial to Recovery — September 23

During my daughter's first years of high school I did not realize that I was denying the evidence before me that she had a problem with drugs and alcohol. I would find alcohol in her room and remove it, or dump out vodka and replace it with water. I never said anything, because I was uncomfortable with confrontation. Once I did confront her about a marijuana pipe I found in her room, and she told me she was holding it for a friend. I believed her despite the fact that I knew she was drinking and had even received a minor in possession of alcohol ticket. I just assumed that all teens experimented a little. Then one day I was called to her school and told she was in possession of ecstasy. The school penalty was two weeks suspension, but only one week if a student went for a drug evaluation. It was near final exam time and I did not want my daughter's academic standing to suffer, so I said I'd take her for the evaluation. The school counselor asked me if I knew that my daughter had been at a rave that weekend. My daughter had told me she was at a friend's house, and I had believed her. Shortly thereafter my husband and I enrolled our daughter in an Enthusiastic Sobriety program.

I faithfully attended the parent meetings and joined a parent prayer group. After awhile I understood that the parent meetings were for *me*, not my kids. I got a sponsor, worked the steps—including writing an inventory in Al-Anon's *Blueprint for Progress*—shared it with my sponsor, got onto steering committee for the parent group, and started sponsoring other parents. I was amazed at how this helped my own recovery. Applying the steps on a daily basis to my life, I now have an incredible relationship with my children.

Today's Reminder

Once I am able to see reality, I can take steps to deal with it. Today I will do my best to see clearly and apply the steps to my life.

Teaching Responsibility   September 24

I detach from my adult son by letting go and letting him take care of his life. Instead of nagging him about his obligations, I focus on having a connection with him as another adult. By focusing on the good in him and letting the world bring about consequences, I can preserve my relationship with him. I still find myself wanting to help. Yet I know that saying something once is a reminder. Twice is nagging.

This does not mean that we parents can't give our kids the benefit of our knowledge. At one point my son had a legal obligation to meet and he asked my husband and me about the possible consequences for failing to take care of it. His stepdad did not lecture him. Instead, he told him about the experience of an acquaintance who had failed to take care of a legal obligation ten years earlier. One day this acquaintance was found fishing without a license, not a major offense. However, because of an outstanding warrant for the unmet obligation, he was arrested immediately, incarcerated and had to serve three months in jail. Because our son asked us, he was receptive to hearing what we said and benefiting from our knowledge.

Today's Reminder
I don't have to bring down consequences on my adult child. He can learn these from life. I will simply be available to lend moral support and answer questions he may ask.

Love Means Not Accepting Wrong Behavior[19]

September 25

I have always loved my children unconditionally, but I sometimes confused love with overprotection. During the period of their early drug and alcohol use, I was in such denial that I did not realize they were drinking and drugging. I simply thought they were ditching school. I often intervened and bargained with teachers to try to prevent their getting poor grades.

As their behavior continued, I finally suspected and confirmed marijuana use by my son and alcohol use by my daughter. I brushed it off as "normal." I thought, "Everyone drinks in high school or everyone tries a little pot; it's just pot." The behavior continued. My husband and I continued to try to save them from the mounting consequences. We negotiated with teachers, coaches, and, administrators. Both kids were bright, former honor roll students and star athletes. My husband and I did not understand that our overprotective behavior was crippling our children. They were not experiencing the consequences of their actions and continued using.

Finally our daughter was arrested, got suspended from school, and entered the local Enthusiastic Sobriety program two days later. At the time, I thought this was one of the worst things that could have happened. Four months later, I realized it was the best thing. She had been on a self-destructive path. Had it not happened, she might not have survived. She has now been clean and sober for over two years. She returned to high school, graduated, and is now entering college.

---

[19] "Love means not accepting wrong behavior..." *Beyond the Yellow Brick Road.*

My son never entered a program. He still uses. He graduated from high school but also from pot to coke to opiates. Currently, he is not allowed to live at home. I love him, but I do not accept his drug use in my house.

Today's Reminder
I no longer save my teens from the consequences of their poor choices. I do not accept unacceptable behavior in my home

Right Here Right Now September 26

Once our son entered high school, his life unfolded in a way totally different from what we had expected and hoped for. Instead of being on the honor roll and playing a high school sport, he dropped off the team, started skipping classes and getting high and/or drunk. After several months, we became painfully aware of his drug and alcohol addiction. Getting angry with him, ourselves, or the "unfairness of life" was an unhealthy vicious cycle which we had to break if we wanted relief from this painful situation. The path out was painful, but it has led to comfort and peace of mind.

We intervened, got our son into treatment, and started working the Twelve Steps ourselves. Instead of dwelling on what would not happen—we're no longer concerned with his getting into Harvard—we began, each day, to focus on the here and now. Now each day I tell myself after prayer and meditation, "Today is going to be a good day. What can I do to help myself today? How can I help—not rescue—my family members?" Often the answer is simply go to work, do the best job I can while I'm there, and perhaps pick up clothing from the dry cleaners on the way home that night. Nothing earth shattering. Today I keep it simple.

Today's Reminder
I choose to focus on today and do my part to have as good a day as I can.

Luxury Concerns   September 27

When dealing with a newly recovering addict, I had to let go of household rules that got in the way of recovery. I know the frustration of wanting him to mow the lawn, pick up his dishes, clean his room, etc., but today I also realize that these are luxury concerns. When I temporarily gave up on those "luxuries" for his early recovery, he was able to focus on sobriety. Meanwhile, I focused on putting into practice the slogans, "First things first" and "How important is it?" Sobriety had to come first, because without it, my kid would accomplish nothing else.

Today while I do not take sobriety for granted, I am grateful that my family is at the stage in our recoveries to be considering luxury concerns. Today life is good.

Today's Reminder
If my child is early in his recovery, I will be patient and put first things first. Household chores take a back seat to sobriety. If my child has long-term sobriety, I will be grateful that I can now consider "luxury" problems.

Maintaining a Three-to-One Ratio — September 28

It seems that most of us Enthusiastic Sobriety parents have lived in atmospheres of perfectionism and extensive criticism. In fact, before going to a Twelve Step group, I usually focused on the negative. I saw a glass as "half empty" instead of "half full." This is called "stinking thinking" in Twelve Step groups.

One hot summer day my son and I were out in the yard pruning bushes. I called his name (to ask him if he wanted some lemonade), and he immediately responded defensively to explain why he hadn't pruned the limbs of one of the bushes. Realizing that he was expecting to hear criticism from me when I spoke his name, I felt terrible. How many times had I criticized him or complained that he hadn't done a household chore? I remembered hearing at a parent meeting a remedy for this negativity. Say at least three positive, nurturing, and encouraging statements to a child for each critical statement. So from that moment, I became more aware and made a point of acknowledging the good in him. I started with, "You're working so hard and doing a good and careful job. How about some lemonade?" He was relieved and pleased.

Today's Reminder

I shall focus on the positive in my teen and be careful to maintain a three-to-one ratio of positive remarks to each criticism.

Trust in God's Will, Not Mine — September 29

I have had two sons in an Enthusiastic Sobriety program. My first son is alive and prison is his life support. My second son is alive and the program is his life support. When my first son relapsed, he left the program and our home and was eventually arrested. Our family had endured the consequences of his drug abuse for years. My second son just entered the intensive outpatient program, which I consider a true blessing.

Despite the consequences for my first son and my heartbreak over his sentence, my prayers and belief that God is with us has never faltered. In fact, instead of feeling abandoned by God, I have learned to accept this suffering and misfortune. I know I cannot understand it or explain it, but I have decided to trust God to protect my family and me. My daily prayer and meditation has brought me peace and acceptance. Trust is not always easy; the end result is not always what *I* want, but I truly believe that God is at work in all of our lives. I continually strive to let go and let God.

Today's Reminder
Today I will remember to pray for acceptance of things I cannot change and for courage to change the things I can.

"It is better to trust in the Lord than to put confidence in man." Psalm 118:8

Scientific Evidence of Benefit — September 30

I especially love the slogan, "Let go and let God," which I have used frequently to calm myself down. One day I was amazed to find scientific evidence of its benefit. While on the way to a doctor's office, I had a near car accident, so I was upset. My blood pressure was higher than it's ever been. Then I decided to think, "Let go and let God." After thinking this for a few minutes, the nurse came back and took my blood pressure again—it was near normal! Now I know that when I think, "Let go and let God," it not only calms me emotionally but promotes my physical well-being.

Today's Reminder
Twelve Step programs benefit us spiritually, emotionally, mentally and physically. I will use a program tool today to promote my overall health.

OCTOBER

Hitting Rock Bottom   October 1

It is so hard to let go and allow our children to hit rock bottom. However, sometimes that ends up being the best thing for our children, because it is a wake-up call. Removing the natural consequences (i.e. trying to protect our children) keeps them from learning.

Without any accident, my underage child was pulled over for a DUI. She had a very high blood alcohol level. The policeman suggested that I not bail her out immediately but allow her to stay in jail for a day to realize the seriousness of her crime. However, that short stay was not enough. When her day in court came, she was miraculously given only non-reporting probation and a small fine. Her probation officer was astonished. She predicted that with such a small punishment my daughter was likely to repeat the offense. Within weeks, she was caught again. By violating probation, she was looking at some serious jail time. The probation officer graciously said that if she completed rehab successfully, the officer would ask the judge to dismiss the jail time. It was only then that my daughter agreed to get the help she needed.

I am filled with gratitude for the wisdom of those public servants and our Enthusiastic Sobriety program. By refraining from rescuing my daughter, I allowed her to experience the natural consequences of her actions, which motivated her to receive help.

Today's Reminder
Today, if necessary, I will "get off the asphalt" and not cushion my child's fall. I will not intervene and will let her experience real world consequences for her actions.

Changed Attitudes and the Powers of Positive Parenting

October 2

At a women's retreat, one of the meeting topics was "Changed Attitudes." We talked about how many of us tend to see the worst in a situation. So how can we change these negative views? We all agreed that we have to admit the problem and cultivate willingness to change. One idea for developing a more positive perspective is practicing gratitude. Writing gratitude lists has helped many of us. As we write, we become more able to see the good in the situations we face, and we stop seeing ourselves as victims. We become empowered by seeing that we can make choices that affect our lives.

In *Bumper Stickers* Bob Meehan has a chapter entitled, "P.O.P.P." (Powers of Positive Parenting) and he asks, "Do we understand that the management of ourselves is a form of parenting?" After two years in recovery, I realized that my gratitude lists have paid off. I am more likely to see the positive aspects of a situation and acknowledge the good in myself. I am less likely to berate myself for my mistakes or to blame others. I know that all human beings make mistakes. As for mine, I consider: 1) In the present, what can I do to correct any harm caused by my mistake? and 2) How I can do better in the future? The amazing discovery I made is that by being gentler with myself, I have also become much gentler with my drug addicted-child as well as everyone else. As a result life goes more smoothly and less harshly for all of us. I am truly grateful for the benefits of my changed attitude.

Today's Reminder
Instead of wasting energy on self-recrimination or blame, I will change my attitude, be gentle with myself, and take appropriate action.

No Victims   October 3

To me, the saying, "There are no victims, only volunteers," means that I always have the power of choice in my life. I can choose to wallow in self-pity about my life circumstances or my child's substance abuse problem, or I can take charge of *my* life and do what I want with *my* life. I can also set boundaries, with logical and enforceable consequences for my children. Logical, enforceable consequences are those which I have the power to do, such as to refrain from giving my misbehaving child a reward or privilege. I cannot actually *make* my child do something he doesn't want to do, so any consequence requiring that I have my child affirmatively do something is unworkable. Today I will stand tall, accept my life as it is, work toward achieving my own life goals, and—as for parenting—set enforceable consequences.

When my son was using drugs, even logical, enforceable consequences did not get him to stop using or engaging in related misbehavior. I have learned that drugs, especially marijuana, completely clouded his judgment and made it difficult for him to learn. Now that he's been in recovery for a while and I am clear on how to create enforceable consequences, he rarely oversteps boundaries. When he does, I enforce consequences and he refrains from similar behavior in the future.

Today's Reminder
I have chosen to be a parent, so I will take this responsibility seriously. I will set boundaries and implement enforceable consequences, as necessary.

Control Freak   October 4

One thing became clear to me at parent meetings: although my kid had a drug problem, I also had a problem because I wanted to control him. I was going crazy because I couldn't make him stop doing drugs, go to school, study, get good grades, act politely and respectfully. I wallowed in self-pity, "Oh, where did I go wrong?"

Yet repeating the same actions and expecting different results is insane. I had to change my way of thinking and acting. It became clear that I was powerless over other people, places and things. Instead of trying to control everything, I had to let go. Once our son was in an Enthusiastic Sobriety program and listening to the counselors and his peers in recovery, I felt better about letting go. At least he was listening to people telling him to get and stay sober. Now I could focus on my *own* life. I found it interesting to watch how my daily activities changed as I let go of trying to control both of my teenagers, the drug addict and the "normal" one. I stopped trying to "fix everything" for them when their actions might cause them pain. For example, I stopped calling the school to excuse their tardiness and I didn't stay up late and help them when they had school projects due the next day. I had so much more time and energy to do my own work. At first, I felt selfish, but I soon saw that my teenagers were doing more for themselves and becoming more self-reliant. It was a win-win situation!

Today's Reminder
Today I will not try to fix anything or control anyone but myself.

Being Right   October 5

I've been in the program long enough to know I'm in trouble when I know I'm right about something. Being right always costs me. I don't listen to others. I simply think of how I'll respond to show them I'm right. I become focused on winning and start to value that over the relationship with the other person. Being right means I'm not being open-minded. Twelve Step programs tell us to be: Honest, Open-minded, and Willing. When I don't listen, it usually results in a protracted argument and hurt feelings between me and a family member.

I have also learned that each of us perceives situations differently and all perceptions have some truth. Even when there may be a lot of truth in my beliefs about something, there may be some aspect of the situation—vitally important to another—hat I haven't considered at all. Truly listening to my loved ones, finding out what's most important to each of us, and being willing to work toward a solution which addresses what we each value, leads to a more satisfying and longer-lasting outcome.

Today's Reminder
I'd rather be open and listen than be right. This is the key to better relationships.

Sober Living Facility, Step 2   October 6

Letting go of the constant worrying about our son was a great gift of the program for us. Because he had not been successful with our local Enthusiastic Sobriety outpatient program, the counselors recommended he go to Step 2, the sober living facility. Although dubious at first, we agreed to let him enter the facility. This experience was very beneficial for us as well as our son.

It was quite an adjustment. One rule of Step 2 is no communication between parents and child. This was the first time he had been away from home by himself. Yet, as hard as it was not to have contact with him, we found it restful for us. We did not have to worry during this time. We knew he was safe and not using drugs. We began getting some good nights' sleep.

Eventually, some communication via faxes was permitted. He told us that he loved the place, the people, and the program. When we flew to Atlanta for the S.O.,[20] we saw our son—the respectful and good young man we had known before drugs—had returned. A week later he came home. The change in his behavior has persisted since his return. He is more sensitive and

---

[20] The S. O. (Significant Others ceremony) is a meeting held in both the outpatient program and Step 2 sober living facility. The parents meet with their child, others in the program, and the counselors after the program is near completion. During the S.O. the child states how he harmed his parents by his use of drugs or alcohol and tells how he will make amends to his family. It is a very emotional and healing experience.

aware of the effect of his actions on others. Our life at home has improved dramatically and we are grateful.

Today's Reminder
I will let go of worry about my child. I will obtain appropriate treatment for him and then have faith

The Power of Sticking with Winners October 7

There is a connection between powerlessness and sticking with winners. I am powerless over *some* things –not *every* thing. I have no power to change other people, things, or situations to be as I want them to be. Yet, I do have power to change myself. If I want to have a more balanced outlook toward life and not obsess about my kid's drinking, drugging, or sobriety, I can talk with other people who spend their time thinking more about the things I want to think about and less about the things I don't want to. At 2 a.m. when I wake with worry and fearful thoughts, I can read Twelve Step literature. Turning my mind away from worry and obsession is a healthy choice that I have the power, every second of every day, to make. When I join with other parents or loved ones of alcoholics and/or drug addicts who are also choosing a healthier outlook for themselves, I am using my power of choice to improve my own life and am sticking with winners.

Today's Reminder
Today I make healthy choices: to turn my thoughts to the solution, not the problem and to spend my time with like-minded persons.

Why I Kept Coming Back to Meetings After My Son Left   **October 8**

I know that some parents choose to stop coming to parent meetings after their kid bails from an Enthusiastic Sobriety program, but I did not. I was sick with worry about my son who suddenly left the program and drove away with his girlfriend to places unknown. They were gone and did not return for several months. To keep from going insane with worry, I read Melody Beattie's *The Language of Letting Go* each morning and repeated the Serenity Prayer to myself many times a day. I called other parents for moral support. I went to our Enthusiastic Sobriety parent meetings weekly and also went to Al-Anon meetings. I shared my painful experience and it seemed to help. I also listened to other people share and gained hope. Eventually, my son did return home. My husband and I stuck to our household rules, and eventually our son became sober after his extensive relapse. I understand that the parent meetings are for *us*, not our kids. Having an active drug addict child was too much for me to bear alone; meetings and talking with others in similar situations helped immensely.

Today's Reminder
Parent meetings and Al-Anon meetings are for *me*, not my kid. I will take advantage of my resources and get help to cope with my drug addict/alcoholic child.

EWOP (pronounced E-wop)   October 9

This is my personal mantra and it stands for *Everything's Working Out Perfectly*. This has been enormously helpful, especially on the days when I'm stuck in the muck and mire of my child's drama. I know it's hard to see a child's addiction as a blessing, but when I remember that everything is happening for a reason and that God has a plan, I find it easier to get through some of the rough patches. Also remembering the saying, "God doesn't give us any more than we can handle," has always been a comfort.

Today's Reminder
Despite what I think should be happening, I will remember that God has a better idea. Everything is working out perfectly.

"AA has an actual bumper sticker that reads, 'Expect a Miracle.' It doesn't tell us that we *deserve* a miracle, it says we can *expect* one. There is a difference. Expecting a miracle means that we expect something wonderful is going to happen—we aren't putting a specific expectation on some 'thing.' We are not expecting it not to rain tomorrow. We are expecting a good day, no matter the weather." ~*Bumper Stickers*

Changed Actions   October 10

"God grant me the serenity to accept the things I cannot change, the courage to change the things I can, and the wisdom to know it's me!" This variation on the Serenity Prayer helps me remember that truly I have no control over other people. The only person I can change is myself. I can choose to think, say, and do things differently in the future. The definition of "insanity" is doing the same thing over and over again and expecting a different result. Once I began experimenting and handling situations with my kids differently—sometimes using suggestions from other parents, sometimes using ideas that came to me after quiet prayer or meditation—things changed, usually for the better. Even when the situation itself remained the same, I felt calmer, more confident and capable as a parent. It was surprising how often *not* doing anything for or not saying anything to my teen helped the situation! Perhaps the reason for this was that I had too often in the past done for my teen what he needed to do for himself.

Today's Reminder
I have no control over other people, but I *do* control my own words and deeds. Today I choose to be open to new ways of handling old situations, including doing nothing.

I Can't Control, but I Can Complicate   October 11

While I've heard the three C's of Al-Anon: "I didn't cause it, I can't control it, and I can't cure it," I was also warned that I *can* complicate it. That is, my response to my child's alcoholism and/or drug addiction can make matters worse. How?

First, I can return his angry remarks with my own angry reactions, resulting in a home filled with discord. Second, if I get anxious because I fear bad consequences will follow from my child's latest non-sober behavior, I may jump to do everything I can to prevent those consequences. For example, I may pay overcharge fees on his debit or credit card, pay a fine, or offer an adult child his old room in the family home rent-free after he's lost a job or been evicted from his apartment. I jump in to "help" not only because of my fear for my child, but if I am honest with myself, it's because of the reflection on *me*. I don't want people to think ill of *me* and *my* child. Yet, I am merely "enabling" my child to continue his non-sober behavior without suffering the consequences which might cause him to reach "bottom" and actually become motivated to change. My behavior can *prolong* the active stage of this disease.

Equally important, as a parent of a young person, my job is to encourage independence. When I do something to "help" my teen or young adult, I am furthering his dependence on me. In the past my "helping" was instinctual, to protect my young child. Now my help is inappropriate and counterproductive. Before I do anything, I need to stop and think. Am I planning to do something to prevent a bad consequence for undesirable behavior on the part of my child? Is this a problem my child should face and learn to handle?

Today's Reminder

Because my behavior can make a difference, today I will stop before doing anything for my child. I will consider: is this something which will further his dependence on me or encourage him to become the independent adult I want to see him become?

Family Meetings   October 12

My wife and I agree with the Enthusiastic Sobriety acronym, "C.R.A.P.," Communication Resolves All Problems. We use scheduled family meetings to aid communication. We begin with a prayer followed by a brief statement by each person of how he or she feels now. ("Fine" or "good" is an unacceptable answer. Actual feelings need to be acknowledged.) Next are the meeting topics. These can be pre-arranged or determined at the time of the meeting. Examples of topics we have discussed are: our son's getting a job, buying cigarettes, and having more family time together. The topics are agreed upon by everyone. Each person speaks about the topic for no more than ten minutes while the others listen completely. The speaker uses "I" statements, speaking solely about what he or she has said or done and what he or she feels and needs. All listeners acknowledge what they have heard by repeating the idea back in their own words. Once everyone has spoken on the topic and has been acknowledged, we explore and brainstorm possible solutions. Exploration usually leads to creation of a plan on which we all agree. Next we make sure that each person understands the plan and finds it acceptable. We close with each person telling the rest of the family how he or she feels now.

Family meetings benefit us in many ways. We all show respect for each other's feelings and needs. Harms to family members can be addressed, admitted, and amends made. Together we work to build family harmony.

Today's Reminder
Today I will speak respectfully, listen to and acknowledge others' feelings and needs, and be open to hearing others' ideas for solving conflicts

Feeding the Sobriety Dog   October 13

My son relapsed after three month's sobriety in an Enthusiastic Sobriety group. During his relapse I realized the power of addiction. As much as our son loves his friends in the group, understands the program, and knows what he has to lose if he uses, he relapsed. He told me that once the drug was in his system, the cravings came back and *all* he could think about was using; nothing else mattered.

The kids say that you can either feed your addiction dog or your sobriety dog, but not both. Whichever one you feed gets bigger and stronger. At first I didn't understand why he couldn't work or take a few classes. Now I understand that the kids in the group need to spend time together and build support. Addiction is so strong that it can be a full-time job until the sobriety dog is bigger and stronger. My son could not work or go to school until his sobriety dog was well fed.

I also learned to control my responses to my son: I stand fast to the lines I am not willing to cross. When my son relapsed, I told him he could not stay at home that night because he was using. If he returned to working his program, he could keep his car, but if he left the program, he would lose his car and money. I learned not to bail my son out. If I were to do everything for him, he might get the message that he is not capable. Instead, I want to give him the message that I'll be there for him in difficult times, but he is responsible for his actions. Letting him live with consequences and taking responsibility helps him grow up.

Today's Reminder
Am I helping my child feed his sobriety dog? Am I holding fast to the lines I have drawn? Am I giving my child the opportunity to take responsibility for his actions?

Giving Up Control — October 14

Letting go was the hardest thing I have ever had to learn. I was always the master controller of the family, the fixer. That was my role, and I thought I did it really well. I really believed that my family would not be able to function without me always solving the day's problems.

Finally I learned to step back and let the cards fall, to love, to encourage, and to support without doing it all for them. Our family became healthy, happy, and strong. I became a better parent, a better wife, and a better friend. I have learned how to give without controlling. I got this from the parent group and from working the steps.

When God leads you to the edge of the cliff, trust Him fully and let go. Only one of two things will happen: either He'll catch you when you fall, or He'll teach you how to fly!

Today's Reminder
By letting go of the desire to "fix" everything and solve all my family member's problems, I am better able to be there for them. When I step back and let everyone handle his or her own problems, I am ready to congratulate them when they succeed and provide moral support should they not.

Forgiveness: It's about Me   October 15

My understanding of forgiveness has changed since working the Twelve Steps. I used to think that when I forgave people, I was telling them that I no longer held ill feelings toward them. The forgiven persons could then feel absolved of guilt.

Yet, I have seen that forgiveness goes beyond this. When I forgive, I benefit more than the people I forgive. True forgiveness removes or precludes resentment, the most devastating of emotions. When I truly forgive others, I tell *myself* that I no longer want to hold any resentment toward them. I relieve myself of the all-consuming feelings that will destroy my relationships with other people, often including those unrelated to the original events.

Forgiveness is a two-way street, and the most important part is the direction in which I am headed: free of resentment.

Today's Reminder
Today I remember that it is better *for me* to forgive than to hold on to resentment.

"Forgive us our trespasses as we have forgiven those who trespass against us." ~from the Lord's Prayer

Following the Path   October 16

Through this recovery journey with my son, I continued to remind myself to have faith in my Higher Power and my son's Higher Power. I believe everything happens for a reason. I may not know at this moment why things happened as they did, but I continue *now* to have faith and trust that all will work out for my son and me.

When my son first started spiraling down from marijuana use, I tried to "fix" everything; I tried to direct him down a path I wanted. I created more chaos. Through the year of continued chaos I eventually realized that no matter how much I tried, my son had his own free will. He continued to use drugs. His path followed many sharp turns including: running away, police involvement, school suspensions, and finally mandatory attendance in a drug intervention program conducted by an Enthusiastic Sobriety group. Now, reflecting on this, I can see how his Higher Power created a path that my son needed to follow. Without all these connecting life events, he would not have been following the road that guided him to his current happiness and recovery. His path may still have a few bumps, but I rest assured there are reasons for each bump and that we will get through it feeling stronger, happier and more serene.

Today's Reminder
Today should I question any situation in my life or my child's life, I will have faith. Then I will use my Higher Power's guidance to decide how I will respond to each situation.

Learning to Be Vulnerable   October 17

My son began abusing drugs and alcohol in high school. He drank so much wine one holiday that he vomited. Later a neighbor told us that our son had raided his medicine cabinet for prescription drugs. Our son's counselor suggested a local Enthusiastic Sobriety outpatient program.

I started going to the parent meetings and learned about the Twelve Steps. I could understand Step One: "We admitted that mind-changing chemicals have caused at least part of our lives to become unmanageable." My son's life had gone out of control, and as a result, my life had become unmanageable, too. I reflected on the AA and Al-Anon version of Step One: "We admitted we were *powerless* over alcohol—that our lives had become unmanageable." It was this powerlessness over my son, drugs, and alcohol which struck me. I had to admit that this drug problem had me beat. I couldn't control it or my son's behavior.

The steps gave me a way to cope. The Enthusiastic Sobriety Programs' Step Two, stick with winners, encouraged me to rely on other parents—especially my sponsor—for moral support. Next I turned to a higher power for help. For me, this meant that I had to strengthen my existing faith in the flow of life and karma. When I meet a challenge in life, I need to work through it. I realized that I can be my own worst enemy, expecting myself to be perfect. I needed my faith to fill and strengthen me. I came to believe that the higher power is indeed within each person, in the external world, and between each of us as we interact. With this connection, I no longer feel so vulnerable. Today I do the best I can, which is good enough, in working through my karma.

Today's Reminder

I need not fear to admit defeat over drugs and alcohol; a higher power is ready to help me.

"The path to paradise begins in hell." Dante

Would You Like to Hear My Opinion About That?

October 18

Letting my teen "own" his behavior means I let him make his own decisions, act accordingly, and experience the consequences of his actions. By doing this, I show my respect for him and treat him with dignity as a capable person. Since following the Twelve Steps, I have stopped giving unsolicited advice to my teen. I confess that I want to, but I bite my tongue. Sometimes, should he mention a troubling situation to me, I simply say, "That *is* a tough situation. Would you like to hear my opinion about that?" Usually he declines my offer, deciding he can handle it himself.

One day when he mentioned a dilemma he was facing, I asked him if he wanted to hear my opinion. He actually said, "Yes." This time he actually *wanted* to hear my suggestions and was truly listening to me! I was so honored and gently told him my ideas. He seemed to take it all in and used this information to help him make his *own* decision. It was truly a "win-win" experience for both of us.

Today's Reminder

I bite my tongue when I want to give my child advice. If he mentions a dilemma to me, I will ask, "Would you like to hear my opinion about that?" and if he says, "No," I will honor his choice.

Work the Program as Hard As You Want Your Kid To

October 19

Like most of the parents I met in the program, our family experienced a crisis before we got our son into treatment. The Dean and School Resource Officer recommended that I get my son into a drug treatment program as soon as possible before he was expelled from school. A local Enthusiastic Sobriety program was on the list that they provided and one of our neighbor's sons was in that program, so we entered our son shortly thereafter.

I'll never forget what the counselor said during our first meeting, "You need to work the program as hard as you want your son to work it." I wanted my kid to get and stay sober, so I jumped into the program with both feet.

It was amazing how much I learned, including a whole new set of coping skills. Today whenever I revert to my old ways of doing things, I question myself, "How's that working for you?" Then I think of an applicable slogan[21] or the Serenity Prayer to help guide my thinking and behavior.

My working the program does not in any way assure that my son will, but it helps me cope much better with daily life challenges. I have learned better ways of interacting with each member of my family, and I feel healthier and happier today.

Today's Reminder

Today I will recall slogans and the Serenity Prayer to help me through every day challenges.

---

[21] Slogans are explained in Appendix C: A Spiritual Toolkit. Also see the index for entries on the slogans in general as well as references to specific slogans.

No Unearned Highs — October 20

Part of teaching my teenager responsibility is teaching her that there are "no unearned highs." In life, good things happen to those who prepare, plan, and work for them. As Bob Meehan said in his book, *Beyond the Yellow Brick Road*, "everybody is looking for highs in life." Setting and achieving goals helps us feel good about ourselves and enhances our self-esteem. However, a drug gives a person the same feeling without the work or accomplishment, and according to Meehan, "[N]ot only do you gain unearned highs when you use drugs, you lose the real ones."

After undergoing treatment, my daughter set a goal to graduate with her high school class, despite the time she had missed from school for treatment. She returned to high school and completed 11 courses in one semester. She worked very hard and met her goal. For her graduation present, other relatives gave her their old car which needed some repair. I paid for the repair and the first three months of her car insurance, letting her know I was happy for her accomplishment. She also knew that she would have to earn money to pay for gas, maintenance, subsequent insurance, and any other car-related expenses. She experienced an "earned high" and learned that there are occasionally unexpected rewards from hard work.

Today's Reminder

I will support my child by allowing her to feel the consequences of her choices. When she reaches a substantial goal, I will acknowledge her accomplishment in a way that feels right for me

Life Balance and Levity   October 21

An insight I received from our Enthusiastic Sobriety parent meetings is that before entering the program I was unable to laugh about anything. I realized why. Subconsciously I hoped that by devoting all my energy to my son's addiction and not letting myself be "distracted" by other things in life, I could solve the problem faster. I believed there was no time for enjoyment or levity. My seriousness reflected self-centeredness and a refusal to believe that I could not solve the problem of my son's addiction. At first I was not letting God (and/or the parent group) help me cope.

Now I don't have to constantly wrestle with my son's addiction or other challenges I face. I can keep balance in my life by focusing for a while on steps I can take to face an issue and then letting go and having some fun each day.

Today's Reminder
I cannot cure my teen's addiction no matter how seriously I treat it. I accept what I cannot change today and spend my time changing what I can, me!

Higher Power   October 22

I was always religious, so when I was told that I had to believe in a higher power for this Twelve Step program to work for me, I thought that it was "no problem." Yet, as I did my best to "Let go and let God," I found that I really had a hard time doing this. Why? I believed in a punitive god. I also believed that I was only worthy of punishment. Once I realized that, I had to challenge both ideas. I began to visualize God as a more loving, nurturing parent who *gently* helps His children learn about life. I also realized that I deserved good things as much as anyone else. I began by not expecting the worst to happen and having faith that God would help me in all situations.

Today I believe that God may not prevent all "bad" things from happening, but He certainly helps me cope with anything that comes along. Also, I believe that God often acts through people—my family, friends, and others. With this newer concept of God, I am feeling less fearful these days and more trusting of God, myself, and others. I also am gentler and less punitive with my children. I give them opportunities to learn from their own mistakes and support them through the process.

Today's Reminder
Should I begin to worry about my children, myself, or others, I will remember that our Higher Power is taking care of us.

Self-Esteem   October 23

I can build my self-esteem by doing esteem-able acts. Substance abuse is a family disease; the addict can only think about his next fix while we family members can only think of ways to get the addict to stop. As a result, the self-esteem of all family members suffers. Working the Twelve Steps involves looking at my part in each resentment I hold, admitting this to another person, and—after becoming ready and willing to have God remove my character defects—making appropriate amends to people. This behavior takes faith and courage and helps me "bank" esteem-able acts to build my self-esteem. Regardless of the person's response to my admission of wrongdoing and efforts to repair the harm, I can feel good about my behavior in trying to make the situation right and restore harmony. There are many benefits to working the Twelve Steps, and feeling better about myself is just one of them. Today I pray that my Higher Power will give me the courage to admit my wrongs promptly and repair any resulting damage to others.

Today's Reminder
I feel good about myself by doing my best to repair any harm I have caused another and restoring harmony in my relationships with others.

Logical Consequences and Reaching Bottom   October 24

Our older son was in high school when we realized he was regularly drinking and smoking pot. We were tired of worrying about him when he did not come home until the wee hours of the morning. Plus we were concerned about the effect on our other son. My husband and I imposed logical consequences to help him reach a bottom. We told him that if he continued to drink alcohol and smoke pot, he was no longer welcome in our home. He could return any time he chose to stop drinking and smoking pot and agreed to go into treatment.

Our son left home and lived with another teen. His mother was so busy with a demanding job that she never realized that her son and ours were usually drunk or stoned and not going to school. Finally, our son was arrested for drug possession, and the court ordered him to stop using drugs—a weekly urine sample was required—and to live at home. Once the law got involved, our son suddenly found getting sober and living with us attractive. We were fortunate that he liked the local Enthusiastic Sobriety outpatient program, enjoyed the social functions, and found the meetings helpful. He discovered that being sober could be fun, and he even began to get along better with his brother and us again. At the Enthusiastic Sobriety parent meetings, other parents were impressed with my husband and me for setting limits and enforcing them.

Today's Reminder
I set limits and enforce them to encourage my child to stay on the right path.

Supporting My Teen in His Recovery   October 25

I believe all parents have a duty to set a good example. Obviously, to support my child in his recovery from alcoholism, I myself need to be sober. Also, I want to set a good example of how to accept life's problems and work through them to find solutions. When my son gets discouraged about a problem *and asks for my help*, I can show compassion and provide him the benefit of my experience.

For example, the first time his car broke down, our son called his father and me for help. We explained how to call for a tow truck. We reminded him that his car insurance would reimburse him for the cost of the towing. Because we had been through this process before, and it was a new experience for him, we walked him through it, so that he could learn how to handle it in the future. We empathized with him and helped him see that by taking certain steps, he could take care of the problem. By giving him aid and comfort *when he asked for it* and giving him the opportunity to take the necessary actions to solve his own problem, we provided moral support but did not "rescue" him.

Now when he has car problems, he takes it in stride, knows what to do, and does it.

Today's Reminder
When my young adult asks for my help, I can support him in his recovery by sharing my life experience with him.

Not Just a Bad Spell — October 26

The reality of my son's problem really struck my husband and me one evening. We were talking with one of the Enthusiastic Sobriety fathers at a party. He was sad and told us, "I have a twenty-six-year old son who has relapsed." Our son is also in his 20's. Our local Enthusiastic Sobriety program was his second treatment program, and right now our son is sober. Although he began using drugs in seventh grade, we were unaware of it. We did not realize he had a problem until he called us from college and asked for help. That father's statement helped us see that drugs and alcohol were not just a "bad spell" in my son's life that he could get over like the flu.

I analogize my son's condition to cancer. It is something that goes into remission but may reappear at any time. I can't dwell on this aspect of the disease. I need to live in the present moment and appreciate life as it is.

Today's Reminder
While I have a healthy respect for the disease of addiction, I do live my life one day at a time and enjoy the good I have today.

Teen Rebellion is not About Me! October 27

There was nothing working in my life before coming to our Enthusiastic Sobriety program. My teenager was a mess, so my life was a mess. Nothing I did to help him seemed to work. As a matter of fact, he seemed bound and determined to undermine my every good attempt to fix things. I was constantly trying to figure out why he was doing drugs even though they seemed to make him feel worse and worse, even though he was losing his friends and family, and especially since he now had legal trouble. My thoughts kept telling me that he was looking for ways to make me miserable, and it was working. I was miserable. Why didn't he just stop?

It was only after coming to meetings and hearing other parents describe this same kind of hell that I began to realize it was less about me and more about being a teenage addict. He still had all the normal teenage needs to rebel. He still had a need to make fun his primary goal in life. Drugs and alcohol had gotten in the way of normalcy. What I began to see as my son got clean and sober was that he still acted like a teenager. That was something I could learn to understand and live with, "normal" teen behavior. I had to give him time to grow up and trust everything would work out. With the help of clean, sober friends in the group he would learn and grow. I, too, could learn to accept, trust and encourage healthy growth.

Each sober day I see a little more maturity and a little less teenager. "One day at a time." It is enough!

Today's Reminder
A teenager, not under the influence of drugs or alcohol, is still a teenager. I will avoid unrealistic expectations for my teenager.

Speak Your Truth Kindly   October 28

Working the steps and going to meetings, I saw that I prefer to keep quiet rather than tell people what I need or want. For example, while I'm driving the car, one of my teens may put the radio on at a very high volume and listen to music I find discordant and irritating. In the past, I said nothing. Even worse, on a long drive after an hour or so of feeling miserable and getting angrier but not saying anything, I would suddenly explode, "Shut off that awful racket!"

Now I'm learning more effective ways of dealing with my feelings, needs, and wants. Ignoring them doesn't work and turns me into a human time bomb. Today I've learned I can "speak my truth kindly" *as soon as* I am aware of my needs or wants. Such as, "I'd really rather not listen to the radio now. Would you mind shutting it off?" The kids may shut the radio off or protest. We may discuss it and negotiate, but either way my needs are recognized.

The more I practiced this new behavior with little things, the more confident I felt with more important matters. The most important was telling my son to move out when he wasn't going to his intensive outpatient treatment sessions regularly. I couldn't live with him and watch him slowly sink. I warned him that if he missed another session, he would have to find another place to live. He missed another session, and I followed through, telling him that he was welcome back if he could attend for 30 days without missing any sessions, meetings, or functions. He gathered a few things in a small bag and left. Ultimately, he put together the 30 days and returned home. I am grateful that by working the program I gained the skills that helped me and benefited our family.

Today's Reminder
I do not ignore my feelings, needs, and wants to avoid conflict. Today I speak my truth kindly. Sometimes I negotiate with others so everyone's feelings, needs and wants can be considered.

Love Means Not Accepting Lies — October 29

There's a riddle, "How do you know when your teen is lying to you?" Answer: "When her lips are moving." Teens, alcoholics/drug addicts or not, lie to their parents. It's a fact. But we parents don't have to believe their lies.

One of the Enthusiastic Sobriety counselors at a recent parents meeting shared and assured us parents, "'Hanging out all night'" is not part of the program. It is not one of the [twelve] steps. Don't believe your kid if he tells you differently. Also, if you have a curfew, be sure to hold your kid to it. Don't believe your kid if he says you can't take away his cell phone because he needs it to call his sponsor. It may be hard to imagine, but people *did* get sober before cell phones!"

Our teens have not stopped being teens. They will try to use everything at their disposal—even the Twelve Step program—to attempt to manipulate us and avoid consequences for breaking household rules. We have to be ready and work our own program so that they don't pull the wool over our eyes.

Today's Reminder
If my teen tells me something that I suspect is untrue, I will check it out. If he lied, I will discuss it with him later and set appropriate consequences.

Sibling Issues   October 30

I recall other Enthusiastic Sobriety parents telling me about their response to sibling complaints about the amount of time and attention the drug addict/alcoholic in the family was receiving when the family first entered the program. They analogized the addict's condition to that of a cancer patient needing intensive treatment. For a while, it is important for the parents to give more time and attention to the child with the life-threatening disease. I did plan some special time with my other child to help him not feel neglected.

Further, it is important to remind my non-addict son that he, too, needs to think before he interacts with his addicted brother. When he asked me if he should lend money to his brother, I asked him questions such as, "What do you think your brother will do with the money?" "Why do you think your dad and I have refused to give him any money?" and "Do you think he will pay you back?" In this way, he begins to understand the need to set boundaries, too, so that he protects himself and does not enable his brother's drug use.

Raising two teens, one a drug and alcohol abuser and one not, presents many challenges, but none that cannot be faced calmly with the help of the Twelve Step program and other parents.

Today's Reminder

Each of my children is unique. I do my best to provide for their individual needs and guide them toward tools to handle situations they face.

One Day at a Time and Keep the Focus on Me   October 31

Just as the addict must restrain himself from taking a drink or drug one day at a time, we also need to take life one day at a time. We often get upset with our kids, spend much of our days mentally reliving our children's mistakes, and fear they will repeat their mistakes. We need to keep our minds in the present. We, too, can change *our* habit of worrying.

Even when my mind stays in the present, I find I sometimes worry about what my kids are doing right now, rather than focusing on what *I* need to do right now. Worrying about my son doesn't help him stay sober; instead it draws my mind away from what I need to do now. When I can focus on what I need to do, moment by moment, I find, at the end of the day, I feel less tired and am pleased with my productivity.

Today's Reminder
There is no time like the present. I will focus on what *I* am doing today, be a good example for my children, and let go of worry and fear.

NOVEMBER

Step One: Admitting the Problem November 1

Enthusiastic Sobriety Programs' Step One reads: "We admitted that mind-changing chemicals have caused at least part of our lives to become unmanageable."

As a parent in an Enthusiastic Sobriety program, I have found it helpful also to attend Al-Anon meetings. Al-Anon (and AA) Step One reads: "We admitted we were powerless over alcohol—that our lives had become unmanageable."

I was told that the reason that Bob Meehan got permission from the AA World Service Headquarters to slightly modify the wording of the AA steps was to make it more applicable to people addicted to all drugs, including alcohol. Also, specifically with regard to Step One, he wanted to make it more amenable to teenagers, who tend to believe they are invincible, but are willing to admit that having their parents, school officials, police, and/or other adults "on their back" can make at least part of their lives unmanageable.

The Al-Anon (and Alcoholics Anonymous) Step One helps me remember that I am powerless to control my child, his addiction, or his sobriety. My efforts to keep him from his drug-using friends did not stop him from using drugs. He and his Higher Power are in charge of his sobriety, not me. I only have control over my own actions, so I focus on my role as a parent.

Today's Reminder
I cannot orchestrate my child's life to prevent his ever being anywhere where drugs or alcohol are found, so I let go of trying. Instead, I focus on what *I*, as a parent, can do.

Step Two: Stick with Winners — November 2

Enthusiastic Sobriety Programs' Step Two reads: "We have found it necessary to stick with winners in order to grow."

The question we parents usually ask is, "Who are the winners?" One answer is other families who are working the program. As a parent, I found it most helpful to talk with other parents whom I saw every week at the meetings and who, during their sharing time, talked about working the steps or successfully applying ideas they had learned from meetings to situations with their teens.

It took trial and error to learn who the other winners were. Winners included: 1) the people who were kind and encouraging and who told us about their own family members who had a drug or alcohol problem, 2) other friends who did not judge or criticize, admitted they knew nothing about alcoholism and addiction, and were kind and non-judgmental. I also learned from experience who were *not* winners for me or my family, such as: 1) "friends" who inquired about our son, but lost interest as soon as the "drama" (and fuel for gossip) was over, 2) extended family members who were unwilling or unable to participate in sober family get-togethers for holidays or special occasions, 3) well-meaning friends who criticized the late hours of the meetings and functions. Soon, I realized that the way to cope with "friends" was to avoid them and spend more time with winners.

Today's Reminder
I will avoid people who gossip, judge and criticize. Instead, I will spend time with people who are kind and accepting and who encourage our family in our recovery.

Step Three: Higher Power — November 3

Enthusiastic Sobriety Programs' Step Three reads: "We realized that a Higher Power, expressed through our love for each other, can help restore us to sanity."

I had never been a very religious person, so I struggled with Step Three when I reached it. How would I know what a higher power is? Many said you could feel the higher power work through the parent group. In the group I felt accepted, knew others suffer as I do, and shared each week at the meeting. I started to feel a higher power when I let go of my control and started accepting things as they are. My day-to-day life became more peaceful.

However, when my serenity was interrupted by chaos, I tended to go back to my old ways of control. Once while my family vacationed at Lake Powell, a huge wind and lightning storm came in. Other family members were moving the houseboat to a more secure location, and we could not fasten the ski boat to it until the houseboat was secure. So I was driving the ski boat around in circles and becoming increasingly anxious as the storm intensified. I was angry and irritated that they couldn't get the houseboat secure more quickly. I was resentful that my expectations were not being met. Then I realized that I could continue my madness of trying to control and resent the situation or I could ask my higher power for help. I stopped the boat and prayed. Suddenly a huge calm washed over me and I knew my higher power was helping me, letting me know everything would be ok. The slogan, "Let go and let God", now made sense. I became calm. The houseboat got safely tethered. I am grateful for my higher power, the unconditional love of the parent group, and the kids in our local Enthusiastic Sobriety program.

Today's Reminder
Today I will remember that my higher power is there to guide me whenever I let go. "Let go and let God" is now part of my daily prayers.

Step Four: Turn It Over to God — November 4

Enthusiastic Sobriety Programs' Step Four reads: "We made a decision to turn our will and our lives over to the care of God as we understand Him."

We often hear in meetings, "turn it over to God." Yet, sometimes, when I "turned it over," I wondered if we were just postponing our parental role. For example, when our son first entered the program, I was relieved to have him spending so much time with the group and staying at other Enthusiastic Sobriety kids' homes. It gave my husband and me a nice break from the tension that had built when our son had been using drugs.

Shortly after out-patient treatment, we felt guided to play a more active parental role again. We still had a duty to raise our son, which, for us, meant showing him by example that we were working the steps to the best of our ability. We also suggested that he return to school, get a job, and save money to buy his own car. We discovered that we didn't have to convince him to do these things, because—through the influence of the other teens and his own Higher Power—he already had decided that he wanted these things. We were able to help him by answering specific questions he asked about how to open a bank account and reconcile it, how to shop for a car, etc. We were acting as sane parents: guiding and assisting our child to navigate life's challenges and being ready to help when asked.

Today's Reminder
As a parent I will set a good example for my child. I will let him make his own decisions and show up for him when he asks for my advice.

Step Five: Inventory   November 5
Enthusiastic Sobriety Programs' Step Five reads: "We made a searching and fearless moral inventory of ourselves."

Some people say that the hardest part of doing an inventory is admitting their faults to another. Yet for me, the hardest part was uncovering or discovering my faults. I began listening carefully at meetings to others who revealed their faults or character defects; did I share any of these? I realized that I had some weaknesses or poor coping mechanisms that I had been unable to see before. For example, I was not as honest as I had thought. I had shielded my son from the consequences of his poor choices. I became aware of other unhealthy behaviors or "character defects." The more I considered this, the more I saw the potential for growth by working the steps.

Today's Reminder
Today I will take a good look at my actions and uncover any self-deceptions. I cannot do my part in changing poor coping mechanisms if I am not aware of them.

Step Six: Honesty with Self and Another   November 6

Enthusiastic Sobriety Programs' Step Six reads: "We admit to God, to ourselves, and to another human being the exact nature of our wrongs."

Initially one of the greatest deterrents to working Step Five for me was the thought of Step Six. The fear of disclosing my inventory to another person inhibited me from even beginning to write my inventory. However, the really scary part of Step Five was the process of becoming honest with myself. My sponsor told me that he had experienced a lifting of a weight after he shared his inventory. So, I had to trust that this would happen for me.

The inventory process includes listing resentments. My tendency at first was to focus on acts or omissions, since I easily recalled those. It was easy to see how they had caused pain or harm to someone. Ironically, I discovered that some of my resentments were towards persons who were completely unaware of them. These resentments were double trouble because they hurt me without the desired benefit of revenge against the other persons. It has been said that resentment is like taking poison and expecting someone else to die.

In writing my inventory I saw that when I focused on the resentment, I dwelled on the other person. I needed to focus on *my own role* in the situation. I also saw that resentment often hides behind anger, fear, envy, and many other emotions, so that I had to dig deep to uncover its true nature.

Ultimately, I did find that sharing my inventory with my sponsor led to a sense of relief, rather than embarrassment or condemnation, as I had feared. By flushing out the things that had weighed upon me for a long time, I found that they no longer haunted me.

Today's Reminder
When writing my inventory, I do not worry about the next step. After completing my inventory, I share it with my sponsor and trust that I will benefit from the experience.

"And you will know the truth, and the truth will set you free." John 8:32

Step Seven: Enmeshed Families and Change — November 7

Enthusiastic Sobriety Programs' Step Seven reads: "We became willing to allow our Higher Power, through the love of the group, to help change our way of thinking and humbly ask Him to help us change."

After listening in parent meetings and doing my own inventory, I became aware of an unhealthy behavior pattern of mine called "triangulating." When I had a dispute with a family member, I would stew about it and convince myself I was "right" and the other person was "wrong." Then I'd talk with another family member—not the one with whom I had the problem—and try to solicit his or her "support." Depending on how "hurt" I was, I might gather other "support" from additional family members. I might even orchestrate a time when my "supporter" would talk with the offending person about my problem. The potential for misunderstandings and resentments grew with each indirect communication and each additional party drawn into the fray. This was crazy-making, and I didn't even realize it!

It was the love and support of the parent group and my sponsor that helped me become aware of this pattern and recognize it as destructive. Today when I have a conflict with a person, I ask my Higher Power for the courage to talk honestly and directly with the person and try to resolve it.

Today's Reminder
If I have a conflict with someone, I will go directly to that person and discuss it. Also, I will not listen to another family member complaining to me about a third. Instead, I will suggest the speaker communicate directly with the source.

Step Eight: Willingness   **November 8**
Enthusiastic Sobriety Programs' Step Eight reads: We made a list of all persons we have harmed and became willing to make amends to such people, whenever possible, except when to do so would injure them, others, or ourselves."

An important point to recognize is that Step Eight has two parts: making a list and *becoming willing* to make amends. No amends are actually made in this step. Most people check their list with their sponsor who helps them determine which persons on the list were *actually* harmed. (For many of us, that usually means a *shorter* list than the one we started with.)

The time-consuming part of the step is the *becoming willing* part. I found that praying daily for the people on my list helped me become willing and see them all as more approachable. Also surprising to me was that life often placed these people, whom I may not have seen for awhile, in my path at just the right time.

Today's Reminder
When working Step Eight, I make a list, consult my sponsor, revise the list if necessary, and then pray for the willingness to make amends to the persons on my revised list.

Step Nine: Making Amends — November 9
Enthusiastic Sobriety Programs' Step Nine reads: "We made direct amends to such people, whenever possible, except when to do so would injure them, others, or ourselves."

While creating an inventory we become aware of harms we have caused. Step Eight tells us to make a list of the persons we harmed and become willing to "make amends" to them; Step Nine says we make amends. Amends are not simple apologies. They are *behavioral changes* that we become willing to make.

In making my list, I found that the most significant harms were not material harms, such as failure to pay a debt, but the emotional harms I caused. For example, I often told my kids what to do when they had a problem; I never let them solve it. Plus I often said nothing when they treated each other (and me) rudely and disrespectfully. Today, I am much more conscious of these situations. I keep quiet instead of offering unsolicited advice. I listen to their proposed solution and later compliment them once they have solved the problem. I now enforce limits about disrespectful and rude behavior. I calmly and quietly state that I do not appreciate their rude or disrespectful tone. In these ways I am making changes on a day-to-day basis that help me feel better about my actions and improve my family life.

Today's Reminder
I realize apologies are insufficient. I begin to make changes in the way I interact with others.

Step Ten: November 10
A Balanced, Regular Self-Appraisal

Enthusiastic Sobriety Programs' Step Ten reads: "We have continued to look at ourselves and when wrong, promptly admitted it."

At first, this step scared me. New parents are encouraged to read the book, *Alcoholics Anonymous*, commonly referred to as the "Big Book." In that book, it talks about taking a moral inventory every evening before retiring. Having to take a "searching and fearless moral inventory" once was bad enough, but did I really have to do that all the time? I had always been a perfectionist who daily held many critical thoughts about myself and others. When my son entered treatment, I felt depressed and believed I was a "failure" as a parent. So, Step Ten evoked images of nightly mental self-whippings, which I felt I needed like the plague!

In *Beyond the Yellow Brick Road*, Bob Meehan assured me that "It's only halftime" and that I could do more to help my son. I clung to that thought. I continued to go to parent meetings and heard from others doing inventory and the self-discoveries they made. I eventually realized that I was a good mother who deeply loved my children and had expended a great deal of energy to show them my love. Unfortunately, that energy had been channeled into ineffective actions: rescuing them from the consequences of their missteps and "helping" them to perform tasks which they needed to do for themselves. Hearing about others' positive experiences, I realized that the inventory steps could be a positive learning experience.

Today, I try to take Step Ten every day. My sponsor suggested I ask these questions: 1) What did I do right today?) 2) Who did I help today? 3) Where did I have trouble today? (i.e. Where was I dishonest, selfish, resentful, or afraid?) 4) What am I grateful for?

Today's Reminder
At the end of the day I will look at what I did well and acknowledge my character assets. I will also look at what I did not do well and consider how to improve in the future. I will finish my contemplation by counting my blessings.

Step Eleven: **November 11**
   Contact with Our Higher Power
The Enthusiastic Sobriety Programs' Step Eleven is: "We have sought through prayer and meditation to improve our conscious contact with our Higher Power, that which we have chosen to call God, praying only for knowledge of His will for us and the courage to carry that out."

Everyone has his or her own unique view of a Higher Power and unique way of praying and meditating. In our parent group we have people from all religious faiths as well as agnostics and atheists. For some, the Higher Power is the collective power of the parent group. Some use the prayers or meditation styles of their faiths and others try different styles at different times.

When my husband and I first became members of the parent group, I was exhausted and frantic over our son's drug addiction. We had tried everything to stop him and nothing had worked. I recalled feeling equally exhausted years earlier when we had two toddlers at home. At that time I had heard about the Friends' (Quakers') meetings which were one hour of "sitting in the silence." Because I never had an hour of silence during the day at home, the Friends' meeting sounded like heaven on earth to me! I went, placed my kids in the childcare room, and enjoyed the silence an hour each week. Recalling the respite I felt from that experience, I decided that this Higher Power thing was definitely something I could use to rest my rattled nerves. I was open and willing to try anything for some peace of mind.

The parents in our group have found that all ways of connecting with a Higher Power work if we are making an honest effort. I have become calmer and a better listener. Now I frequently enjoy the silence in our home that didn't exist before our son got into treatment. Step Eleven works.

Today's Reminder
Today I will use whatever method works for me to connect with my Higher Power.

Step Twelve: November 12
Sharing with Those Who Want to Hear

The Enthusiastic Sobriety Programs' Step Twelve reads: "We, having had a spiritual awakening as a result of these steps, tried to carry our love and understanding to others, and to practice these principles in our daily lives."

As we parents feel the power of the application of the Twelve Steps in our lives, we are naturally excited and want to share this wonderful program with others. Yet, talking with everyone we know at the office, health club, PTA, or in the neighborhood about the Twelve Steps is not the most effective way to "carry our love and understanding." The best way to help other parents of drug addicts and alcoholics is to reach out to newcomers after a meeting. These are people who have come to a meeting to investigate and see if the Twelve Steps are for them.

We do not want to get into the bad habit of trying to "save" and "rescue" someone who does not want to be "saved" and "rescued." But, if someone from the office, club, PTA, or neighborhood *initiates* a conversation with us and asks about our experience, we can certainly tell them. We want to help those who want help.

Today's Reminder
I work the steps, share my recovery at meetings, and answer people's questions about the program. I no longer try to save or rescue anyone.

Help with the Holidays   November 13

As parents we want to support and encourage our children in their sobriety by providing a sober home environment for them during the holidays. To do this some families have had a family round table discussion to plan their holiday events and environment. Our family decided to give up some of the tradition, at least for now. Fortunately, to fill the gap we have some help from our Enthusiastic Sobriety program itself. Kicking off the holiday season is the traditional Gratitude meeting on the eve of Thanksgiving. This "must attend" event, open to extended families, helps center us about the important things in our lives. It also helps us think about the upcoming holidays.

For me, the Round Robin New Year's Eve event in particular was a life saver, because it provided a reason *not* to attend the traditional neighborhood celebrations, which invariably centered around alcohol. In addition, the Round Robin is filled with fun activities and with people who share a deep common experience. It is something to run to, rather than simply running away from a former family experience that included alcohol.

Most importantly, we are not alone; there are parents and counselors who can help us deal with and plan for the holidays, no matter what our situations. Sometimes, just knowing that others are there for us gives us the strength and courage to forge ahead in a new, positive direction.

Today's Reminder
I want to support my child in sobriety. The entire family will discuss and plan our holidays so everyone can enjoy them. I will also talk with other parents in the program to learn from their experience and gather new ideas to help us during the holiday season.

Open-Mindedness and Humility   November 14

The first time we took our son to an Enthusiastic Sobriety program, I was not very receptive to the parent meetings. I felt angry and defensive. I was frustrated that I had no control over my son or my own life. I went to meetings and rarely saw very much positive I could gain from them. Our son got some sobriety under his belt, left the drug treatment program, returned to school and graduated.

However, he eventually returned to drugs, and after a brush with the law, he was desperate and ready to work the program with renewed vigor. This time I was less fearful, more relaxed, and more open-minded about the program. I realized there were things I could share. I embraced the concept of humility. My child taught me to laugh at my frailties and learn from them. With open-mindedness and humility, this second time around in the program has been a blessing for all of us.

Today's Reminder
Today I accept my life as it is. I am open-minded about where I may receive help in overcoming my life challenges.

"Seest thou a man wise in his own conceit? There is more hope of a fool than of him."
Proverbs 26:12

Forgiving Myself   November 15

As I worked my steps I discovered that I had often been hardest on myself. In my inventory I was harder on myself than on others. For instance, I was unsure of whether my sharing was "good enough" in meetings, because I somehow felt responsible for motivating and enlightening others. I worried that I said the wrong things at functions and that others would somehow judge me. After being in the group for over a year, I learned that when you speak from the heart and are sincere, others will listen and embrace the good while understanding the rest. I learned to love myself for who I was and to forgive myself for minor missteps. After all, I easily forgave others, because I knew that many of the things that they did, I had also done, often by accident and never with malice.

Since I had always apologized when I thought I was wrong, and even sometimes when I didn't think I was wrong, I ended up making amends mainly to myself in Steps Eight and Nine. Although I have a caregiver personality and enjoy doing things for other people, I realized that I couldn't do for others at my own expense. I had made time to eat right and exercise, but never fully developed my spiritual being. Now while going through the Twelve Steps a second time, I am exploring ways to be more spiritual. I have mostly forgiven myself for things I did without malice. I have learned that each of us does the best we can and that we each have our own particular gifts to share.

Today's Reminder
We are all imperfect humans doing the best we can. I forgive myself and others for not being perfect.

Cleanliness is Next to Godliness?   November 16

A common complaint of parents after our kids have gotten sober is their messiness. Although we are grateful that our kids are sober and more polite, we find it frustrating that they leave messes in the home and don't keep their rooms clean. Why is cleanliness so important to us? I don't think that most of us believe the old adage, "cleanliness is next to godliness." I do believe that my son's keeping things in order is a symbol of being a mature person who can function successfully in the world.

Yet, when I scrutinize this belief, I see it is false. I know a number of successful adults whose work areas seem disorderly.

Yet, these people function perfectly well in the world. So, for today, I will continue to be grateful for my son's sobriety and not despair about his messiness. I will lower my expectations and only ask that he keep the common living areas picked up. He may keep his room as he pleases.

Today's Reminder
Today I will focus on what is good in my child and in my world.

God's Got Their Backs! November 17

The primary lesson I seem to experience repeatedly from working the Enthusiastic Sobriety parent program is to let my children run their own lives. By the time they are teens and young adults, I have done everything I can to provide the background they need to live a happy life. It's not my job to tell them how to live their lives. As a recovered alcoholic, I know that the grace of God got me sober and is there for everyone else, too.

One recent example of my being reminded to let go involves my oldest son. He is very bright and yet has chosen to work at a fast food restaurant. He has been there for a few years and is quite happy, despite the fact that I feel he could do so much more. I tried to steer him into a school and career, but he really did not want that. He said to me, "I'm happy. Why can't you be happy for me?" I realized my ego was getting in the way of being happy for him. Now I do my best to let go and be glad he is enjoying his life.

Today's Reminder
My life is my business; my children's lives are their business.

Marijuana and Logical Consequences   November 18

When we first discovered our son was addicted to marijuana, our family physician explained that it stays in a person's system for six weeks. The detective from our local police department told us that, in his experience, once a parent finds evidence of marijuana paraphernalia in a teen's belongings, the teen has most likely been smoking for a while. At some point the teen gets sloppy and forgets to be secretive about his illegal behavior. THC, the active ingredient in marijuana, distorts a person's perception of reality.

In *Beyond the Yellow Brick Road,* Bob Meehan talks about a teenager, Johnny, who starts smoking marijuana and within six months walks down a street in broad daylight rolling a joint and offering a hit to a person at a bus stop. Meehan says that when treating young marijuana addicts, the counselor has to "straighten their devious thought patterns" and "make them understand logical consequences."

This explained why our efforts to employ logical consequences with our son hadn't worked. Smoking marijuana had interfered with his ability to understand. This was a powerful lesson. We could not "control" or "cure" our son. We were indeed powerless over his drug abuse and had to turn to other sources for help.

Today's Reminder

As a parent, I cannot "cure" my teenager of addiction; yet I have a duty to seek medical treatment for my minor child. To learn more about my child's disease and to help me cope with the challenges of raising a drug-addicted child, I will attend Enthusiastic Sobriety parent and/or Al-Anon meetings.

Freedom from Insanity   November 19

I do not believe in chance; I believe that each of us is in his or her own situation in life for a reason. Each has the opportunity to realize this reason and to gain his or her own personal enlightenment from each and every life situation that is presented. Being people of free will, we do not have to find freedom in these challenging situations, but we can. We can be free from the insanity that the effects of mind-altering chemicals have brought into our lives. We can find and experience the truth of our lives. We can make a difference in the lives of our children, our family members and our fellow parents in the group. The Twelve Steps of recovery are a path of discovery. The Twelve Steps can be entered into at any level of participation that you desire; there is no requirement to have an intense experience or even a mild experience. Take the steps at your own pace and from your own place in life and see what comes up for you. Each of us is unique and each of us has his or her own truth.

Today's Reminder
I will take the steps at my own pace, savor each moment, and enjoy the view.

Setting Our Priorities for the Holidays   November 20

It's that time of year that we used to look forward to with positive anticipation. It was a family gathering time, a time of celebration, a time of relaxation, a time of thankfulness. But all of that changed when our son fell down the hole of substance abuse. Now the thought of celebration sometimes conjures fears of our son's relapse. Also we realize that some family members just don't get it about our son who struggles around people celebrating with alcohol. One year we were dumb and happy; the next year we were aware and worried. What did we do?

The first year that my wife and I were in the parent program we listed all of our priorities and ranked them. We found that sobriety topped them all, for without sobriety, nothing else works. So during the holidays, sobriety was at the forefront of our minds when making decisions about what to do, where to go, and with whom to be. That meant forgoing traditions, including a traditional family gathering and a neighborhood "progressive" dinner which often involved alcohol. Once aware of our situation, many relatives and friends were able to adapt to an alcohol-free celebration. But for those relatives and friends who were not, it meant excluding them from our holidays or excluding ourselves from theirs. Over the years we have found that celebrating the holidays with understanding relatives and friends, as well as participating in the Gratitude meeting on Thanksgiving Eve and the New Years' Round Robin event with our local Enthusiastic Sobriety "family," has brought us much love, joy, and peace of mind.

Today's Reminder
I will support my child in his recovery by providing alcohol-free celebrations in our home.

Mean What You Say   November 21

There is a saying: "Mean what you say, say what you mean, and don't say it mean." Parents in our program have found this very important – albeit sometimes hard to follow.

My husband and I talked about our son's behavior and agreed on consequences so we could provide a united front. In the past when his usual ways of manipulating his way out of consequences weren't working, he threatened suicide if he didn't get what he wanted. We always backed down, failed to enforce consequences, and walked on eggshells to protect him. This time, though, we suspected it was a manipulation. Erring on the side of safety, we called 911 and had our son committed to a hospital for a (mandatory) 48 hour evaluation on the grounds that he might be a danger to himself or others. After that incident the next time he began to threaten suicide, we reminded him that we would take it seriously and have him committed again. He stopped the behavior.

Today's Reminder
My spouse and I will present a united front of consequences for unacceptable behavior. We will take threats of suicide seriously and not allow them to be used as manipulation.

I Came for My Daughter and Stayed for Myself — November 22

When my bright, athletic high school student started using marijuana, her behavior changed drastically. She was "hanging out" all hours of the day and night. My friends and I would chase her down. This made me crazy. Eventually, she ran away. When she returned, I got her into various treatments; we tried psychiatrists, group therapy, a troubled teens' group, but nothing seemed to work. A friend heard of an Enthusiastic Sobriety program in our area, so I tricked my daughter into going to see a counselor there. She started the program but had a rocky time the first year and relapsed several times. She went to Step 2, the sober living facility. She eventually chose sobriety.

The Enthusiastic Sobriety programs require parents to attend weekly parent meetings and suggest that parents work their own Twelve Step program so as not to sabotage the kids' success. I learned many things from working the steps and attending parent meetings. One important result for me was that I stopped living my life out of fear. I talk with my sponsor regularly and also have sponsees—other fathers in the program with whom I share my experience, strength, and hope and whom I assist in working the steps. I have found that by working the steps in all aspects of my life, I enjoy a deeper, better life. Today I am thankful that my daughter's addiction brought us into a program of working the Twelve Steps for a saner, happier life that we share.

Today's Reminder
The purpose of the parent group is to help me with *my* life. I will take advantage of this opportunity to enrich my life and improve my relationship with my child.

No Longer a Victim — November 23

I had a habit of feeling like a victim of circumstances. I let my kids control things at home. When my husband wasn't home, they often heard me say, "Wait till your father gets home." Of course, by the time he got home, I was too tired and exhausted to remember all the transgressions which had caused that familiar refrain. Rarely would anything happen. Although I felt like a victim, after some soul-searching, I realized *I* was the *adult* and *I* had failed to take control. I had let the kids control me because I had trouble making unpopular decisions.

Once we got into an Enthusiastic Sobriety program and I started working the Twelve Steps in earnest, I realized my shortcoming and how it had affected our family. I also heard from the counselors that it is very important for our teens to be held accountable for their behavior. They need to have someone to answer to, so it is good to have them "check in" with phone calls about where they are, with whom, and when they plan to get home. My son began "checking in" and I began holding him to the agreements we made over the phone about what time he would get home. If he didn't meet our household curfew, he lost privileges and could not go out or use our car. Although he was not pleased when I enforced a curfew violation, he accepted it. Today I no longer feel like a victim. I feel like a responsible parent and it feels good.

Today's Reminder
I am the parent and it is my duty to set limits and enforce them with logical consequences. Today I will do my duty to the best of my ability, and if I need help I will call my sponsor or another parent in the program.

"...[L]ogical consequences that create real feelings make people change; that's what forces teenagers to grow up." ~*Beyond the Yellow Brick Road*

Let Life Unfold   November 24

I was frightened and I wanted to "fix" my son, but I realized that I could not. It was important for me to focus on how much I love my son and how much he loved me. Even though he frequently did not act as if he loved me when he was using drugs, I knew how deep and strong our love had been. It was this love which motivated me to find a treatment program for him.

At the same time my son entered an Enthusiastic Sobriety program, I began to attend parent meetings where I was introduced to the Twelve Steps. I was also studying Eastern philosophy. Both teach that there is much an individual cannot control, and it is best to let go and let life unfold. Although this message is simple, it is not easy to follow. I made a decision to leave my son's treatment to the program and let go of my ideas of how a program should be. I can only control my own actions, so I got a sponsor and worked the Twelve Steps myself. Eventually, I let go of fear and my son let go of drugs. Today, I see how the love my son and I share, along with our working of the Twelve Steps, helped us reunite.

Today's Reminder
I do what I can to guide my child into a treatment program and let go of the outcome. At the same time, I work the Twelve Steps and let life unfold.

The Power of the Group   November 25

My son, like many teens, had poor social skills. In middle school he felt like a misfit and had difficulty making friends. By high school, he was suffering both academically and socially and started experimenting with drugs, so I sought out an alternative school for him. He did better for a while at this school, but he struggled again with drugs in the summer.

Because of this I insisted that my son enter and stay in a drug treatment program. I did some research and found an Enthusiastic Sobriety program in our area. Driving there, I could see my son was feeling negative about looking at a possible treatment program. Once we arrived at the Enthusiastic Sobriety shop, my son saw a schoolmate there. His spirits brightened and he happily went to the teens' meeting; meanwhile I attended the parents' meeting. As I walked into the other room to meet him at the end of the evening, I saw my son surrounded by many teens that really were happy to have him join the group. They all said, "Love you, man," and I could tell they meant it. It was the first time in his life my son had experienced unconditional love from his peer group. I knew that being loved unconditionally by this peer group was a strong power; if anything could help my son get sober, this was it. It has been almost one year since he entered the program and he has almost a year of sobriety.

Today's Reminder
I do not underestimate the power of the group. Just as my teen uses his group to help him, I will use the power of the Enthusiastic Sobriety parent group and Al-Anon groups to help me. If I am uncertain about handling some situation with my teen, I will call a member of my group to talk it over and reason things out.

The Serenity Prayer — November 26

When our family entered an Enthusiastic Sobriety program, I became aware of the tradition of closing each meeting with The Serenity Prayer. Certainly, I had heard this prayer before but it held no true meaning for me.

Now, this prayer is posted on my bathroom mirror. It is the first thing I see when I wake and the last thing I see before I retire.

The Serenity Prayer is a constant source of peace and inspiration for me. I find myself consciously saying it each day as a reminder that God's will surrounds me. I find myself saying it unconsciously at times when I am going about my day, whether it be taking a walk, driving to work or facing a difficult moment when I need guidance.

The Serenity Prayer is a source of strength, wisdom and hope for me each and every day.

The Serenity Prayer
God grant me the serenity to accept the things I cannot change, the courage to change the things I can, and the wisdom to know the difference.

Treating My Children with More Objectivity   November 27

Deeply invested in my children's lives, I have found it hard to be objective about them and let them make their own choices. I am not alone, though, because I saw the very same difficulty in the character, Indiana Jones, in the movie, *Indiana Jones and the Kingdom of the Crystal Skull*. Indiana Jones meets a young man in his twenties, and they strike up a friendship. The young man tells Indiana that everyone—especially his mother—tells him he should go to college and get his degree. However, he has no interest in school.

Indiana tells him to follow his heart and not let anyone pressure him into doing anything he doesn't want to do. "School isn't what it's made out to be," Indiana counsels. Of course, this is just what the boy wants to hear, and it strengthens his bond with Indiana.

However, later in the movie, Indiana learns that the boy is actually his son. Literally the first thing out of his mouth when he next sees the lad is, "Forget everything I said about not going to school. You need to get your *** in school right now!"

Why is it that we can objectively counsel other people's children, but not our own? Our motivations are deep and complicated. Of course we want the best for our children, but isn't there a little selfishness there too? If we are truly honest with ourselves, we may find a subconscious motivation such as, "It will reflect well on me and my parenting skills."

Through working the steps and attending parent meetings, I have found it actually counter-productive to give my children advice and try to influence their decisions. As I start to let go, I find everything works out.

Today's Reminder
Today I practice viewing my children with the same objectivity that I would my neighbor's children. I let go and avoid giving advice.

Happy Holidays — November 28

For many years the holidays were happy for us. We spent time with family and continued traditions. Then it hit. Our daughter, who used to be fun and outgoing, became sullen and withdrawn. She attended family functions only because we insisted. Her goal was to figure out how soon she could leave. At first we believed it was teenage rebellion. In reality she was using drugs. For several years all I wanted for Christmas was peace in my house; it seemed impossible.

Our daughter entered an Enthusiastic Sobriety program just before Thanksgiving one year. By Thanksgiving Day she was starting to feel the effects of withdrawal. By Christmas she had relapsed. We were all well on the way to accepting the fact that addiction had made our lives unmanageable. We were also well on our way in the Enthusiastic Sobriety parent program that would help support and guide us over the next months and years as we healed and grew to understand our daughter and ourselves.

We now let our daughter take the lead. Our traditions—which never required alcohol—continue. As long as she is sober, she will always be welcome. The difference is that she is not held to a command attendance. This has helped her realize that she has a base of loving support from the generations. Today she truly does want to be a part of building the traditions for our newest family members.

Today's Reminder
I want holidays in my home to be filled with peace. I set boundaries and refuse to accept unacceptable behavior today. All sober family members are welcome to participate in holiday planning and events. Those who are not sober are not welcome. If I need to, I will call other parents who have set these boundaries to gain their support.

True Confessions: I was a Wimpy Parent   November 29

When my kids spoke to me in a disrespectful tone, I was unable to respond with a calm voice. I would get very upset and either walk away or raise my own voice. It took doing my inventory and sharing it with another parent to understand why.

After working these steps I began to be emotionally ready to set my limits in a calm voice.

What had I felt when one of my kids spoke disrespectfully to me? I was afraid that if I said anything, disrespectful remarks would likely escalate. I feared and avoided conflict, because I thought that if my kids rebelled against my rules, I wasn't doing my job right. In fact, my whole life, I had avoided conflict with everyone and tried to make peace, which often meant not standing up for myself and caving in to others.

Talking about this with another parent, I realized that kids naturally rebel against the rules (also called "testing their limits") and that coping with this is part of the parenting process. I had to *expect* misbehavior, and *not see it as a sign of my failure, but as a sign that it was time to do my job* as a parent: have very few rules but be firm about them, be sure my children know the consequences of breaking them, and be ready to invoke those consequences if necessary. Doing this is doing my job and being a good parent.

Today's Reminder
Rebellion is a natural part of childhood and dealing with it is a normal part of parenting. Today I will use all available resources to help me set and maintain firm, appropriate limits.

Walking the Tightrope of Raising Teens   November 30

I remember going to some Al-Anon meetings and seeing only spouses of alcoholics and drug addicts. It was hard to relate. One can divorce a spouse. One cannot divorce a child. I believed that my situation was different. I had a minor child, a high school student, who was an alcoholic and drug addict. As a parent, I had both a legal and moral responsibility to take care of him and teach him to become a good citizen. How could I "let go?" How could I meet my parental responsibilities and, at the same time, not "enable" him by providing basic care for him?

Luckily, I found our local Enthusiastic Sobriety program for my son and I went to Enthusiastic Sobriety parent meetings. By talking with other parents of teens, I learned how to walk the tightrope of meeting my parental responsibilities and, at the same time, not enabling my child to use drugs and drink alcohol. Later, with some time and tools under my belt, I was able to return to Al-Anon meetings and identify (not compare) myself with others. I soon realized that I could learn things from other relatives of alcoholics.

Today's Reminder
Practicing the Twelve Steps works, regardless of what our specific relationship with the addict is. Today I will read recovery literature, attend a Twelve Step meeting, or call someone in a Twelve Step group for support.

DECEMBER

We are Not Alone

December 1

While my son was actively using drugs, I felt resentful that my life was being co-opted by him. I spent hours driving around looking for him and knowing that he was doing something harmful to himself. I felt like an addict myself because *everything in my life was taking second place to my efforts to save him*—and drag him from the vortex he was being sucked into. I missed appointments, ignored business phone calls, and tried to catch him "in the act." It was awful; my wife and I felt so alone. I couldn't believe that anyone else was going through the kind of hell we were going through.

From our very first Enthusiastic Sobriety parent meeting, I felt that healing was taking place. Looking around the room and seeing other parents, we knew we were not alone. Listening to their stories, we realized we were simply parents of drug-addicted teens, somewhere on the continuum of experiences. Today we have a support group of loving parents. We show up. We care, not only about our kids, but about each other. We help each other by sharing our experience, strength, and hope. We work the steps.

I have attended some Al-Anon meetings. Although I believe that any Twelve Step meeting helps, I found that it was harder for me to relate to spouses of alcoholics. Unique to Enthusiastic Sobriety parent meetings is the opportunity for fathers to talk with many fathers and mothers to talk with many mothers. For me, it helps to hear from another father how he handled specific situations with his son. The fellowship of our Enthusiastic

Sobriety program has helped my son learn that sobriety can be fun and has helped me cope with the challenging experiences of raising a drug-addicted teenager.

Today's Reminder
I am not alone. There are other parents going through similar experiences. Today I will seek them out in a Twelve Step program near me.

One of the Greatest Gifts December 2

One of the greatest gifts, among so many that I have learned from our local Enthusiastic Sobriety group, is what an absolute joy and relief it is to get off the path that society dictates to us. When we first came to the group, I had a timeline and an established path for each of my children. There were certain boxes to be checked, certain colleges that were acceptable, certain objectives that had to be satisfied no later than… Although it was explained to me on day one that the program was really a two-year program, I knew that in our case, it really would only be three months, and then we would be on our way, back on our predetermined path.

A year later I know that we are on our *predestined* path, the one our Higher Power has ordained, not me! Wow, what an ego I had! I look back now not with loathing at myself, but instead with amazement at how much I've grown and changed. Now I know what really matters: our relationships with our Higher Power, our loved ones, and the joy of living.

To be off "the path" is one of the most liberating gifts in the world. It is the journey that matters, not the end. There are a number of paths to take unique for each person. My child has been sober for a year and is actively involved in the group. He is taking what he has learned and continues to learn out to the real world each day. But for this journey, my child would not have the relationship with his Higher Power that he has today, and I would never have learned how to live and love each day, versus checking each day off the calendar.

Today's Reminder
Today when I get concerned that my "list of things to do" will not get done, I will remember that my Higher Power has a better plan and I can choose to enjoy it.

"There Ain't No Victims— Only Volunteers"   December 3

I was always feeling responsible for everything that happened in my family. It was *my* fault if the kids were late to school, if they forgot their lunch, or if my husband missed his dentist appointment. I felt I should have reminded everyone and been sure they knew what they were supposed to do that day. Yet, I began to feel resentful that no one else seemed to remember these things and would blame me when they forgot something.

Reading in *Bumper Stickers* that there are no victims, only volunteers, I began to see that by always reminding everyone of their tasks for the day and getting things ready for them—as if I were personal secretary to two teen-agers and an adult—I had created the situation in which my family members had come to expect me to take care of all their needs. I had volunteered for all that extra work and criticism!

So, just as I had volunteered, I decided I could un-volunteer. I let them know that I was changing my behavior and letting them prepare and handle their own daily tasks. I occasionally had to stop myself from reminding them about something, but the more I did this, the more I felt empowered. I was helping my teens take responsibility for their lives and they were developing more confidence. Plus, I had more time for my own projects.

Today's Reminder
I let go of self-pity and managing other family member's lives. I manage only my own.

Volume Does Not Convey Authority December 4

My mother was raised in a household dominated by an alcoholic father who yelled at everyone often. Her reaction was to yell back. When I was a child and failed to obey her, she would yell at me, and then I would cower in fear and comply with whatever she wanted. In this way I learned that the louder you yell, the more of an authority figure you are.

This did not bode well for raising my own kids. I yelled when my kids were little and did not obey. Yet, this technique only worked with one of my children; the other would simply yell back louder! Life was quite unpleasant, long before one of our kids—the more compliant and quiet one—turned to drugs and alcohol.

Today I see that the volume of my voice is *inversely* proportional to the authority I have in my household. When I feel angry because a kid has misbehaved, I can calm myself down by breathing, reciting the Serenity Prayer or an applicable slogan, or leaving the room and calling another parent in the program. Once I feel calm, I can tell my kid in a moderate voice what the consequence is for the misbehavior.

Today's Reminder
If agitated by my kid's disobedience, I find a way to calm down so that I can speak in a natural and quiet voice when I tell him the consequence.

F.E.A.R. December 5

There are a few acronyms for *fear*: "False Events Appearing Real," "Forget Everything And Run," and "Face Everything And Recover." I have a "gift" for imagining all the worst possible outcomes for any situation. I made a conscious decision to turn that "gift" on its head. Now, whenever I start to visualize worst outcomes, I stop and "delete" those mental pictures—like deleting an image on a computer screen. Next, I imagine some attractive colors and draw good, better, and best possible outcomes. Once I've drawn my new mental pictures, I no longer want to "Forget Everything And Run." I face my fear. I have more confidence in dealing with the situation. Also, it's amazing how often one of the better outcomes actually materializes! Now I am able to "Face Everything And Recover."

Today's Reminder
There are many possible outcomes to situations. Today I will visualize outcomes I hope for, not those I dread.

Don't Take It Personally December 6

My daughter's sober teenaged behavior drives me nuts! We often are having a calm, pleasant conversation when she suddenly erupts like a volcano. I have said something which has upset her. Recently I mentioned that I had seen one of her former classmates who told me that she has a circle of friends from a couple of towns in the area. My child went ballistic. She yelled at me and stomped to another room. Shocked, I did nothing. I did not take her behavior personally. She was being a teenager. (I later learned that she perceived my comment as indirect criticism of her for not having as large a circle of friends!)

In that case, it was easy not to react, but there are other times when I have to stop, think, and remember—"One, two three; it's not about me!" Then I can refrain from reacting with indignant, self-righteous anger. Instead I can remain calm and, if necessary, physically remove myself from her and wait until the teenaged storm dissipates.

Today's Reminder
Should my teen fly off the handle today, I will stop, and recall, "One, two, three; it's not about me!" Exercising self-restraint and remaining calm, I model the behavior I want my teen to emulate and I preserve calm in my home.

Stick With Winners December 7

Many of us find that the parents with whom we shared our children's trials and triumphs in the past are no longer "winners" for us. These parents are discussing which AP courses their teens are taking or whether their kids will apply to Harvard or Yale and have no idea what we are going through. Some are genuine friends; others are acquaintances that like to gossip and criticize. How do I deal with them?

It has been suggested by parents at Enthusiastic Sobriety meetings that it is a good idea to minimize contact with judgmental types as much as possible. If one of them asks how your child is doing, respond with a generic, "Fine. Things are really working out for him." With more specific questions about school or work, a parent may respond, "No, he's not back in school [or working] yet. He will be, when he's ready."

It is very important for our own recovery as parents to avoid judgment; most of us have already harshly (and *incorrectly!*) judged ourselves for our children's addiction. It's time to focus on solutions, move forward with what is within our power to do each day, keep working the steps, and set a good example for our children. It is not helpful to wallow in the guilt game.

Today's Reminder
I avoid parents who gossip and judge. I find strength from other parents going through similar experiences.

A Perspective on the Holidays — December 8

We are in year two of being a family in recovery. Last year we were all apprehensive about unknowns and creating new traditions to replace those that included alcohol.

This year our son has over a year of sobriety, is living on his own with buddies from the group, and attends college. Gone from our holidays was last year's awkwardness. We have settled into new routines, working our programs, and enjoying time together.

There are occasional flare-ups. Holidays bring the challenge of blending in returning family members, including non-addict siblings and visiting grandparents who can't wait for an evening cocktail. But each member has lovingly learned to make small adjustments such as not having that glass of wine.

Also I gave up the notion that we had to keep all the old traditions; some didn't matter and others made Christmas more stressful than joyful. If our son felt the need to leave a family or neighborhood gathering, he had a pre-planned exit strategy. A quiet departure worked great. I also realized that my relationship with God is not dependent upon our son sitting next to me in church. He is in control of his relationship with his Higher Power and I am in control of mine. I even was calm and patient as I stood in a store line for 45 minutes on the day after Christmas. That was a first!

The love of our group, what I have learned from others, my faith, my readings, and my working the program have made each day more meaningful and restored my serenity.

Today's Reminder
When I feel stress during the holiday season, I will remember that I can create new traditions to replace old ones. Letting my children have time to be with supportive friends instead of spending all their time with the family relieves stress for everyone.

Improving My Spiritual Health   December 9

To support my son in his recovery, I agreed to attend Enthusiastic Sobriety parent meetings and work the Twelve Steps myself. I have come to embrace the steps, especially Steps Ten, Eleven, and Twelve. I have found that working these steps gives me an awesome boost to my own spiritual health. Just as the alcoholic maintains his sobriety by looking daily at any 1) dishonesty, 2) resentment, 3) fear or 4) selfishness which crops up and makes amends for any harms caused by these, I find that when I do the same, I also am able to maintain a closer relationship with God. (This is Step Ten.) I make sure to spend time daily in prayer and meditation (Step Eleven) and when confused, doubtful, or agitated, I pause and relax, knowing that God will give me an idea to handle the situation. Many times during the day I find myself thinking, "Thy will, not mine, be done." Thus, I practice the principles daily in all my affairs (Step Twelve). Working the steps fits very well with my Christian faith and has brought me peace of mind.

Today's Reminder
At the end of the day I will review my actions for dishonesty, resentment, fear, or selfishness. Where appropriate, I will discuss this with someone else and make amends. Then I will be grateful that I have another day to improve my spiritual health.

Where are the Walls? December 10

Today's society seems to tolerate much more outrageous behavior than in the past. Both daytime and evening television programs contain a lot of violence, sexual situations and drug use. Years ago less explicit references would have been cause for a network to lose its FCC license. On various screens: television, video games, movies, and the Internet, our kids see and hear all kinds of very rude behavior. Without parental guidance, kids may think that everything they see on a screen is acceptable; they may think that "everyone does it." "It" might include: cursing, acting rudely and disrespectfully toward others, fighting, cheating, stealing, having sex indiscriminately, drinking alcohol, taking drugs, etc.

Our responsibility as parents is to care for our children. They need to learn how to get along in the world and live happy, successful lives. Being aware of the negative influences that our kids are being exposed to, we parents want to provide examples of socially desirable behavior at home. We cannot shelter our kids from the world, but we can let them know what we think about the behavior shown on a screen. Most importantly, in our home we can set boundaries for acceptable behavior.

Today's Reminder
I will tell my kids what behavior is acceptable in our home and I will let them know what I think of certain behaviors seen on television, in video games, in the movies, or on the Internet.

Should I Go to Meetings If My Kid Is Not in the Program?   December 11

Parents whose kids chose to leave one of the Enthusiastic Sobriety programs, are still welcome at parent meetings. Some parents choose to come to parent meetings, some go to Al-Anon meetings, and some go to neither. Personally, I find both Enthusiastic Sobriety and Al-Anon meetings helpful. In both types of meetings I hear how others are applying the steps to help them cope with their loved ones, some who are sober, some who have relapsed after a period of sobriety, and some who have no interest in sobriety. This is a regular reminder that alcoholism and drug addiction last a lifetime; there is no known cure. My kid will always be an addict, and I will always be his mother. So I have decided that I can always use the Twelve Steps, the support of the groups, and my Higher Power to help relate to him in a healthy way.

Today's Reminder
Today I will go to a meeting and listen. I will consciously consider and apply a step to a situation involving my child.

"God helps those who help themselves." ~Benjamin Franklin

To Thine Own Self Be True December 12

In his book, *Bumper Stickers,* Bob Meehan uses the Shakespearian phrase, "To Thine Own Self Be True," as a reminder that self-deception can prevent us from reaching our goals. Perhaps we are unwilling to see a shortcoming which prevents our progress. I thought about my situation. What are the things I find most irritating about my kids? They don't plan ahead, are not punctual, and say they want to achieve something but do not work consistently and persistently toward that goal. When I looked at my own behavior, I saw the same thing! I was narrowly arriving on time and sometimes late for meetings, not planning ahead sufficiently, and being haphazard about performing necessary steps toward my desired career goals. By being honest with myself, I could no longer look at my kids and criticize them for behavior I also engaged in. I had to focus on correcting myself. In doing this, I set a good example for them and increase the likelihood that I will achieve my own goals.

Today's Reminder
Instead of judging my kids, I will look at my own shortcomings and address them. My actions speak louder than words.

Where Are All the Miracles? December 13

A small group of parents in our support group made a commitment to read "The God Memo" chapter from Og Mandino's book, *The Greatest Miracle in the World,* for 100 days. The first time I took on this project I read it with my daughter. We would read it aloud to each other, and on the nights she read aloud, I heard something new each time. But it wasn't until I was sitting in the waiting room at our Enthusiastic Sobriety program that I really understood.

One young man, who had graduated from the sobriety program, came to visit and see who was hanging out. After walking around for a minute he came back through the waiting room exclaiming in his well-known humorous manner, "Where are all the miracles?" He knew what I realized at that moment. Our miracles are working hard each day to stay sober; our miracles are reaching out to newcomers; our miracles are giving hope to those in despair; our miracles are all around us. I am so grateful that I have come to know them.

Today's Reminder
Dear Lord, thank you for surrounding me with miracles.

How Do I Love Thee? December 14
Let Me Count the Ways

In reviewing my resentments while doing an inventory, I saw that I was quite attached to them. It feels good to feel right and feel that others are wrong. So it was hard for me to let go of some resentments, especially the one against the school staff who suspected my son was smoking marijuana in the boys' room but did nothing about it and did not inform me. When I found out through other means, I was so angry that I did not want to deal with the school at all. Later I realized that my reluctance to communicate with the school was not serving my family's best interest. I knew that I had to let go of my resentments in order to help myself and my family.

With the help of my sponsor, with whom I discussed my resentments and my part in situations giving rise to them, I was able to drop most of them and begin to take steps to solve my problems. Once my son returned to school after completing the intensive outpatient program, I communicated with teachers and told them about my son's drug problem and asked them to let me know not only his academic progress but also if they witnessed any strange behavior by him. I found that people, approached individually, were quite kind and willing to help. Blame of others or myself had not helped. Honest appraisal of the situation, doing the next right thing, and being honest with others did help me obtain peace of mind and make my life more manageable.

Today's Reminder

I get in touch with what I get out of my resentments and then I am better able to let them go. Once I do, a weight is lifted and my mind is free to solve my problems.

How to Eliminate Obsession and Perfectionism During the Holidays

December 15

It's getting close to December 25th and I am beginning to see a pattern of thoughts and behavior that disrupted my peace of mind when my son was using drugs. I have been obsessing about the presents I am planning to give each person on my list. I have been worrying that I must have the same number of gifts under the tree for each of my children. The total cost of gifts for each child should be about the same so it does not look like I favor one. Plus, all gifts cannot exceed my budget. Meanwhile, the dinner I plan has to be just right, eliminating the alcohol in the recipe and using the *Cooking Light* substitutions. Of course there has to be something in the menu that is elegant or exotic, to show it is a special treat. These obsessive thoughts with creating a perfect holiday destroy my serenity.

I love the program, because I can apply the principles to *all* aspects of my life. I remember the slogan, "Easy does it." I let go of my efforts to control people, places and things. Instead of getting into frenzy, I stop and think, "How important is it?" When in doubt, I pray and meditate for guidance from my Higher Power. Sometimes I call another person in program to get a "reality check" to see if my concerns are realistic or blown out of proportion. Then I do the next right thing and relax, leaving the outcome to a power greater than myself.

Today's Reminder
I can apply the program to all aspects of my life and eliminate habits that disrupt my serenity. Should I begin to feel upset about something today, I will remind myself, "Easy does it." I will also consider, "How important is it?"

Breaking Through My Fears   December 16

I know that addiction is a disease. I was afraid to express my feelings of anger and despair so as not to upset my addicted son. I believed that these feelings were mine to contend with or to work out with my sponsor. Although I didn't enable him financially or rescue him from the consequences of his behavior, such as jail and fines, I did believe that showing feelings other than love and support might be destructive for our suffering child.

The rehabilitation program our son participated in when he finally became willing to get help encouraged me to share my deepest feelings with him. I specifically was able to share about things that bothered me, such as seeing his child, my grandchild, not properly bathed or clothed and dragging a dirty blanket. I was afraid that actually sharing my feelings (not just talking about them) would hurt him too much and undercut his efforts at sobriety. The program acknowledged the validity of my fears about hurting our son but assured my husband and me that he was in a safe place and could benefit from hearing them. I fell apart when I shared the years of grief from my heart. My son listened to me. It was empowering for both of us. I was no longer acting the protective parent, shielding him from my truth, keeping myself invulnerable and distant. Also I was showing respect for him that he could handle my truth. We can now communicate openly with each other.

Today's Reminder

I will not allow fear to prevent open and honest communication with my child and all my family members when the time is right.

Keeping Busy — December 17

Working the steps is something we do to keep busy while God works His magic on us. Because I tend to prefer keeping busy, I have no difficulty "working the steps." For me, once I went through the steps in order with a sponsor, I began studying each one and attended a step study. Now I know them by heart. Most importantly, when I feel confused, frustrated, or unclear how to handle circumstances, I can think of the steps. For a particularly thorny problem, I take a few slow, deep breaths, and consider all Twelve Steps. Sometimes I write them down, describing how I can apply each one to the particular concern. Other times, if I am in too much of a tizzy to calm myself down, I call my sponsor or another person in the program. In lieu of thinking over and over again about my problem and its magnitude, I keep busy thinking of the steps and using them to find solutions to my problems.

Today's Reminder
I let go of my problem and focus my attention on the steps and how to use them to solve my problem.

Respect is an Inside Job — December 18

A common refrain from parents of all teens is that kids have no respect. Yet, my experience has been that once I started acting respectfully *toward myself,* my teenagers began to reflect and show that respect for themselves and me.

Before working the Twelve Step program, I was a doormat my kids could walk on whenever they wished. After beginning program, I started to set boundaries with my teens and enforce them. I treated myself as a person worthy of being treated well. And my teens got the message. Moreover, I noticed that my sponsor—from the very beginning of our relationship—kindly listened to me and never interrupted, criticized, or gave advice. She affirmed my worth as a person by listening, occasionally reminding me of a step or a slogan, and letting me arrive at my own conclusions and make my own decisions. This kind of affirmation of my worth is exactly what I needed to experience and exactly what I needed to give to my teens. I began to listen kindly without interrupting, criticizing, or offering unsolicited advice. I gave them the opportunity to make their own decisions. Our family is more respectful and more harmonious.

Today's Reminder
I listen without interrupting. I affirm my children's worth and let them make their own decisions. Most importantly, I only give advice if they ask for it.

Teaching Your Child about Making Amends   December 19

I recently had an experience with a younger child in which I put the Twelve Steps into action and taught the child about responsibility and accountability. This, I must confess, was new behavior for me. My nephew ran across a hall in our home and a wooden picture frame fell and broke. In the past, I would have said, "Oh that's all right, dear, you didn't mean it. Don't worry about it. I'll take care of it later." I would have glossed over the harm to spare his feelings. Yet, I now see what a disservice that is to a child. If I frequently make excuses for his behavior and don't have him experience any consequences for his actions, he begins to think he can do anything he wishes with impunity!

The changed behavior for me was to say, "Oh, no! My picture frame! Well, the break is in a place where it can be repaired. So, let's get the wood glue and you can fix it." Being guided, he was able to fix the frame. He learned much from the experience, and so did I. With the help of the Twelve Steps, an old dog like me can learn new tricks!

Today's Reminder
When a child makes a mistake, I will acknowledge the harm and, at the same time, give him an opportunity to fix it.

No Unearned Highs or Free Lunches — December 20

Drugs produce "unearned highs" for our children, says Bob Meehan in *Beyond the Yellow Brick Road*. Buying a teen an expensive gift, such as a brand new Jaguar, is also providing him or her with an "unearned high," because this doesn't teach the lesson of working toward goals.

My husband and I decided to follow Meehan's advice. Although we couldn't afford a Jaguar, we had considered giving our son an older car once he got his license. However, we did not. We told him that he would have to save up for a car and buy it when he was able to pay for the car, the insurance, its license plates and registration. He also needed to maintain employment so that he could handle the cost of routine maintenance and put aside a prudent reserve for periodic repairs. It took him awhile, but he did it. Today he is very proud of his car and takes very good care of it. It's an "earned high," the earning of which taught him a wonderful lesson for life: there are no free lunches.

Today's Reminder

I will help my teen learn to set goals and work toward accomplishing them; I will not provide him with "unearned highs." When he accomplishes his goal, he will have achieved a boost in self-confidence that only he could create.

The Purpose of Parenting — December 21

My long-term purpose is to have my children mature into responsible adults who care about others and use their unique talents to contribute to the community. I want them to become the kind of people I would like to associate with.

As a younger teen, our son started to use and abuse alcohol and drugs. He became very self-centered, dishonest, irritable, and rude. After some time in an Enthusiastic Sobriety program, he became polite, considerate, and scrupulously honest. Now, as an adult, he works, goes to school, and is a kind and responsible young man. Although he does not drink alcohol these days, he has a delightful sense of humor which makes him a welcome guest at any party.

Throughout her teen years our daughter was raised with the influence of the Twelve Steps on us, and our parenting. As a younger teen, she was self-centered and threw a fit when she didn't get what she wanted. Now, as a young adult, she thanks us each time we do *anything* for her. She works, goes to school, and does volunteer work. She is honest, perceptive, and confident.

I am glad that by applying the Twelve Steps daily in our lives, my husband and I have influenced our children to become the kind of young adults we are proud to know.

Today's Reminder
I keep sight of my parenting goal before I say or do anything which affects my children. With a clear goal and clear motives for my actions, I do what is best for our family.

Don't Block His Path to Enlightenment! December 22

I have been a spiritual seeker for years, have attended many retreats, and heard many spiritual leaders speak. One day I was worrying about my son who had chosen not to continue in treatment and to move out of our home and in with his girlfriend. I was worrying that he might go through a great deal of pain before he (hopefully) decides on recovery. I recalled numerous times over the years how I had tried to spare him from painful consequences of his alcohol-related actions. Then I remembered a statement I had heard from a spiritual leader, "Pain can be a path to enlightenment." It dawned on me, "Why block his path to enlightenment?" I want him to learn from his experiences and reach a point where he desires enlightenment. I resolved at that point to stop my rescuing behavior and really help my son by letting him learn his own life lessons.

Today's Reminder
I will get out of my child's way so that he can learn his own life lessons.

And a Little Child Shall Lead Them December 23

It is two days before Christmas and our family has gathered to spend the holidays together with our Enthusiastic Sobriety son, who has two and a half years of sobriety! But the pleasant togetherness I had envisioned has turned into hurt feelings. My daughter is crying in her bedroom because, she says, she is irritated with her stepfather's loud voice. I feel bad that I quit a family monopoly game and caused a ruckus. My husband is sulking around, feeling left out.

Meanwhile my son, deeply steeped in the wonders of the steps, moves here and there with a kind smile and tries to make us see ourselves and laugh a bit. I am struck with the insight that I cannot fix everything for the three people I love more than life. So I let go of expectations and decide I'll follow my son's example. I'll laugh kindly at myself and see how things turn out.

Today's Reminder
When I let go of expectations and remember to step back, detach, and look for the humor in the situation, things turn out.

Serenity Prayer (Extended Version) — December 24

I like the extended version of the Serenity Prayer, because it well suits my family's situation as we all work the program. My son's drug-addicted behavior takes time to change, just as my rescuing and "fixing everything" behavior does. By being patient with ourselves, being grateful for every little victory of changed behavior, and taking it one day at time, life improves for all of us.

SERENITY PRAYER (Extended Version)

"God, grant me the serenity to accept the things I cannot change, courage to change the things I can, And wisdom to know the difference."

"Grant me patience with the changes that take time, An appreciation for all that I have, Tolerance for those with different struggles, And the strength to get up and try again, One day at a time."

Our Lives Improved   December 25
When We Worked Our Own Programs

My son met a girl who had a history of methamphetamine use, so I was upset as their relationship developed. He practically moved in with her, but he telephoned me occasionally. In the past my husband and I had suspected that our son had experimented with drugs, but now we could no longer deny the power of drugs over him. When he called home, he would say things like, "I can't come home, because people are following me." (Methamphetamines cause paranoia.) Sometimes his speech was completely irrational.

Seeing a television show about a local young woman, a drug addict who found recovery, I received hope. I contacted the girl from the show and asked her to speak with my son. She did and convinced him to talk with a counselor at the Enthusiastic Sobriety drug treatment program she had participated in. He entered the program. The first two months he ran away a couple of times, but he eventually decided to work the program in earnest. I made a decision to trust the program and leave my son's care to them.

Meanwhile, I became very active in the Enthusiastic Sobriety parent meetings, step study, and women's retreat. I began school to get training in an area in which I had always had an interest. I got certified and have been doing work in the field since. The support of the parent group, working the steps, and my new work helped me get through rough times with my son. Today my son is sober and has returned to the warm, kind, and giving person he was before drugs. I am grateful for this and for the time I took to enhance my own life.

Today's Reminder
As I go to Twelve Step meetings, read recovery literature, and take care of myself, my life improves. I trust that as my child is ready for recovery, the Twelve Steps will work for him, too.

Why We Go to Parent Meetings   December 26

We do not go to parent meetings to complain about our teens or find ways to "make them behave." We do not escalate anger and fear; instead we allow it to dissipate as we focus on compassion for ourselves. We look at ways we can maintain dignity and self-respect during trying times with our teens.

By regular attendance at parent meetings, we listen and learn from each parent's unique story—yet often similar to our own. We identify with their pain, and we help each other find better ways to cope in our families so that *everyone* is treated with respect. We learn that setting boundaries for our teens' behavior and implementing logical consequences for crossing those boundaries is loving and respectful. We give our children the dignity of making their own choices and living with the consequences of those choices. We can do this without anger, because we know that all humans go through a learning curve. This curve is especially steep during the teen and young adult years. We also regain self-respect when we are able to implement consequences that we have set into place calmly before the boundary has been crossed.

Today's Reminder
At meetings I gain insight into ways of handling situations with my teen that provide each of us with dignity and respect.

Self-Respect December 27

While trying to apply the Serenity Prayer in my life, I have become aware of my past habit of not speaking up for my needs and wants. I often used to just "go with the flow", that is, do whatever everyone else in the family wanted. I was such a people-pleaser that I was afraid to do *anything* that might possibly inject additional conflict into our already-disharmonious life with our kid on drugs.

When I consider the second line of the prayer, "the courage to change the things I can," I know that there are times I can state what I need or want. This doesn't always lead to conflict or disharmony. Even when my stating my needs does present a conflict, my Higher Power will see me through it. For example, my son and I share my car. He usually uses the car to get to his Friday night Enthusiastic Sobriety social function, but one Friday I also wanted to go out. In the past I would have said nothing and not gone to my social event. Instead, that night I simply presented my needs to him, and we found a way that we could both get to our respective social functions. He gave me a ride to my event, and I arranged with a friend there to give me a ride home afterwards. In this way, I am learning to have self-respect and not treat myself like a doormat whose needs are unimportant.

Today's Reminder
I respect myself enough today to state my needs and wants and negotiate with another to get them met.

**Inventory— December 28
I am Not Responsible for Everyone!**

Some of the things in my inventory were not actual harms I caused to others, but in my self-centered thinking, I *felt* as if I were responsible for harming them. For example, early in the program my son overslept and did not make it to his outpatient treatment one day. I got a call from the counselor, and I started to apologize for not being home to wake him up. I stopped mid-sentence, realized I am not responsible for getting my son up and to his outpatient treatment, and retracted my apology. At least that particular action did not even make it onto my written inventory! As for other actions that did, my sponsor helped me see that I am not responsible for seeing that every member of my family makes his or her appointments, meets his or her deadlines, and exercises good judgment in the choices he or she makes. This took a big burden off my shoulders.

Today's Reminder
I will let go of my unnecessary burdens and take on my true responsibility, to myself.

Let's All Do Our Own Jobs! December 29

Our son began spending lots of time out of the house with "friends" he would not bring home and whose parents would not return telephone messages. He lost his former interests, other than "hanging out" with these "friends." He quit his high school sports team and did no school work. When home, he hid in his room. This went on for several months. His father and I introduced him to a variety of activities we thought he might like. Nothing worked, and we worried. We asked our daughter to talk with him, find out what was going on, and see if she could help her brother. Ultimately, we learned the problem was drugs.

In coping with our son's crazy-making behavior, our thinking got distorted. After coming to an Enthusiastic Sobriety program, we learned that we had confused family members' roles. By asking our daughter to help her brother, my husband and I had put her in a vulnerable position. We had tried to get our daughter to do *our* job as parents.

Now we know and work hard at fulfilling our parental responsibilities. The job of parents is to love, encourage, and motivate our children to follow the values we model at home. Plus we set limits to discourage them from behavior contrary to our values. Then teens can do *their* own job: to learn, explore their unique talents, and develop into ethical and independent adults.

Today's Reminder
By living my values, I model for my teens how to live. I set limits, as necessary, to encourage them to act consistent with these values. I also encourage and support them in developing their unique potential and becoming independent adults.

I Am Not Alone   December 30

When I first entered an Enthusiastic Sobriety parent meeting, I saw a large group of people who also had been living the anguish of having an alcoholic and/or drug addicted child. Before that day, I felt so alone. Now I have a support group I can talk with, who understand, and who share their experience, strength, and hope with me. I have become a member of a club which I did not want to join—parents of drug addicts and alcoholics—but I thank God it is here!

I am grateful that my initial response to discovery of my son's addiction was compassionate and not angry. This helped me be open-minded and willing to listen to the parent group which has taught me so much: A child's emotional maturity stops at the age he starts using drugs or alcohol. The substance becomes his mistress, the *only* thing he cares about. This is a lifelong disease. Once an alcoholic, he can never have "just one drink" as an adult, because it creates an insatiable craving.

Applying these lessons, I no longer cook anything with alcohol. I have a sponsor. I go to parent meetings. Knowing this is a deadly disease that my son has, I want to be there for him. I want to support him in his recovery without rescuing him. I support him best by not interfering with his program. I focus my attention on my own program which includes receiving support from our parent group. I no longer have to go it alone. Life is better.

Today's Reminder
Today I will remember to focus on myself. When I need some moral support, I will use my resources and talk with another parent in the group.

"A burden shared is half the burden, a joy shared is twice the joy." ~German proverb

Progress Not Perfection   **December 31**

For a reformed, controlling perfectionist, this slogan is my very favorite. I used to feel terrible about myself, because no matter how hard I tried to be a good parent, I never felt I was good enough. Having superhuman levels of perfection as my goal, I now see I was doomed to feel bad about myself. This only made matters worse, because I believe that my kids acquired my perfectionist habits, too.

Now, whenever I review my day or a task I did, I remember, "progress not perfection." First, I look for the good I did and give myself a mental pat on the back. Then I consider if I did something new or different and made further progress because of this new action. I give myself a very hearty mental back pat for anything like this, because change is so hard for me. Then, after I am feeling good about my accomplishments, I can look to see what didn't work so well and where I can improve. Rather than engage in an endless loop of self-criticism, I simply tell myself I'll try to do better in the future. That's it. It feels so much better. It's one of the ways I take care of myself now, by using positive self-talk. Another wonderful benefit is that I find myself looking at the positive in my family members and encouraging them, too.

It really has snowballed into a glorious family of persons with a positive outlook.

Today's Reminder
I look at how far I have come and then my outlook for the rest of the journey brightens.

Appendix A: Enthusiastic Sobriety Program[22] Steps

1. We admitted that mind-changing chemicals have caused at least part of our lives to become unmanageable.
2. We have found it necessary to stick with winners in order to grow.
3. We realize that a Higher Power, expressed through our love for each other, can help restore us to sanity.
4. We made a decision to turn our will and our lives over to the care of God as we understand Him.
5. We made a searching and moral inventory of ourselves.
6. We admit to God, to ourselves, and to another human being the exact nature of our wrongs.
7. We became willing to allow our Higher Power, through the love of the group, to help change our way of thinking and humbly ask Him to help us change.
8. We made a list of all persons we have harmed and became willing to make amends to such people, whenever possible, except when to do so would injure them, others, or ourselves.
9. We made direct amends to such people, whenever possible, except when to do so would injure them, others, or ourselves.
10. We have continued to look at ourselves and when wrong, promptly admitted it.
11. We have sought through prayer and meditation to improve our conscious contact with our Higher Power, that which we have chosen to call God, praying only for knowledge of His will for us and the courage to carry that out.
12. We, having had a spiritual awakening as a result of these steps, tried to carry our love and understanding to others, and to practice these principles in our daily lives.

---

[22] See Appendix G: Enthusiastic Sobriety Programs

Appendix B: Al-Anon[23] Twelve Steps

1. We admitted we were powerless over alcohol—that our lives had become unmanageable.
2. Came to believe that a Power greater than ourselves could restore us to sanity.
3. Made a decision to turn our will and our lives over to the care of God *as we understood Him*.
4. Made a searching and fearless moral inventory of ourselves.
5. Admitted to God, to ourselves, and to another human being the exact nature of our wrongs.
6. Were entirely ready to have God remove all these defects of character.
7. Humbly asked Him to remove our shortcomings.
8. Made a list of all persons we had harmed, and became willing to make amends to them all.
9. Made direct amends to such people wherever possible, except when to do so would injure them or others.
10. Continued to take personal inventory and when we were wrong promptly admitted it.
11. Sought through prayer and meditation to improve our conscious contact with God *as we understood Him*, praying only for knowledge of His will for us and the power to carry that out.
12. Having had a spiritual awakening as the result of these steps, we tried to carry this message to others, and to practice these principles in all our affairs. (Al-Anon)

---

[23] For more information about Al-Anon, see the Al-Anon website: www.al-anon.alateen.org/ or write or call: Al-Anon World Service Office, 1600 Corporate Landing Parkway, Virginia Beach, VA 23454-5617; (757) 563-1600

Appendix C: A.A.[24] Twelve Steps

1. We admitted we were powerless over alcohol—that our lives had become unmanageable.
2. Came to believe that a Power greater than ourselves could restore us to sanity.
3. Made a decision to turn our will and our lives over to the care of God *as we understood Him*.
4. Made a searching and fearless moral inventory of ourselves.
5. Admitted to God, to ourselves, and to another human being the exact nature of our wrongs.
6. Were entirely ready to have God remove all these defects of character.
7. Humbly asked Him to remove our shortcomings.
8. Made a list of all persons we had harmed, and became willing to make amends to them all.
9. Made direct amends to such people wherever possible, except when to do so would injure them or others.
10. Continued to take personal inventory and when we were wrong promptly admitted it.
11. Sought through prayer and meditation to improve our conscious contact with God *as we understood Him*, praying only for knowledge of His will for us and the power to carry that out.
12. Having had a spiritual awakening as the result of these steps, we tried to carry this message to alcoholics, and to practice these principles in all our affairs.

---

[24] For more information about AA, see the AA website: www.aa.org or write or call AA World Services, Inc., PO Box 459, Grand Central Station, New York, NY 10163; (212) 870-3400.

Appendix D: The Twelve Step Spiritual Toolkit

The Twelve Steps is a spiritual program which utilizes many tools. These are: meetings, telephone calls, sponsorship, literature, slogans, the Serenity Prayer, gratitude, journaling, and service.

At Twelve Step groups, such as the Enthusiastic Sobriety parent meetings and Al-Anon and AA[25] meetings, people share their experiences, strength and hope with others. Sharing is kept brief so that every person at a meeting gets a chance to share. Each group creates a list of telephone numbers of members who are willing to receive phone calls in between meetings. Members share what they have learned in the program that has helped them through similar concerns; they may make suggestions but do not give advice. All Twelve Step groups are on a "take what you like and leave the rest" basis.

Sponsorship is a relationship between two people in a Twelve Step program. The sponsor usually has more experience working the Twelve Steps than the sponsee. The sponsee stays in regular contact with the sponsor who helps the sponsee work the Twelve Steps. A sponsor hears the sponsee's entire story and shares ideas about using the Steps and the tools of the program in every day situations.

Literature consists of books and pamphlets. Only Al-Anon Conference-Approved Literature may be mentioned at Al-Anon

---

[25] For information regarding Enthusiastic Sobriety Programs see Appendix G. Al-Anon is a support group for relatives and friends of alcoholics who gather together for mutual aid with no other affiliation and who practice the Twelve Steps of Alcoholics Anonymous (aka A.A.). A.A. is a group of persons with the desire to stop drinking alcohol and who use the Twelve Steps, as outlined in the book *Alcoholics Anonymous*, to recover from alcoholism.

meetings. (See Appendix H: For Further Reading. Al-Anon literature is marked as "CAL".) The Enthusiastic Sobriety groups allow mention of other literature.

Slogans are easy-to-remember phrases that may be used when one is in the midst of a crisis. Examples of slogans are: "Easy does it," "Expectations breed disaster," "First things first," "How important is it?" "Let go and let God," "Let it begin with me," "Live and let live," "One day at a time," "Progress not perfection," and "Trust is a decision." The Serenity Prayer also helps us regain balance when something unsettling occurs.

Gratitude is an attitude which can be cultivated to remove negative thinking and a victim mindset. Journaling is writing down our thoughts and feelings to sort them out, eliminate faulty thinking, and help deal with life situations.

Service is doing anything which helps others in the Twelve Step group, such as setting up chairs for a meeting, answering someone's phone call, being a sponsor, speaking at or chairing a meeting.

Appendix E: Sponsorship

The tradition of the Twelve Steps began with sponsorship. It became apparent early on in the recovery process that only someone who has been through alcoholism or addiction could help someone else going through the same thing. In the Enthusiastic Sobriety Programs' parent groups, one parent who has progressed in the recovery program shares that experience on a continuous, individual basis with another parent who wants help.

Often when we begin to attend parent meetings we are apprehensive, confused, and have many questions. It is advantageous to have an available support person as we learn how to adapt to the recovery process of our child and begin to deal with our own issues as parents.

So, we select a sponsor, another parent from the group, with whom we feel comfortable, someone with whom we can talk freely and confidentially and we ask him or her to be our sponsor. Many people find it easier, initially, to ask someone to be their 'temporary' sponsor to see if they are compatible with the sponsor.

As time goes on and our experience expands, we become a source of help for others in the group. One day we may have the opportunity to be a sponsor for a new parent. We find that sponsorship of another parent helps us by reinforcing what we have learned from the program.

Appendix F: Sobriety and School

Some parents are concerned that the time required by the various Enthusiastic Sobriety intensive outpatient programs (IOPs) may interfere with school. Some teens are able to arrange a modified school schedule while others are unable to remain in school. It is best for each family to speak with the teen's Enthusiastic Sobriety counselor to tailor a plan that best suits their situation. IOP lasts as long as the individual needs it, usually between 8 and 12 weeks.

As parents, our experience has been that after completion of IOP, our teens enter a second phase of their Enthusiastic Sobriety program lasting from 18 to 24 months. This phase involves two evening Twelve Step meetings a week plus two mandatory social functions every weekend which allow the teens to learn that sobriety can be fun. It also helps to build strong relationships with their peers who support them in staying sober. During this second phase, parents often are eager to have their teens resume a normal school schedule. Counselors caution parents that our kids' sobriety is fragile at the beginning, so that the demands of school may be too challenging. Our kids' returning to the high school where they previously obtained drugs is like going into a lion's den.

Many parents, with their teens, look for an alternative school. In some locales there are "sober" high schools where all students have a goal of remaining sober as well as finishing school. There are many other alternative high schools which might be a good fit for a particular teen who has decided to stay sober. In some cases, teens have changed public high schools from one locale to another simply to avoid the group of drug-dealing and drug-using students they used to spend time with. Having at least two sober students attend the same school helps each of them to have a support system. It is a good idea for parents and teens to meet with their school counselor, intervention specialist, or a sympathetic administrator—to let them know that this teen is trying to stay sober and finish school. Many teachers are willing to help by giving parents frequent feedback about their student's performance. A plan can be created to assure a student doesn't fall behind. For example, any missing homework must be completed at school that day during a study hall or extracurricular period after school and given to the appropriate teacher before the student is dismissed.

Parents: one note of caution. While an alcoholic adult may be expected to return to work and function within 30 to 45 days after becoming sober, this same expectation with regard to a teen may be unrealistic. An adult has more maturity and more experience than a teenager in dealing with life's demands. Drugs and alcohol have a very damaging effect on teenagers' developing brains; their higher brain functions are not fully developed and they do not have a well-developed set of tools for dealing with challenging life situations.[26] Therefore, it is very important that a support group be established for sober teens in a school setting.

---

[26] See SAMA (2008-2010), "The Effects of Drugs and Alcohol on the Adolescent Brain," at: http://samafoundation.org/youth-substance-addiction/effects-of-drugs-on-adolescent-brain/

Appendix G: Enthusiastic Sobriety Programs

The Enthusiastic Sobriety Programs are Twelve-Step-based treatment programs with groups in several US cities.

The various programs include:

Cornerstone (Colorado)
   www.thecornerstoneprogram.com
    Centennial (303) 690-0082 or (720) 540-0961

Crossroads (Missouri)
  www.thecrossroadsprogram.com
   Chesterfield (636) 532-9991
   Columbia (573) 256-8020
   Kansas City (816) 941-4000

Insight (Georgia & North Carolina)
  www.theinsightprogram.com
   Atlanta, GA (770) 751-8383
   Augusta, GA (706) 869-0230
   Greensboro, NC (336) 852-3033

Pathway (Arizona)
  www.thepathwayprogram.com
   Gilbert (480) 921-4050
   Glendale (623) 334-4906

Appendix H: Suggestions for Further Reading

Alcoholics Anonymous. New York: Alcoholics Anonymous World Services, Inc., 2000.

Beattie, Melody. *Codependent No More.* New York: HarperCollins Publishers, 1987.

Beattie, Melody. *Codependents' Guide to the Twelve Steps How to Find the Right Program for You and Apply Each of the Twelve Steps to Your Own Issues.* New York: Fireside, 1998.

Beattie, Melody. *The Language of Letting Go.* Center City, Minn.: Hazelden Foundation, 1990.

Blueprint for Progress Al-Anon's Fourth Step Inventory. Virginia Beach, Va.: Al-Anon Family Group Headquarters, Inc., 2004. **(Al-Anon Conference Approved Literature)**

Courage to Change. Virginia Beach, Va.: Al-Anon Family Group Headquarters, Inc., 2004. **(C.A.L.)**

Faber, Adele, and Elaine Mazlish. *How to Talk So Kids Will Listen & Listen So Kids Will Talk.* New York: Avon Books, 1980.

How Al-Anon Works for Families & Friends of Alcoholics. Virginia Beach, Va.: Al-Anon Family Group Headquarters, Inc., 1995. **(C.A.L.)**

Mandino, Og. *The Greatest Miracle in the World*. New York: Bantam, 1977.

Meehan, Bob. *Beyond the Yellow Brick Road: Our Children and Drugs.* Roswell, Ga.: Meek Publishing, 2007.

Meehan, Bob. *Bumper Stickers.* Kersey, Co.: Meek Publishing, 2000.

One Day at a Time in Al-Anon, New York; Al- Al-Anon Family Group Headquarters, Inc., 1979. **(C.A.L.)**

Paths to Recovery Al-Anon's Steps, Traditions, and Concepts. Virginia Beach, Va.: Al-Anon Family Group Headquarters, Inc., 1997. **(C.A.L.)**

Rosenberg, Marshall B. *Nonviolent Communication A Language of Compassion.* Encinitas, Cal.: PuddleDancer Press, 2002.

Twelve Steps and Twelve Traditions. New York: Alcoholics Anonymous World Services, Inc., 2000

A

Acceptable behavior, 383
Acceptance, 18, 77, 166, 193, 233, 237, 272, 286, 289, 303, 330, 343, 356
Accountability, 31, 364
Addiction, 90, 188, 254, 282, 334, 384, 402
Addiction to worry and fear, 73
ADHD, 25
Adult child of alcoholic, traits, 221
Adult children living at home, 226
Adult children of alcoholics, 252
Advice, unsolicited, 52
Advice-giving, 151, 252, 326, 369
Al-Anon, 85, 126
Al-Anon literature, 249
Al-Anon meetings, 75, 134, 140, 146, 265, 282, 367, 372
Alcoholic, is my child an …?, 230
Alcoholics Anonymous, 83, 214, 230, 414
Alcoholism, 83, 223, 230
Amends, 199, 331, 350, 356
Amends list, 114, 198, 349
Anger, 20, 51, 55, 228, 231, 287, 377
Anticipating the worst, 44, 80
Approval seeking, 131
Asking for help, 51, 68, 120, 146, 198, 359
Assertiveness, 144, 336, 399
Attitude, 207, 307
Attitude adjustment, 74, 81, 94, 99, 208
Awareness, 113

B

Balance, 27, 137, 330
Be Here Now, 277
Being gentle, 127, 331
Being gentle with myself, 221, 307
Beyond the Yellow Brick Road, 11, 34, 41, 50, 60, 61, 64, 87, 102, 107, 114, 126, 128, 129, 131, 138, 147, 153, 155, 156, 157, 162, 172, 175, 176, 183, 206, 241, 249, 254, 261, 262, 294, 329, 359, 364, 393, 415,
Big Book. See also Alcoholics Anonymous, See also Alcoholics Anonymous

Bipolar, 90
Blame, 11, 71, 144
Blame and shame, 85
Blueprint for Progress, 295, 414
Bottom, reaching a, 305, 317
Boundaries, 8, 10, 39, 56, 64, 93, 122, 141, 155, 176, 182, 218, 224, 274, 290, 292, 308, 370, 391
Breathe, 69, 266
Bumper Stickers, 17, 40, 162, 183, 307, 342, 385, 393, 415

C

C.R.A.P., 51, 319, 348
Carrying the message, 203, 204, 353
Catharsis, 199
Cell phone, 61, 159, 338
Change, 26, 71, 76, 109, 116, 118, 134, 152, 154, 155, 165, 188, 216, 250, 253, 279, 309, 323, 328, 336, 381, 401
Change of behavior, 7, 275
Changing my thoughts, 73
Chaos, 132
Character assets, 112, 221
Character defects, 345
Children, biological and adopted, 282
Choice, 17, 19, 24, 35, 40, 63, 74, 102, 171, 193, 226, 240, 241, 294, 308, 326, 376
Chores, 64, 271
Christmas, 388
Church, 121
Clean room, 271, 358
Cleaning, 43, 136
Cocaine, 265
Co-dependence, 123, 348
Codependent No More, 172, 414
Codependents' Guide to the Twelve Steps, 182, 414
Coffee, going out for coffee after meetings, 162
Communication, 41, 51, 58, 107, 124, 245, 252, 291, 319, 348, 386, 389, 399
Comparison, 18, 19, 207, 237
Compassion, 85, 127, 223, 398
Compliments, 116
Confidence, 154, 393
Conflict, 348
Conflict avoidance, 107, 131, 189
Consequences, 24, 34, 36, 56, 61, 64, 88, 122, 128, 138, 141, 145, 175, 181, 184, 206, 232, 240, 267, 271, 273, 274, 290, 298, 305, 317, 321, 338, 362, 364, 392, 398

Consequences, teen vs. young adult, 206
Control, 10, 14, 43, 75, 143, 182, 209, 212, 243, 276, 309, 322, 343
Coping skills, 328
Courage, 118, 331
Criticism, 11, 41, 52, 105, 171, 184, 218, 248, 253, 342, 356, 380
Cult, is the program a ...?, 230
Curfew, 56, 64, 124, 364
Curiosity, 287

D

Dead Poets Society, 40
Deadlines, 39
Decision-making, 31
Defining a power greater than myself, 135
Denial, 29, 63, 90, 98, 150, 258, 265
Detachment, 92, 110, 122, 123, 145, 180, 245, 249, 256, 264, 290, 369, 395
Disease, 63, 67, 83, 223
Disease or Choice?, 256
Disrespect, 231, 371
Divorced parents, 88, 183, 222, 288
Does it need to be said? Now? By me?, 212
Doing the next right thing, 58
Don't just do something, sit there., 162
Don't take it personally, 55, 142, 245, 335
Drama, 132
Driving, 60, 103
Driving under the influence, 305
Drug addiction, 83
Drug testing, 122, 274
Dry drunk, 20, 23

E

Earned highs, 60
Egoism, 50
Embarassment, 16
Emotional sobriety, 226, 245
Empathy, 37, 119
Enabling, 8, 9, 24, 57, 93, 141, 209, 224, 317
Enforcing consequences, 129, 131, 144, 189, 308, 332
Enmeshed families, 348
Entering the program, 254
Enthusiastic Sobriety Program shots, 56
Enthusiastic Sobriety Programs' group support, 181
Excuses, not making, 392
Expect a Miracle, 315

Expectations, 11, 40, 136, 153, 172, 335, 358, 376, 395
Expectations breed disaster, 237

F

F.E.A.R., 125, 244, 277, 378, 379
Faith, 44, 150, 190, 209, 315, 324, 331, 358, 375
Family celebrations, 174
Family disease, 188
Family gatherings, *174*
Family meetings, 319
Family roles, 401
Father-son interaction, 52, 66, 103
Fear, 69, 76, 186, 210, 244, 266, 277, 289, 378, 379
Fear of conflict, 371
Feelings, 218
Feelings are not facts, 28
Feelings, needs, and wants, 336
Finances, 26, 60, 91
Financial support of our children, 176, 224, 259, 292, 329, 393
Finding alcohol, 295
Finding drug paraphernalia, 9, 122, 295, 359
First Things First, 272
Flexibility, 77

Focusing on ourselves, 220, 339, 397
Focusing on solutions, 85, 380
Focusing on the good, 296
Foreign management, under, 23
Forgiveness, 97, 199, 252, 323, 356
Freaky Friday, 43
Friends, 177, 193, 265, 342
Funerals, 174

G

"Get Off Your Asphalt", 261
Getting through rough times, 28, 61, 68, 94, 172, 185
Goals, 329, 393
God, 178, 209, 315, 331
God bag, 110
God's will, not mine, 303
Good Orderly Direction, 110
Gossip, 342, 380
Grandchildren, 389
Gratitude, 15, 48, 68, 81, 82, 94, 116, 142, 149, 186, 207, 240, 292, 307, 408
Gratitude lists, 256
Gratitude meeting, 354, 361
Grief, 125, 289
Group support, 374
Guilt, 11, 22, 50, 71, 84, 122, 153, 157, 218, 230, 323

H

Habit, 258
Happiness, 143
Helicopter parent, 186
Higher Power, 14, 118, 209, 210, 315, 324, 331, 375
Holidays, 95, 174, 354, 361, 370, 381, 395
Homework, 77, 281
Honesty, 16, 58, 96, 107, 124, 238, 291, 345, 385
Hope, 49, 54, 82, 84, 100, 185, 249, 368
How Al-Anon Works for Families & Friends of Alcoholics, 162, 414
How do you plan to do that?, 213
Humility, 356
Humor, 11, 330

I

Identify, don't compare, 19, 372, 398
Imagination, 167
Importance of the program for parents, 198, 328, 398, 402
Independence, 31, 45, 226, 228, 262, 317
Indiana Jones, 369
Influence, parental, 243
Insanity, 240, 258, 317
International help, 140
Intervention, 9, 25, 34, 58, 60, 67, 75, 83, 85, 92, 140, 159, 224, 226, 243, 256, 258, 299, 312, 366
Inventory, 97, 184, 197, 221, 253, 275, 289, 345, 356, 386, 400
Inventory process, 346
Inventory, daily, 117, 201, 351, 382
It's not about me, 55

J

Jealousy, 207
Jedi mind trick, 168
Journaling, 142, 234, 408
Judgment, 41, 380
Juvenile detention, 175

K

Kid's requests, 87, 156, 241

L

Leap of faith, 103, 258, 322
Leaving home, 10, 24
Legal consequences, 100, 134, 156, 158, 290, 296, 298, 305, 332

Let Go and Let God, 304, 343
Letting go, 8, 14, 66, 75, 77, 92, 93, 99, 135, 166, 168, 190, 236, 258, 264, 278, 286, 293, 309, 312, 322, 330, 358, 366, 370, 395
Life is good, 81, 208
Limits, 224, 332, 338
Listening, 37, 116, 119, 181, 202, 229, 310
Listing the good in each person, place, or situation, 256
Living amends, 116
Living in the present, 32, 44, 66, 76, 99, 153, 157, 187, 233, 250, 266, 299, 334, 339
Logical consequences, 359
Looking for the good, 233, 237, 307
Love, 54, 178, 338
Love means not accepting wrong behavior, 61, 298
Lying, 29, 96, 98, 134, 164, 265, 295, 338

M

Making healthier choices, 313
Making mistakes, 112, 262
Manipulation, 51

Manipulation by our kids, 21, 87, 128, 158, 164, 230, 254, 262, 338, 362
Marijuana addiction, 359
Martyrdom, 26, 51, 86, 154
Mean what you say, 88, 144, 189, 291, 362
Meditation, 202, 303
Meehan, Bob, 99, 127, 132
Meeting format, 229
Meetings, 9, 49, 146, 147, 181, 185, 220, 332, 363, 402, 408
Mental illness, 90
Methamphetamines, 397
Mothering, 43, 154, 276
Mothers, work experiences, 283
Motives, 169, 226
Motives for questioning our kids, 105
Music, 215

N

Nagging, 217
Needs, 124, 259
Negative behavior patterns, 154, 279
Negative thoughts, 69, 76, 248, 253
New Year's Eve Round Robin, 354, 361
Newcomers' meeting, 162

Ninety meetings in ninety days, 84
Non-addicts, 14

O

Obedience to the unenforceable, 46
Objectivity, 369
Obsession, 48
Ode to Cornerstone Counselors, 149
One Day at a Time, 183, 415
Open-mindedness, 107, 229, 258, 273, 310, 356
Orderliness, 358
Outpatient treatment, end of, 103, 136, 246, 344
Over responsibility, 133
Ownership of one's own life, 12, 33, 41, 43, 45, 52, 57, 86, 105, 158, 162, 176, 186, 212, 217, 262, 264, 271, 276, 281, 285, 289, 290, 293, 321, 326, 369, 395

P

Parent group, 54, 90, 108, 113, 121, 125, 126, 138, 147, 161, 185, 210, 269, 363, 367
Parent meetings, 14, 80, 120, 134, 135, 146, 159, 179, 185, 214, 233, 254, 282, 295, 366, 367, 372, 374, 384, 398, 402
Parent retreat, 103
Parent support group, 120, 177, 214, 246, 247, 258, 402
Parental authority, 377
Parental duty, 45
Parental guidance, 333
Parental lie detector, 170
Parental recovery, 123, 162, 192, 210, 240, 272
Parental relapse, 7, 235, 254
Parental responsibility, 8, 31, 40, 60, 93, 97, 143, 192, 217, 226, 264, 276, 294, 344, 392, 400, 401
Parental responsibility for adult children, 151, 292, 296
Parental responsibility, teen vs. young adult, 161
Parental tools, 21, 168, 184
Parenting, 17, 129, 131, 152, 164, 371
Parenting's purpose, 393
Patience, 103, 125, 282
Patience with the newly sober addict, 293
Peace, 188, 240
People pleasing, 228

Perfectionism, 127, 252, 289, 356, 403,
Perseverance, 54, 269
Phone calls, 68, 95
Positive, being, 11, 48, 80, 215, 302
Power, 313, 367
Powerlessness, 325, 341
Powers of positive parenting, 127, 307
Practice the principles, 15, 142, 162, 181, 388
Prayer, 126, 178, 202, 216, 284, 295, 303
Prayer and meditation, 118, 125, 352, 382
Prayer of St. Francis of Assisi, 223
Prescription drug abuse, 100
Priorities, 272, 375
Problem-solving, 32, 57, 60, 386
Progress not perfection, 125, 289, 403

R

Raising Teenaged Alcoholics/Addicts, 372
Reaching bottom, 100, 121
Reading, 282
Rebellion, 371
Rebuilding our relationship with our kids, 22, 65, 103, 165, 295, 302, 310
Rebuilding trust, 98
Recovery, 7, 9, 64, 84, 107, 132, 137, 169, 188, 254, 265, 319, 333, 360, 384, 386, 396, 402
Regret, 76
Relapse, 28, 34, 68, 82, 102, 121, 150, 156, 169, 172, 206, 223, 269, 321, 334, 338
Relief, 197
Reminder, 217
Rent, adult children paying, 122, 161, 226
Rescuing, 57, 91, 155, 209, 258, 261, 298, 305, 317, 395
Resentment, 22, 74, 86, 154, 186, 198, 207, 228, 287, 323, 386
Respect, 171, 326, 391, 398, 399
Responsibility, 158, 192, 217, 276, 285, 376, 400, 401
Responsibility, teen vs. young adult, 224
Right Here Right Now, 99, 299
Risking our relationship with our kids, 158, 389
Rules, 34, 35, 54, 56, 61, 64, 65, 88, 102, 122, 129, 131, 141, 144, 181, 182, 206,

222, 240, 267, 273, 290, 300, 321, 364, 383

S

Sanctuary, 223
Sanity, 102
School, 16, 137, 265, 267, 281, 295, 298, 328, 386, 411
Self-care, 133
Self-centeredness, 152
Self-destructive behavior, 119
Self-esteem, 285
Self-forgiveness, 197
Self-pity, 26, 74, 152, 187, 207, 228, 237
Self-recrimination, 71
Self-reflection, 385
Self-reliance, 228
Self-restraint, 91, 252, 262
Self-righteousness, 154, 310
Self-sufficiency, 146, 198
Self-talk, 127, 403
Serenity, 343
Serenity Prayer, 82, 88, 167, 216, 247, 317, 368, 377, 396, 399
Serenity Prayer, extended, 16
Service, 408
Setting an example, 60, 231, 383, 385
Setting boundaries, 383, 398

Setting limits, 64, 128, 274, 371
Shame, 84
Sharing at meetings, 47
Shortcomings, 385
Shots, 8, 25, 34, 36, 39, 40, 54, 56, 61, 64, 71, 88, 93, 102, 128, 129, 131, 141, 155, 175, 181, 206, 267, 273, 290, 298, 321, 332
Siblings, 104, 338
Silence, 55, 91, 217
Slogans, 408
   Easy Does It., 37, 105, 388
   Expectations Breed Disaster., 136
   Fake It Until You Make It., 82
   First Things First., 272, 300
   How Important Is It?, 95, 136, 142, 186, 238, 300, 388
   In general, 82, 142
   Let Go and Let God., 69, 150, 186, 235, 303, 304
   Live and Let Live., 105, 180
   One Day at a Time, 18, 82, 339
   Right Here Right Now, 99
   Think, 31, 86, 248
   This Too Shall Pass, 256
Smoking cigarettes, 64

Sober living facility, 33, 137, 150, 168, 267, 312, 363
Sobriety, 8, 64, 93, 159, 226, 272, 386, 411
Sobriety, early, 321
Solving my problems through the Twelve Steps, 135, 142
Spiritual toolkit, 37, 215, 408
Sponsor, 80, 175, 177, 194, 201, 386
Sponsors, 147, 280, 390, 402
Sponsorship, 47, 95, 156, 280, 295, 363, 391, 408, 410
Staying on our kid's side, 241
Stealing, 26, 63, 134, 175, 249
Step meetings, 146
Steps
   In general, 13, 194, 235, 360, 393
   Step One, 79, 192, 210
   Step One, Al-Anon, 325, 341
   Step One, Enthusiastic Sobriety Programs', 107, 325, 341
   Steps One - Four, Enthusiastic Sobriety Programs', 73
   Step Two, Al-Anon, 79, 109, 343
   Step Two, Enthusiastic Sobriety Programs', 108, 193, 279, 325, 342
   Step Three, Al-Anon, 79, 110, 213, 236, 246, 344
   Step Three, Enthusiastic Sobriety Programs', 109, 343, 348
   Step Four, Al-Anon, 345, 346
   Step Four, Enthusiastic Sobriety Programs', 110, 213, 236, 246, 344
   Step Five, Al-Anon, 112, 197, 346
   Step Five, Enthusiastic Sobriety Programs', 345, 346
   Step Six, Enthusiastic Sobriety Programs, 112, 197, 346
   Steps Six and Seven, Al-Anon, 113
   Step Seven, Enthusiastic Sobriety Programs, 113, 198, 348
   Step Eight, 114, 349
   Step Eight, Enthusiastic Sobriety Programs, 198
   Step Nine, 116, 199, 350
   Step Ten, 58, 117, 201, 220, 351, 382, 403

Step Eleven, 118, 202, 284, 352, 382
Step Twelve, 119, 203, 204, 353, 382
Stick with winners, 108, 138, 313, 342, 380
Strength, 185, 368
Strengthening faith, 214
Substance abuse, 67, 83
Suicide threat, 362
Support group, 386
Supporting and encouraging our kids in recovery, 31, 98, 166, 174, 191, 223, 232, 238, 259, 296, 333
Supporting vs. enabling our children, 224

T

Taking care of myself, 162
Taking care of ourselves, 27, 75, 126, 133, 169, 180, 182, 228, 282, 292
Teaching your child about making amends, 392
Teenage behavior, 20, 55
Teenaged mood swings, 278
Teenagers, 41
Telephone calls, 408
The 4th "C", 151
The Greatest Miracle in the World, 386, 415
Think, 15, 31, 86, 238, 252, 317

This too shall pass., 218, 223
Three C's, 17, 25, 50, 75, 83, 97, 151, 217, 250, 282, 317
Three F's, 273
Thy will, not mine, be done., 284
To thine own self be true., 385
Tools of the program, 61, 95, 128, 172, 187, 234, 269, 388
Tough love, 85, 145
Traditions, 381
Treatment, 9, 18, 34, 67, 100, 140, 159, 224, 256
Trust, 22, 29, 65, 96, 98, 103, 190, 324, 331, 397
Trust but verify, 170
Trust in a Higher Power, 236
Trust is a decision., 22, 35
Trust your instinct, 29, 170, 270
Turning it over, 110, 344
Turning over our worries, 213, 278
Twelve Steps, 83
Type A personality, 37, 233

U

Unacceptable behavior, 10, 64
Unconditional love, 105

Under foreign management, 249
Understanding, 119, 185
Unearned highs, 60, 329, 393
United front, 21, 54, 56, 65, 87, 128, 156, 222, 246, 254, 262, 288, 362
United front between home and school, 267
Unmanageability, 134, 210, 266, 325, 363, 374

V

Values, 102
Victims, 26, 171, 275, 308, 364, 376
Visualizations, 378, 379
Volunteers, 26, 275

W

Waking up our kids, 12
Walking on eggshells, 158, 389
Walls, 8, 36, 54, 56, 61, 64, 71, 88, 93, 128, 129, 131, 141, 155, 175, 176, 181, 206, 232, 262, 267, 290, 300, 321, 338, 364, 383
Wants, 259
Weddings, 174
What's your plan?, 31

Why me?, 250
Willing to go to any lengths, 159
Willingness, 107, 198
Willingness to make amends, 114, 349
Winning, 310
Wisdom, 368
Working the program, 104, 126, 153, 185, 222, 226
Working the program as hard as you want your kid to, 328
Working the program, how to, 73
Working the steps, 13, 46, 79, 147, 159, 165, 166, 177, 188, 194, 209, 214, 220, 235, 238, 250, 279, 288, 294, 331, 363, 366, 374, 382, 390, 397
Worry, 44, 69, 75, 76, 167, 180, 210, 244, 266, 277, 312
Would you like to hear my opinion about that?, 326

Y

Yelling, 377
Young person's group, 121
Younger group, 367